The Economics of Privacy

National Bureau of Economic Research

Conference Report

The Economics of Privacy

Edited by **Avi Goldfarb and Catherine E. Tucker**

The University of Chicago Press

Chicago and London

The University of Chicago Press, Chicago 60637
The University of Chicago Press, Ltd., London

Published 2024
Printed in the United States of America

33 32 31 30 29 28 27 26 25 24   1 2 3 4 5

ISBN-13: 978-0-226-83407-8 (cloth)

ISBN-13: 978-0-226-83408-5 (e-book)

DOI: https://doi.org/10.7208/chicago/9780226834085.001.0001

Library of Congress Cataloging-in-Publication Data

Names: Goldfarb, Avi, editor. | Tucker, Catherine (Catherine Elizabeth), editor.
Title: The economics of privacy / edited by Avi Goldfarb and Catherine E. Tucker.
Other titles: National Bureau of Economic Research conference report.
Description: Chicago : The University of Chicago Press, 2024. | Series: National Bureau of Economic Research conference report | Includes bibliographical references and index.
Identifiers: LCCN 2023055007 | ISBN 9780226834078 (cloth) | ISBN 9780226834085 (ebook)
Subjects: LCSH: Privacy, Right of—Economic aspects. | Privacy, Right of—Economic aspects—United States. | Data protection—Law and legislation. | European Parliament. General Data Protection Regulation.
Classification: LCC K3264.C65 E36 2024 | DDC 322.44/8—dc23/eng/20231207
LC record available at https://lccn.loc.gov/2023055007

♾ This paper meets the requirements of ANSI/NISO Z39.48-1992 (Permanence of Paper).

Relation of the Directors to the Work and Publications of the NBER

1. The object of the NBER is to ascertain and present to the economics profession, and to the public more generally, important economic facts and their interpretation in a scientific manner without policy recommendations. The Board of Directors is charged with the responsibility of ensuring that the work of the NBER is carried on in strict conformity with this object.

2. The President shall establish an internal review process to ensure that book manuscripts proposed for publication DO NOT contain policy recommendations. This shall apply both to the proceedings of conferences and to manuscripts by a single author or by one or more co-authors but shall not apply to authors of comments at NBER conferences who are not NBER affiliates.

3. No book manuscript reporting research shall be published by the NBER until the President has sent to each member of the Board a notice that a manuscript is recommended for publication and that in the President's opinion it is suitable for publication in accordance with the above principles of the NBER. Such notification will include a table of contents and an abstract or summary of the manuscript's content, a list of contributors if applicable, and a response form for use by Directors who desire a copy of the manuscript for review. Each manuscript shall contain a summary drawing attention to the nature and treatment of the problem studied and the main conclusions reached.

4. No volume shall be published until forty-five days have elapsed from the above notification of intention to publish it. During this period a copy shall be sent to any Director requesting it, and if any Director objects to publication on the grounds that the manuscript contains policy recommendations, the objection will be presented to the author(s) or editor(s). In case of dispute, all members of the Board shall be notified, and the President shall appoint an ad hoc committee of the Board to decide the matter; thirty days additional shall be granted for this purpose.

5. The President shall present annually to the Board a report describing the internal manuscript review process, any objections made by Directors before publication or by anyone after publication, any disputes about such matters, and how they were handled.

6. Publications of the NBER issued for informational purposes concerning the work of the Bureau, or issued to inform the public of the activities at the Bureau, including but not limited to the NBER Digest and Reporter, shall be consistent with the object stated in paragraph 1. They shall contain a specific disclaimer noting that they have not passed through the review procedures required in this resolution. The Executive Committee of the Board is charged with the review of all such publications from time to time.

7. NBER working papers and manuscripts distributed on the Bureau's web site are not deemed to be publications for the purpose of this resolution, but they shall be consistent with the object stated in paragraph 1. Working papers shall contain a specific disclaimer noting that they have not passed through the review procedures required in this resolution. The NBER's web site shall contain a similar disclaimer. The President shall establish an internal review process to ensure that the working papers and the web site do not contain policy recommendations, and shall report annually to the Board on this process and any concerns raised in connection with it.

8. Unless otherwise determined by the Board or exempted by the terms of paragraphs 6 and 7, a copy of this resolution shall be printed in each NBER publication as described in paragraph 2 above.

Contents

Acknowledgments

This volume was made possible by a generous grant from the Alfred P. Sloan Foundation (grant #G-2020-12662) to the National Bureau of Economic Research. It is part of a multi-year research initiative at the NBER on the economics of digitization. We are grateful to Daniel Goroff of the Sloan Foundation for his interest in and support for this project. We would also like to thank Helena Fitz-Patrick for outstanding assistance in the editorial process, Denis Healy for expert management of the Sloan Foundation grant, and Rob Shannon for excellent administration of the meeting at which the papers in this volume were presented.

Introduction

Avi Goldfarb and Catherine E. Tucker

Digital economics focuses on how the economy is transformed when information can be stored in bits and not atoms. This advance has reduced the cost of collecting, storing, and processing data. Firms and governments can observe individual-level behavior at a detailed level and use this information to provide better products and services; however, the ability to access this information raises privacy concerns.

This volume provides a summary of the research to date on the economics of privacy and identifies a number of open questions. The five chapters in this volume are based on presentations that the authors gave to the NBER PhD tutorial on the Economics of Privacy, held in October 2022. They provide different perspectives on the role of economists and economics research in understanding the benefits of privacy and the benefits of data flows.

Several common themes emerge across the chapters.

One common theme is the challenge in applying the Coase theorem to privacy. To many economists, it is compelling to assume that privacy concerns can be solved by the market because the parties should be able to negotiate a price for exchange of data if property rights are well defined and transaction costs are low. Each chapter describes situations where the Coase theorem breaks down.

Avi Goldfarb is the Rotman Chair in Artificial Intelligence and Healthcare and a professor of marketing at the Rotman School of Management, University of Toronto, and a research associate of the National Bureau of Economic Research.

Catherine Tucker is the Sloan Distinguished Professor of Management Science and Professor of Marketing at MIT Sloan, and a research associate of the National Bureau of Economic Research.

For acknowledgments, sources of research support, and disclosure of the authors' material financial relationships, if any, please see https://www.nber.org/books-and-chapters/economics-privacy/introduction-economics-privacy.

A second common theme relates to measurement. It is relatively easy to measure the costs of privacy in terms of innovation or competition and so much of the existing literature has documented such costs. It is more difficult to measure the benefits of privacy, particularly when those benefits are about intrinsic preferences rather than a direct and measurable market harm.

A third common theme is the difficulty in defining privacy through an economics lens. The broader academic and legal literature includes many distinct definitions of privacy. With our emphasis on formal models, economists must select a definition and formalize it. This creates challenges in the literature as people use the same word, *privacy*, to mean different things.

We next briefly describe each chapter in turn.

In Chapter 1, Catherine Tucker focuses on identifying the open research questions, linking the economics perspective to changes in other fields. The chapter defines privacy using the definition from Warren and Brandeis (1890) as "The right to be let alone." The chapter comprehensively lists a set of outstanding questions and discusses the role of the economist's perspective for addressing these questions. Key open questions include the value of privacy, the role of property rights and data markets, the relationship between privacy and inequality, and the political economy of privacy.

Alessandro Acquisti takes a different approach in Chapter 2, arguing that the typical economic approach is flawed in the context of privacy. While the chapter's core point matches a point made by Tucker—that we need more research on the benefits of privacy—Acquisti argues that the economic approach is limited because it focuses on what we can measure and what markets can solve. The chapter defines privacy using Altman's (1976) definition as "a dynamic and dialective process through which individuals contextually manage the boundaries between the self and others." Ultimately, the chapter concludes that economists would benefit more from reading the privacy literature outside of economics and provides a brief summary of key ideas in that literature.

In Chapter 3, Alessandro Bonatti provides a formal approach to understanding how privacy, defined as a restriction on data flows, affects market outcomes. The chapter begins by providing a comprehensive theoretical framework for understanding privacy. Then the chapter explains how the broader economics literature on privacy can be interpreted using this model. A key idea emerging in this literature, and central to the chapter, is the role of data externalities. The provision of data by one person can affect others. One aspect of this is the social dimension of data, as data about other people can be informative about one's own behavior. Like Tucker in Chapter 1, this chapter identifies open questions related to markets for privacy and to political economy.

Garrett Johnson's chapter provides a detailed analysis of a particular regulation: the European Union's General Data Protection Regulation (or GDPR). The chapter provides a detailed description of what is likely the most important digital privacy regulation to date. In the process, it highlights several ongoing challenges in empirical privacy research. Regulation has benefits and costs, and because costs are more straightforward to measure in terms of reduced competition and reduced innovation. The chapter highlights how the regulation as written can be different from the regulation as implemented. This distinction between the law and its enforcement can lead to a misinterpretation of the effects of privacy regulation on behavior and on market outcomes. Overall, the chapter provides a useful framework for economists looking to examine how changes in privacy policies by firms or governments might affect economic outcomes.

Fifth, and finally, Amalia Miller describes the role of privacy in healthcare. She notes that health is a particularly interesting area to study privacy because there are extraordinary benefits of data flows and an extraordinary potential for harm. The benefits are clear as improved healthcare means longer and healthier lives. Better information about individual patients could lead to improved care. Better aggregated health information could lead to better diagnostics and treatments. The chapter also lists a variety of harms. Direct harms include a feeling of shame or embarrassment, a feeling of betrayal, and a feeling of invasion or loss of freedom. Indirect market harms include labor market harms, insurance, personalized pricing (if higher), and targeted advertising (if manipulative, annoying, or intrusive). Indirect nonmarket harms include social stigma, harms to reputation, increased risk of identity theft or fraud, and increased legal risk. While the chapter emphasizes these harms in the context of health information, the division into direct harms, indirect market harms, and indirect nonmarket harms provides a useful framework for the broader economics of privacy literature. This perspective is grounded in economic models of the costs and benefits of data flows, and the potential for externalities to undermine standard economic approaches. The chapter also notes that there is a great deal of health privacy regulation in place in the US and around the world, making health a fruitful area for empirical work. The conclusion of Chapter 5 summarizes the challenges for decision-making around privacy, highlighting the "fundamental trade-offs between preserving privacy and harnessing the value of IT and data-driven innovation."

This volume aims to summarize the key open questions in the economics of privacy as of 2023. In doing so, the chapters provide different frameworks that economists can use to undertake research on privacy.

1

The Economics of Privacy
An Agenda

Catherine E. Tucker

1.1 The Challenge of Privacy for Economics

The economics of privacy is a challenging field in which to be an economist. There are two reasons for this.

The first challenge stems from the definition of privacy. What is privacy? My favorite definition is "freedom from unwarranted intrusion." This definition stems from Warren and Brandeis (1890), who defined privacy as the "right to be left alone." They were famously inspired to write their influential essay by the rise of gossip columnists capturing photos with the new technology of portable cameras. This is important, as I will argue in this essay that our conceptions of privacy, and therefore what is important to study as economists, are inextricably tied up with progress in technology. Concepts of privacy are constantly challenged by new technologies that parse personal information in new and unexpected ways. Therefore, unlike a field such as labor economics where the definition of what labor supply is is relatively unchanging, our ideas of what privacy is and should be are in constant flux.

The second challenge stems from our need as economists to at essence conceptualize any question in economics through the lens of a utility function. Farrell (2012) describes the issue very usefully. Typically, in the theoretical literature in economics we tend to think about intermediate preferences for privacy—these reflect the anticipation that if we share our data with a firm, it can be used potentially for things that harm us, like price discrimina-

Catherine Tucker is the Sloan Distinguished Professor of Management Science and Professor of Marketing at MIT Sloan, and a research associate of the National Bureau of Economic Research.

For acknowledgments, sources of research support, and disclosure of the author's material financial relationships, if any, please see https://www.nber.org/books-and-chapters/economics-privacy/economics-privacy-agenda.

tion. By contrast, the vast majority of the literature outside of economics thinks about privacy as a right or something where people should just have a fixed intrinsic taste for keeping certain types of information privacy. Indeed, often the descriptions of tastes for privacy outside of economics suggest a distaste for creepiness (Richards and Hartzog 2015), or a taste for data being only used in the same context (Nissenbaum 2004). While of course a taste for anything can be included in a utility function, it is unsatisfactory for a discipline that has tried to always model utility functions based on first principles.

1.2 The Focus of the Economics of Privacy Literature So Far

When trying to write an essay on the economics of privacy, it is important to highlight that this has already been done stupendously well by Professor Alessandro Acquisti of Carnegie Mellon University and co-authors, culminating in an essay published in the *Journal of Economic Literature* (Acquisti, Taylor, and Wagman 2016). What is attractive about this conception of the history of privacy is that they define a variety of decades of schools of thought and how this has progressed over time.

The first wave identified by Acquisti et al. (2016) is that of the Chicago School in the 1970s, led by theorists such as Stigler and Posner. In this literature, privacy was defined as a propensity toward secrecy—and in a world where information is generally beneficial to welfare, these models evaluated how tastes for privacy itself could lead to harm to welfare (Posner 1978, 1981; Stigler 1980). Of course, the wave of information economics that characterized theory in the 1980s in economics, itself questioned the idea that more information is always beneficial initiated by some of the idea in theories of signaling and information cascades (Spence 1973; Hirshleifer 1971).

The second wave identified by Acquisti et al. (2016) is also a theoretical literature but this time led by information economists who were interested in questions of technology. Varian (2002) shifted the question of privacy from being one of simply secrecy in what information is shared with other people, to being one firmly about data. This led to new questions such as what should be secondary use rights associated with data. As such it gave rise to what Acquisti et al. (2016) describe as the third wave of theoretical literature, which is interested in questions such as price discrimination (through the use of cookies) (Acquisti and Varian 2005) and targeting effects in online advertising (Johnson 2013; Bergemann and Bonatti 2011, 2015).

The other large shift in the last decade of research has been a proliferation of empirical work in privacy. As described by Goldfarb and Tucker (2012a), much of this work has tried to quantify the effects of privacy regulation on the economy, with much of the literature asking questions about advertising markets (Goldfarb and Tucker 2011; Chiou and Tucker 2012; Johnson, Shriver, and Du 2020; Jia, Jin, and Wagman 2018; Peukert et al. 2020; Johnson, Shriver, and Goldberg 2022; Godinho de Matos and Adjerid

2022), though some of the literature also asks about online behavior (Zhao et al. 2021), financial markets (Kim and Wagman 2015), and health markets (Miller and Tucker 2009, 2011; Adjerid et al. 2016; Miller and Tucker 2017).

These few brief paragraphs do not of course do justice to the literature on the economics of privacy. However, it is fair to say that as yet the number of researchers and number of publications are relatively small given its potential importance in the digital economy. Recently recognizing this, the NBER, and with support from the Sloan Foundation, has instituted a one-off conference on the economics of privacy and also a PhD tutorial to try and inspire more work in this area. This chapter of the handbook that reflects this work tries to offer some suggestions about how economists might be able to deepen and broaden this current literature.

1.3 Outstanding Questions

This handbook is aimed at young researchers who are starting off their careers. Therefore, it makes sense to focus on some of the big questions that researchers in economics have not yet tackled (or have only tackled in part).

1.3.1 The Value of Privacy

1.3.1.1 Measuring Positive Consequences of Privacy Regulation

Much of the empirical wave of research on privacy has focused on the question of how privacy regulation hurts economic outcomes—by restricting advertising effectiveness (Goldfarb and Tucker 2011; Johnson, Shriver, and Du 2020), leading to market concentration (Peukert et al. 2020; Johnson, Shriver, and Goldberg 2022), exacerbating inequality (Kim and Wagman 2015), or hurting health outcomes (Miller and Tucker 2009; Adjerid et al. 2016; Miller and Tucker 2017). However, given the large literature on how privacy regulation has large negative economic consequences, the paucity of literature on the benefits of privacy regulation is surprising.

Therefore, it may make sense for researchers to also think about situations or contexts where privacy rights and regulations might have clear positive consequences for individuals. Some I have thought of include:

- Data concerning reproductive health
- Data concerning mental illness
- Data concerning disability that might be used to disqualify potential employees from jobs they could do well
- Data concerning past crimes that are orthogonal to a current question that requires judgment

One thing which all these things have in common is that they concern questions where a stigma exists that is unrelated to potential economic output or the economic quality of a match. In such cases, if privacy regulation tempers data diffusion about something that has an irrational stigma, then it must be the case that privacy regulation benefits individuals. If this is the case, privacy regulation or privacy protections should have positive effects on consumer welfare.

Other occasions where it should be straightforward to document benefits from privacy regulation include instances where data itself might be used for coercion: This might include:

- Targeting those who suffer from addictive behavior to pursue their addiction
- Targeting those who have struggled managing their credit in the past, with further unwise credit offerings
- Targeting those who suffer eating disorders, with weight loss products

These examples share the theme that if prompted, an individual might pursue a course that is not ultimately utility-maximizing for them. As such a restriction of data that means they are not likely to be targeted with prompts may benefit them.

1.3.1.2 Measuring Tastes for Privacy

If we are to truly understand, though, whether privacy regulation has benefits to consumers, we have to return to measurement of key parameters in the utility function. If we assume that a taste for privacy is built into a consumer's utility function, then by definition any regulation that caters to this taste improves consumer welfare. However, this implies we have to actually measure relative intrinsic tastes for privacy. One of the first empirical papers that has attempted to do so is Lin (2022). This paper finds that in general there is a lot of heterogeneity in intrinsic tastes for privacy and perhaps the magnitudes are smaller than might be expected given the privacy literature.

It is clear that the more that can be inferred about underlying tastes for privacy, given observed consumer choices over privacy decisions regarding their data, the more informed this debate can be.

One issue that has thwarted attempts at measuring preferences for privacy is something known as the privacy paradox (Athey et al. 2017). This reflects the observed phenomenon that often while consumers express a desire for privacy when asked about it, it appears they are willing to share their data very readily in a way which seems to contradict this. Of course, in economics tension between stated preferences and revealed preferences are not new, and economists by disposition tend to trust more revealed preferences. But privacy is a domain where trying to unpack this tension appears worthwhile. How is the privacy paradox moderated by the knowledge of consumers? Does the privacy paradox ever reflect consumers engaging in some type of behavioral distortion, which means their stated preferences are closer to the truth? In what domains is the privacy paradox most important, and how does that affect our attempts to evaluate privacy regulation?

In general, what is clear is that from an economics perspective the more we can examine and model actual consumer behavior regarding privacy data using individual-level decisions, the more we will be able to model and parse individual privacy preferences. In particular, the more we could have data on an individual's decision-making regarding the privacy of their data across different domains, the more informative this may be.

1.3.1.3 Privacy Preferences and Context

An appealing theory for understanding some apparent disconnects in privacy preferences is that of the idea of contextual integrity (Nissenbaum 2010). This states that privacy preferences or intrinsic tastes for privacy can be understood as reflecting five contextual parameters that help shape the view of privacy of the individual. These span who the sender of the data is; who the subject of the data is; who the recipient of the data is; the type of data that is sent; and what is referred to as the "transmission" principle, which reflects whether the data was obtained via consent, coercion, or by sale, or by law. Dr Nissenbaum is a philosopher, meaning much of the work is conceptual. As such it reflects a potentially rich testing ground for different theories of tastes for privacy (Bleier, Goldfarb, and Tucker 2020): For example:

1. How much does the same person have different tastes for privacy depending on the recipient? Or the type of data?
2. How does the original context in which data was given affect privacy principles?
3. Do we have similar privacy preferences over our associates' data as we do our own?

Mapping out all these parameters that affect privacy preferences conceptually seems a very useful exercise for empirical analysis.

1.3.1.4 Time-Inconsistency and Privacy Preferences

One important question that appears to have been neglected in the literature is the question of how privacy preferences evolve over time. This is particularly striking because the drop in costs of storing and parsing digital data means that it is virtually costless to store an individual's history of actions over time, rather than periodically deleting it. In other words, there is no reason to think that costs of storage will necessitate the deletion of data. However, there is evidence (Goldfarb and Tucker 2012b) that people's privacy preferences evolve as they grow older; as people get older, they get more privacy conscious. This means that data that young people create today may not reflect their privacy preferences when they get older, which may have negative consequences. In addition, it is of course possible that there are technology shocks, which means that there are unanticipated consequences of sharing data. For example, I might have made decisions about sharing video footage of myself without predicting that advances in machine learning could lead such data to be decomposed in a manner that allows seamless prediction.

1.3.1.5 Inferential Privacy

Much of the privacy debate has focused on issues of data. And indeed this reflects lawmaking—most laws regarding privacy do not mention the use of algorithms or how that might affect privacy considerations. However, this could be an artifact of laws generally being backwards-looking rather than a prediction of the future.

If I was to speculate, I would argue that in the future we may see a realization that many potential privacy concerns are not a result of the data itself being transferred but instead a result of predictions that are made using this data. For example, though I might be happy to share my photos publicly, and the photos themselves do not cause me any privacy concerns, if algorithms were able to make predictions from these photos about my health, my financial status, my fertility, or other domains of data that I considered private, then I might want to object to using the data in that manner.

If this prediction comes to pass then, this opens up multiple different avenues for research. Indeed, there are already theory papers that are exploring these topics (Acemoglu et al. 2022; Bergemann, Bonatti, and Gan 2020; Goldfarb et al. 2020).

1.3.2 Markets and Privacy

1.3.2.1 Property Rights and Privacy

Whenever economists who have not studied the economics of privacy give interviews about privacy they tend to immediately and instinctively talk about property rights. After all, one of the central tenets of economics is the Coase theorem (Coase 1960), which suggests that many instances of inefficiencies in information markets can be solved by simply clarifying property rights (Farrell 1987). And the idea that all the tensions involved by trying to optimize privacy protections can be best solved by property rights is superficially an attractive one. And indeed my own research has shown that giving controls to people over their privacy—perhaps akin to property rights—helps address privacy concerns (Tucker 2014; Miller and Tucker 2017).

However, there are ultimately obvious flaws in thinking that property rights alone can address privacy concerns, which are themselves worth exploring as potential research topics:

- The idea that data is neatly binary does not fit current data markets. Instead, it makes sense in a world of spreadsheets where each person's data is neatly encased in a single row of data. Take, for example, a photo

I take of myself in a shopping center. This photo might—through facial recognition technologies—also place other individuals at that shopping center. However, even though I might have taken the data and therefore own the data, it is not clear that I have property rights over anyone else's image that might appear in the photo.

- When I take a genetic test, and create data, I am creating data that might affect my ancestors and my descendants. Though I might be able to sell my genetic data to an interested firm, what should be done about the spillovers this has and inferences that are created for my family members?
- Often my data is not particularly valuable, however, inferences from it may be (Miklós-Thal et al. 2023). Let us suppose I liked curly fries on Facebook and researchers were able to infer that this implied I was clever. Do I as the owner of the data also own rights to this inference—or do property rights to that inference belong to the researchers? As an aside, this correlation is based on real-life research (Kosinski, Stillwell, and Graepel 2013).

Therefore, perhaps a way for research in this area to succeed is to study the differences between data where there is a clear property right, and data where there is not. And understand the economic implications of both. This is an area where it seems to be that the talents of theorists would be particularly helpful.

1.3.2.2 Individual Data Markets

Though it is possible to think that the fuzziness of property rights when it comes to data could be one potential explanation for why current approaches to privacy have failed, it is also possible to think of more traditional sources of market failure, such as moral hazard and adverse selection. A useful place to study this is in current efforts to build up individual data markets. There are plenty of firms that have sought to set up businesses which would allow individuals to own their data and trade it for monetary value. For example, firms like CitizenMe, Streamlytics, and Clture have tried to establish individual data markets along these lines (see https://www.citizenme.com/, https://www.streamlytics.co/, and https://www.clture.io/). Firms like brave offer to pay people for their attention and data.[1] However, as of yet none of these efforts have thrived.

There is a fledgling literature that tries to understand some of the limitations from a privacy perspective of these markets (Spiekermann et al. 2015). There is also a theoretical literature that explores the consequences of these markets not existing (Jones and Tonetti 2020), being distorted by regulation (Fainmesser, Galeotti, and Momot 2022), or being plagued by externalities

1. See: https://brave.com/compare/chrome/earning/.

(Ichihashi 2021). But it seems clear that more papers are needed that try to study the diffusion of these attempts to create data markets and issues of adverse selection and moral hazard that might intuitively plague attempts to create such markets.

Another explanation that may be worth exploring is that the ubiquity of data and non-rivalry of data have also hampered the successful monetization of an individual's data.

1.3.2.3 Competitive Dynamics and Privacy

It is also useful to think about how privacy regulation or tastes for privacy might affect market dynamics and competition as a whole. Early theoretical work such as Campbell, Goldfarb, and Tucker (2015) sketched out theoretical reasons why privacy regulation might lead to concentration. Since then, a variety of work has appeared to confirm this (Miller and Tucker 2014; Peukert et al. 2020; Johnson, Shriver, and Goldberg 2022; Marthews and Tucker 2019a). However, this doesn't mean that the topic is closed to new research. Instead, it means it is time to broaden the number of contexts that such studies are conducted in—for example extending the insights to less studied industries where privacy matters—such as educational technology.

It is also possible to take this type of research and ask questions that illuminate competitive strategy. For example, it would be useful to study where a differentiation on the privacy dimension is a successful strategy, or whether, as appears to have been the case so far, it is ultimately a niche strategy. What types of privacy regulation might be most successful and curtailing the market power of firms, where their market power stems from data? For example, in the fledgling genetic and genomic health industry, can privacy regulations be designed in a way which will not cement market power for an incumbent?

1.3.2.4 The Market for Privacy-Enhancing Technologies

Just as technology has led to an increase in privacy concerns, there has also been an increase in the use of technologies to help individuals and firms institute privacy protections. In general, the work on economics that has considered the spread and importance of these technologies has focused on ad-blocking software (Shiller, Waldfogel, and Ryan 2018; Gritckevich, Katona, and Sarvary 2022). However, this vastly understates the breadth and depth of these technologies—especially the extent to which they are used by firms. The new suite or stack of technologies is often referred to by the label of "privacy-enhancing" technologies. As the Office of Science and Technology Policy recently said:[2]

2. See: https://www.federalregister.gov/documents/2022/06/09/2022–12432/request-for-information-on-advancing-privacy-enhancing-technologies.

Privacy-Enhancing Technologies (PETs) present a key opportunity to harness the power of data and data analysis techniques in a secure, privacy-protecting manner. This can enable more collaboration across entities, sectors, and borders to help tackle shared challenges, such as healthcare, climate change, financial crime, human trafficking, and pandemic response. PETs can also help promote continued innovation in emerging technologies in a manner that supports human rights and shared values of democratic nations, as highlighted during the Summit for Democracy in December 2021, which included an announcement that the US and the United Kingdom are collaborating to develop bilateral innovation prize challenges focused on advancing PETs.

Such statements make it clear that policy makers believe that these technologies may help unravel the traditional trade-off between privacy regulation and economic efficiency documented by economists. Therefore, it makes sense for economists to both explore the extent to which such privacy-enhancing technologies are successful at achieving these aims and also any barriers that exist to their adoption. Indeed, there are a whole set of technologies designed to help firms manage their privacy internally, such as "consent managers," "privacy assessment managers," and "de-identification tools."[3] Economists are well placed to assess the extent to which these tools actually enhance privacy of customer, grounding such research on the insights of both organizational economics and enterprise-level diffusion of technology. It is also worth exploring the extent to which such tools reflect the deadweight welfare loss of document privacy regulation compliance relative to actual enhancements of privacy protection for consumers.

1.3.2.5 Decentralized Markets

The twin popular waves of cryptoeconomics and web 3 emphasize the emergence of decentralized markets. As such any discussion of markets and data should at least consider the potential consequences of decentralization of markets on privacy.

In general, I have expressed some skepticism about the extent to which many of the underpinning technologies or principles of blockchain technologies are naturally privacy enhancing (Marthews and Tucker 2019b, 2023). In particular the qualities of verifiability of data and immutability of data that are inherent in the blockchain appear to both restrict users' ability to control their data or privacy principles such as the right to be forgotten.

However, it is certainly the case that firms and individuals within this community are hopeful that there are potential ways of using these technologies to enhance privacy. For example, firms like Meeco and Solid are both hoping to establish privacy-compliant data markets and data owner-

3. See: https://www.trustradius.com/data-privacy-management.

ship structures (see https://www.meeco.me/platform and https://github.com/solid/solid). These new technologies and these new settings themselves present opportunities for researchers—given the promise that they themselves will generate data which allow us to study privacy-related behaviors and underlying preferences.

1.3.3 The Broader Economy and Privacy

1.3.3.1 Privacy and Inequality

There appears to be a positive correlation between privacy concerns, the enactment of privacy regulation, and GDP. We also know that when we use proxy measures for privacy concerns such as sign ups to the do-not-call list—an antitelemarketing innovation—this proxy for privacy preferences correlates with household income and is negatively correlated with demographic group indicators that have been historically disadvantaged in the US (Varian, Wallenberg, and Woroch 2005).

However, despite these striking correlations there is little work that tries to understand why there is this relationship between economic prosperity and privacy concerns. Correspondingly, there is little work which investigates whether there are distributional consequences of privacy protections or privacy regulations. For example, one provocative way of thinking about the advertising-supported Internet is that it is hugely redistributional. Rich people's data is valued by advertisers, and it is these high valuations which allow advertising-supported platforms to supply their services for free to many low-income households both domestically and internationally. Privacy regulation might restrict this redistribution. Whether or not the reader agrees with this rather provocative characterization, it does suggest that the question of whether privacy regulation or protection has distributional consequences is an important one to answer. After all, in economics we are interested in studying phenomena that affect both efficiency and equity.

Some initial research in this area has tried to at least establish some facts about the scale and accuracy of data collection (Neumann et al. 2022). This suggests that low-income households, less-educated households, and renters are far less likely to have demographic information accurately filed and also actually have data available to be collected about them.

1.3.3.2 Privacy and Discrimination

In general, as discussed in this agenda, it has been difficult to measure and calibrate privacy harms. This may explain the shift in the policy debate toward questions of algorithmic bias or discrimination. Just by terminology alone, the potential for such phenomena is alarming and also may reflect the untrammeled use of individual data by organizations and corporations. The growing algorithmic fairness literature is beyond the scope of this chapter;

see Cowgill and Tucker (2019) for an overview of the topic from an economics perspective. However, it is useful to think about how and whether privacy regulation reduces, doesn't affect, or augments the potential for algorithmic discrimination. It would seem from a theoretical perspective that any of these outcomes are possible. Privacy regulation might demand that firms reduce the amount of personally identifiable information that is available—this might hinder firms and governments' ability to audit their algorithms and identify instances of bias. Privacy regulation could also restrict the use of data by algorithms which give rise to algorithmic discrimination. Since the direction of the interaction between privacy regulation and algorithmic bias is unclear, this makes it an important area for empirical research.

1.3.3.3 Political Economy: Surveillance and Privacy

A clear gap in the focus of the current economics literature is that it has virtually all been focused on the question of commercial surveillance rather than government surveillance. However, the consequences of these two types of surveillance are not equal—unlike firms, governments can put you in jail and confiscate your property. As such understanding how the digital revolution has affected our conclusions about government and privacy is important.

There are two exceptions to this gap which are instructive. The first is a paper that explores the extent to which government surveillance of commercial searches associated with the PRISM scandal had chilling effects on customer behavior (Marthews and Tucker 2017). This area of work is important as it suggests that knowledge and fear of government surveillance actions can shape the commercial landscape, putting this topic squarely in the realm of microeconomics and industrial organization. Recent work by Beraja, Yang, and Yuchtman (2020) examined the relationship between government surveillance and economic success but taking more of a macroeconomics perspective. This is useful as it suggests that understanding government surveillance can help shape our understanding of important macroeconomic questions such as growth and trade.

Indeed, there appear to be many questions to uncover when it comes to privacy and trade. In the US there have been multiple attempts to try and bridge trade barriers with the EU caused by government surveillance, among other things. Indeed, the Safe Harbor Framework ended up having to be replaced by the Privacy Shield Framework due to the inadequacy of the current regime in complying with EU privacy regulations.[4] This uncertainty over trade and compliance has almost certainly had consequences that are important to study but have not yet been evaluated by economists.

4. See: https://www.ftc.gov/business-guidance/privacy-security/us-eu-safe-harbor-framework.

1.4 The Future

This chapter has been an attempt to set an agenda on privacy. However, it is written by a researcher who has been working on these topics for two decades. She anticipates both that she has missed things that are important and also made many wrong predictions about what is important. As a result, this chapter concludes by expressing excitement about what the research that young researchers who read this paper will do in the future.

Appendix

The FTC recently shared an Advance Notice of Proposed Rulemaking. Here are some illustrative questions. Answering these questions would indeed move the field forward:

1. Which practices do companies use to surveil consumers?
2. Which measures do companies use to protect consumer data?
3. Which of these measures or practices are prevalent?
4. Are some practices more prevalent in some sectors than in others?
5. How, if at all, do these commercial surveillance practices harm consumers or increase the risk of harm to consumers?
6. Are there some harms that consumers may not easily discern or identify? Which are they?
7. Are there some harms that consumers may not easily quantify or measure? Which are they?
8. How should the Commission identify and evaluate these commercial surveillance harms or potential harms? On which evidence or measures should the Commission rely to substantiate its claims of harm or risk of harm?
9. Which areas or kinds of harm, if any, has the Commission failed to address through its enforcement actions?
10. Has the Commission adequately addressed indirect pecuniary harms, including potential physical harms, psychological harms, reputational injuries, and unwanted intrusions?
11. Which kinds of data should be subject to a potential trade regulation rule? Should it be limited to, for example, personally identifiable data, sensitive data, data about protected categories and their proxies, data that is linkable to a device, or non-aggregated data? Or should a potential rule be agnostic about kinds of data?
12. Which, if any, commercial incentives and business models lead to lax data security measures or harmful commercial surveillance practices? Are some commercial incentives and business models more likely to protect

consumers than others? On which checks, if any, do companies rely to ensure that they do not cause harm to consumers?

13. Lax data security measures and harmful commercial surveillance injure different kinds of consumers (e.g., young people, workers, franchisees, small businesses, women, victims of stalking or domestic violence, racial minorities, the elderly) in different sectors (e.g., health, finance, employment) or in different segments or "stacks" of the Internet economy. For example, harms arising from data security breaches in finance or healthcare may be different from those concerning discriminatory advertising on social media, which may be different from those involving education technology. How, if at all, should potential new trade regulation rules address harms to different consumers across different sectors? Which commercial surveillance practices, if any, are unlawful such that new trade regulation rules should set out clear limitations or prohibitions on them? To what extent, if any, is a comprehensive regulatory approach better than a sectoral one for any given harm?

References

Acemoglu, D., A. Makhdoumi, A. Malekian, and A. Ozdaglar. 2022. "Too Much Data: Prices and Inefficiencies in Data Markets." *American Economic Journal: Microeconomics* 14 (4): 218–56.

Acquisti, Alessandro, Curtis Taylor, and Liad Wagman. 2016. "The Economics of Privacy." *Journal of Economic Literature* 54 (2): 442–92.

Acquisti, A., and H. R. Varian. 2005. "Conditioning Prices on Purchase History." *Marketing Science* 24 (3): 367–381.

Adjerid, I., A. Acquisti, R. Telang, R. Padman, and J. Adler-Milstein. 2016. "The Impact of Privacy Regulation and Technology Incentives: The Case of Health Information Exchanges." *Management Science* 62 (4): 1042–1063.

Athey, S., C. Catalini, A. Moehring, and C. Tucker. 2023. "The Digital Privacy Paradox: Small Money, Small Costs, Small Talk." NBER Working Paper 23488. Cambridge, MA: National Bureau of Economic Research.

Beraja, M., D. Y. Yang, and N. Yuchtman. 2020. "Data-Intensive Innovation and the State: Evidence from AI Firms in China." NBER Working Paper 27723. Cambridge, MA: National Bureau of Economic Research.

Bergemann, D., and A. Bonatti. 2011. "Targeting in Advertising Markets: Implications for Offline versus Online Media." *RAND Journal of Economics* 42 (3): 417–443.

Bergemann, D., and A. Bonatti. 2015. "Selling Cookies." *American Economic Journal: Microeconomics* 7 (3): 259–294.

Bergemann, D., A. Bonatti, and T. Gan. 2020. "The Economics of Social Data." arXiv preprint arXiv:2004.03107.

Bleier, A., A. Goldfarb, and C. Tucker. 2020. "Consumer Privacy and the Future of Data-Based Innovation and Marketing." *International Journal of Research in Marketing* 37 (3): 466–480.

Buckman, J. R., I. Adjerid, and C. Tucker. 2023. "Privacy Regulation and Barriers to Public Health." *Management Science* 69 (1): 342–350.

Campbell, J., A. Goldfarb, and C. Tucker. 2015. "Privacy Regulation and Market Structure." *Journal of Economics & Management Strategy* 24 (1): 47–73.

Chiou, L., and C. Tucker. 2012. "Data Storage, Data Privacy and Search Engines." Mimeo, MIT.

Coase, R. H. 1960. "The Problem of Social Cost." *The Journal of Law and Economics* 56 (3): 1–40.

Cowgill, B., and C. E. Tucker. 2019. "Economics, Fairness and Algorithmic Bias." Mimeo, MIT.

Fainmesser, I. P., A. Galeotti, and R. Momot. 2022. "Digital Privacy." *Management Science* 69 (6): 3157–3173.

Farrell, J. 1987. "Information and the Coase Theorem." *Journal of Economic Perspectives* 1 (2): 113–129.

Farrell, J. 2012. "Can Privacy Be Just Another Good?" *Journal of Telecommunications and High Technology Law* 10: 251.

Godinho de Matos, M., and I. Adjerid. 2022. "Consumer Consent and Firm Targeting after GDPR: The Case of a Large Telecom Provider." *Management Science* 68 (5): 3330–3378.

Goldfarb, A., A. Haviv, J. Miklos-Thal, and C. Tucker. 2020. "Digital Hermits." Mimeo, Rochester University.

Goldfarb, A., and C. Tucker. 2012a. "Privacy and Innovation." *Innovation Policy and the Economy* 12 (1): 65–90.

Goldfarb, A., and C. Tucker. 2012b. "Shifts in Privacy Concerns." *American Economic Review: Papers and Proceedings* 102 (3): 349–53.

Goldfarb, A., and C. E. Tucker. 2011. "Privacy Regulation and Online Advertising." *Management Science* 57 (1): 57–71.

Gritckevich, A., Z. Katona, and M. Sarvary. 2022. "Ad Blocking." *Management Science* 68 (6): 4703–4724.

Hirshleifer, Jack. 1971. "The Private and Social Value of Information and the Reward to Inventive Activity." *American Economic Review* 61 (4): 561–74.

Ichihashi, S. 2021. "The Economics of Data Externalities." *Journal of Economic Theory* 196: 105316.

Jia, J., G. Z. Jin, and L. Wagman. 2018. "The Short-Run Effects of GDPR on Technology Venture Investment." NBER Working Paper 25248. Cambridge, MA: National Bureau of Economic Research.

Johnson, G., S. Shriver, and S. Goldberg. 2022. "Privacy & Market Concentration: Intended & Unintended Consequences of the GDPR." Available at SSRN 3477686.

Johnson, G. A., S. K. Shriver, and S. Du. 2020. "Consumer Privacy Choice in Online Advertising: Who Opts Out and At What Cost to Industry?" *Marketing Science* 39 (1): 33–51.

Johnson, J. P. 2013. "Targeted Advertising and Advertising Avoidance." *RAND Journal of Economics* 44 (1): 128–144.

Jones, C. I., and C. Tonetti. 2020. "Nonrivalry and the Economics of Data." *American Economic Review* 110 (9): 2819–58.

Kim, J.-H., and L. Wagman. 2015. "Screening Incentives and Privacy Protection in Financial Markets: A Theoretical and Empirical Analysis." *RAND Journal of Economics* 46 (1): 1–22.

Kosinski, M., D. Stillwell, and T. Graepel. 2013. "Private Traits and Attributes Are Predictable from Digital Records of Human Behavior." *Proceedings of the National Academy of Sciences* 110 (15): 5802–5805.

Lin, T. 2022. "Valuing Intrinsic and Instrumental Preferences for Privacy." *Marketing Science* 41 (4): 663–681.

Marthews, A., and C. Tucker. 2019a. "Privacy Policy and Competition." Brookings Paper.

Marthews, A., and C. Tucker. 2023. "What Blockchain Can and Can't Do: Applications to Marketing and Privacy." *International Journal of Research in Marketing* 40 (1): 49–53.

Marthews, A., and C. Tucker. 2017. "The Impact of Online Surveillance on Behavior." In *The Cambridge Handbook of Surveillance Law*, edited by D. Gray and S. Henderson. Cambridge: Cambridge University Press. doi:10.1017/9781316481127.019.

Marthews, A., and C. E. Tucker. 2019b. "Blockchain and Identity Persistence." In *Cryptoassets: Legal, Regulatory, and Monetary Perspectives*, edited by Chris Brummer. New York: Oxford Academic online edition Oct. 24, 2019. Accessed Oct. 29, 2023. https://doi.org/10.1093/oso/9780190077310.001.0001.

Miklós-Thal, J., A. Goldfarb, A. M. Haviv, and C. Tucker. 2023. "Digital Hermits." NBER Working Paper 30920. Cambridge, MA: National Bureau of Economic Research.

Miller, A., and C. Tucker. 2011. "Can Health Care Information Technology Save Babies?" *Journal of Political Economy* 119 (2): 289–324.

Miller, A., and C. Tucker. 2014. "Health Information Exchange, System Size and Information Silos. *Journal of Health Economics* 33 (2): 28–42.

Miller, A., and C. Tucker. 2017. "Privacy Protection, Personalized Medicine, and Genetic Testing." *Management Science* 64 (10): 4648–4668.

Miller, A. R., and C. Tucker. 2009. "Privacy Protection and Technology Diffusion: The Case of Electronic Medical Records." *Management Science* 55 (7): 1077–1093.

Neumann, N., C. E. Tucker, L. Kaplan, A. Mislove, and P. Sapiezynski. 2022. "Data Deserts and Black Boxes: The Impact of Socio-Economic Status on Consumer Profiling." Mimeo, MIT.

Nissenbaum, H. 2004. "Privacy as Contextual Integrity." Symposium. *Washington Law Review* 79: 119. Available at: https://digitalcommons.law.uw.edu/wlr/vol79/iss1/10.

Nissenbaum, H. 2010. *Privacy in Context: Technology, Policy, and the Integrity of Social Life*. Stanford Law Books. Stanford: Stanford University Press.

Peukert, C., S. Bechtold, M. Batikas, and T. Kretschmer. 2020. "European Privacy Law and Global Markets for Data." Marketing Science 41(4): 663–869.

Posner, R. A. 1979. "Privacy, Secrecy, and Reputation." *Buffalo Law Review* 1: 28.

Posner, R. A. 1981. "The Economics of Privacy." *American Economic Review* 71 (2): 405–409.

Richards, N., and W. Hartzog. 2015. "Taking Trust Seriously in Privacy Law." *Stanford Technology Law Review* 19: 431.

Shiller, B., J. Waldfogel, and J. Ryan. 2018. "The Effect of Ad Blocking on Website Traffic and Quality." *RAND Journal of Economics* 49 (1): 43–63.

Spence, M. 1973. "Job Market Signaling." *Quarterly Journal of Economics* 87 (3): 355 –374.

Spiekermann, S., A. Acquisti, R. Böhme, and K.-L. Hui. 2015. "The Challenges of Personal Data Markets and Privacy." *Electronic Markets* 25 (2): 161–167.

Stigler, G. J. 1980. "An Introduction to Privacy in Economics and Politics." *Journal of Legal Studies* 9 (4): 623–644.

Tucker, C. 2014. "Social Networks, Personalized Advertising, and Privacy Controls." *Journal of Marketing Research* 51 (5): 546–562.

Varian, H., F. Wallenberg, and G. Woroch. 2005. "The Demographics of the Do-Not-Call List [Security of Data]." *IEEE Security & Privacy* 3 (1): 34–39.

Varian, H. R. 2002. "Economic Aspects of Personal Privacy." In *Cyber Policy and Economics in an Internet Age*, 127–137. Boston, MA: Springer.

Warren, S. D., and L. D. Brandeis. 1890. "The Right to Privacy." *Harvard Law Review* 4 (5): 193–220.

Zhao, Y., P. Yildirim, and P. K. Chintagunta. 2021. "Privacy Regulations and Online Search Friction: Evidence from GDPR." Available at SSRN 3903599.

2

The Economics of Privacy at a Crossroads

Alessandro Acquisti

By several accounts, the economics of privacy has grown into a remarkably successful field of research. As the means of collecting and using individuals' data have expanded, so has the body of work investigating trade-offs associated with those data flows. The number of scholars working in the area has grown, much like the breadth of topics investigated. References to the economic value of personal data have become common in policy and regulation, and so have mentions of economic dimensions of privacy problems.

Thinly veiled underneath those successes, however, lies a less encouraging trend. In this manuscript, I argue that the very success of the economics of privacy has laid the foundation for a potentially adverse effect on the public debate around privacy. Economic arguments have become central to the debate around privacy. When used as complements to considerations less amenable to economic quantification, those arguments are valuable tools: they capture a portion of the multiform implications of evolving privacy boundaries. When, instead, economic arguments crowd out those other

Alessandro Acquisti is the Trustees Professor of Information Technology and Public Policy at Carnegie Mellon University's Heinz College.

I gratefully acknowledge support from the MacArthur Foundation through grant 22–2203–156318-TPI. I am also grateful to several scholars for comments and critiques, including Idris Adjerid, Laura Brandimarte, Cristobal Cheyre, James Cooper, Brett Frischmann, Avi Goldfarb, Chris Hoofnagle, Brian Kovak, Michael Kummer, Tesary Lin, Jonathan Mayer, Klaus Miller, Verina Que, Ananya Sen, Priya Shah, Daniel Solove, Ryan Steed, Andrew Stivers, Lior Strahilevitz, Catherine Tucker, Joel Waldfogel, Frederik Zuiderveen Borgesius, one reviewer, and participants in workshops and seminars at HEC Paris, Massachusetts Institute of Technology, New York University, Princeton University, University of Maryland, University of Minnesota, and the ZEW Conference on the Economics of Information and Communication Technologies. For acknowledgments, sources of research support, and disclosure of the author's material financial relationships, if any, please see https://www.nber.org/books-and-chapters/economics-privacy/economics-privacy-crossroads.

noneconomic considerations from the public discourse around privacy, problematic scenarios arise. In one scenario, the economic analysis of privacy will keep growing in influence, but its overly narrow conception of privacy will impoverish rather than augment the depth of the debate around privacy. In a second scenario, less likely but equally problematic, the economics of privacy will progressively undermine its own relevance by failing to account for the complexity and nuance of modern privacy problems.

There is a third scenario—one this manuscript explores. The economics of privacy may expand its horizons and relevance both by considering economic dimensions and research questions that have so far received limited attention, and by accounting for the broader scholarship on privacy coming from other disciplines. As a complement to the contributions of other fields, rather than a substitute for them, the economics of privacy may keep thriving and remain a useful tool for debate and policy-making.

My argument, and this manuscript, proceed in three steps roughly focusing on the past, present, and possible future of the economics of privacy. In Section 2.1 I focus on the past. I review the rise of this field of research up to the current days and celebrate its successes. In Section 2.2 I take stock of the present and focus on the unintended consequences of those successes. I consider the shortcomings of the economics of privacy arising from its misconstruction or dismissal of critical privacy theories from other social sciences. In Section 2.3, I consider a possible alternative future for the economics of privacy. I propose ways of framing the economic debate around privacy that deviate from the focus of much (albeit not all) current research, which tends to concentrate on the economic costs of privacy protection at the expense of a richer array of yet unanswered questions.

2.1 The Rise of the Economics of Privacy

The economics of privacy is not a novel field of research. It boasts a venerable pedigree.[1] A wave of economic analyses of privacy started appearing near the end of the 1970s and the start of the 1980s. Chicago scholars interested in economics and law, such as Posner and Stigler, produced several of those analyses. They were the intellectual "pioneers"—in Hirshleifer's (1980) wording—who had discovered a "new territory [. . .] the intellectual continent we call 'privacy'" (649). It is not ungenerous to describe (using Hirshleifer 1980's words) those pioneers' views as "hostile" (650) toward privacy. Posner (1977, 1978, 1981) identified privacy, from an economic perspective, as the concealment of information (in particular, *negative* information), and surmised that regulations intended to protect privacy would

1. Others have reviewed its evolution in detail (among them Hui and Png 2006; Acquisti, Taylor, and Wagman 2016; Cecere et al. 2017; Goldfarb and Que 2023). Here, I only highlight a few key milestones.

ultimately be redistributive and result in economic inefficiencies. Stigler (1980) believed that privacy "connotes the *restriction* of the collection or use of information about a person or corporation" (625; emphasis added). He found the spur of new interest in it "paradoxical, for the average citizen has more privacy—more areas of his life in which his behavior is not known by his fellows—than ever before" (623). Not everyone agreed with those views. Hirshleifer (1980) countered that privacy was more than a restriction on data collection; it was about *autonomy within society*. He wondered whether the new continent that economics had discovered was not, in fact, merely a *peninsula* that those economic pioneers had mistaken for the mainland. In some sense, the dispute Posner and Hirshleifer commenced over four decades ago has never been truly resolved. Its relevance to the current debate around privacy will become apparent as this manuscript progresses.

After its first wave of research output, the economics of privacy went largely dormant until the mid-1990s, when a new generation of economists such as Varian, Noam, and Lauden started rediscovering the topic. The reasons why economic interest in privacy reemerged at that time seem clear in retrospect. The information technology revolution was transforming (digitizing) the collection and use of personal data, and the World Wide Web was developing. These scholars captured the impending economic implications of those changes. Varian (1996) diagnosed the link between economics and technology at the root of the modern privacy problem: data that was already theoretically public (or at least accessible) in physical format becomes much cheaper to capture, store, access, and share once digitized, and thus "more" public; as its price lowers, quantity demanded increases. Noam (1997) wrote about the economic interpretation of encryption and data protection. And Laudon (1996) was arguably the first economist to lay out the idea of data markets through which individuals could one day trade rights over their personal data. That idea has taken different manifestations in the roughly 25 or so years since it was first proposed and has been the subject of numerous proposals (from data dividends to data as labor; see Arrieta-Ibarra et al. 2018).[2]

2. In our 2016 review of the economics of privacy in the *Journal of Economic Literature* (Acquisti, Taylor, and Wagman 2016), as well as in other recent pieces (Spiekermann et al. 2015; Acquisti, Brandimarte, and Loewenstein 2020), we discuss some of the reasons why, although consumer data is now an asset explicitly or implicitly traded in a myriad of ways, personal data markets such as those envisioned by Laudon remain elusive—notwithstanding widespread scholarly and commercial interest. Central among those reasons are the absence of regulation creating well-defined property rights over personal information, as well as the fact that most of the more valuable personal data is not static (e.g., a person's gender) but dynamically co-created by the data subject and platforms or services the subject interacts with (e.g., a person's preferences, as revealed by her most recent search query or visited web site). Absent regulation explicitly giving individuals rights over their personal data (including co-created data), platforms maintain economic control over it, undermining consumers' ability to leverage parallel "data markets" to protect (or merely commercially benefit from trades over) their personal information.

The scholars who contributed to the economics of privacy in the mid-1990s added nuances to the minimalist view of privacy espoused by Chicago School scholars in the 1980s. For instance, Varian (1996) noted that individuals may strategically prefer to share some personal information while protecting other, not necessarily negative, information: the same consumer may want her preferences to be shared with a merchant (to get personalized offers), but not her reservation price (to avoid first-degree price discrimination).

Boosted by tectonic changes brought about by the development of the Internet, the field of the economics of privacy eventually took off. Over the last two decades, the costs of data collection, storage, and computation kept falling, while the sophistication of statistical techniques for inferential data analysis kept rising. These combined trends led to the development of strategies for data monetization and to the identification of personal data as an economic asset. This, in turn, spurred novel products and services, which created more data, which generated more value, which attracted more investments, and so forth. As this feedback cycle developed, the data economy grew, and so did the economics of privacy. Economically informed position papers from the 1990s were replaced by analytical models; empirical studies started testing the theories; field and lab experiments became commonplace; and the specific topics of investigation under the vast umbrella of "privacy" economic research started expanding and diversifying—although they remained mostly tied to the informational dimension of privacy. While in the early 2000s much research on this topic focused on data breaches and price discrimination, the topics covered have multiplied over time—from the relationships between data and competition and antitrust to the creation of data markets; from the link between privacy regulation and innovation to data-driven algorithmic bias; from experiments on consumer data valuation to studies of behavioral factors affecting privacy decision-making. The number of scholars authoring manuscripts in this field has increased, and their backgrounds have become more diverse—from mainstream economics to marketing, from information systems to computer science. The number of unique outlets (conferences and journals) publishing work in the field has also increased; it has become more common to see articles published in traditional premiere economic outlets such as the *American Economic Review*, the *Journal of Political Economy*, and the *RAND Journal of Economics*. There are anecdotal yet meaningful signals of relevance, too: the publication in the *Journal of Economic Literature* of a review of the field, and the hosting at the *National Bureau of Economic Research* of a workshop (in May 2022) and a tutorial (in November 2022) on the economics of privacy—both organized by two scholars who have been at the forefront of the revival of the field, Professors Goldfarb and Tucker. In a nutshell, one could say that over the course of four decades, the economics of privacy has attained a meaningful role within the economics mainstream.

2.2 Where Is the Economics of Privacy Going?

As economists, we like to talk about unintended consequences, often referring to undesired ramifications of regulatory interventions in the market. In this section, I discuss the unintended consequences of the success the economics of privacy has experienced as a field of research. I start by comparing the way economists have traditionally construed privacy to the conception of privacy developed by influential privacy scholars who have worked outside of the realm of economics (Section 2.2.1). I argue that as economists we have, by and large, adopted a reductionist view of privacy that overlooks the richness and nuance of the contemporary debate around privacy. Next (Section 2.2.2), I discuss the unintended consequences of that approach. They include an outsized focus on estimating the costs of privacy regulation at the expense of a more comprehensive analysis of the diverse trade-offs of privacy; a lack of attention to the many consumer harms of privacy intrusions; and a misapprehension of the lessons of behavioral privacy research. Ultimately, the rigorous but narrow approach to privacy (pioneered by Posner and Stigler but still—I argue—influential in today's economic research) carries the risk that economic arguments may crowd out of the public debate the discussion of privacy dimensions that are not grounded on economic analysis and yet are no less important.

2.2.1 How Privacy Economists Think of Privacy and How Privacy Scholars Outside Economics Think of Privacy

The essays Posner wrote concerning privacy in 1977, 1978, and 1981 proved over time remarkably influential, and not merely because of their citation count. Notwithstanding the dramatic growth and evolution of this field of research, the influence of those essays can still be detected, today, in the framing and scope of much (but not all) economic research in the field.

Posner makes four remarkable points in the first pages of his 1981 article. First, after having acknowledged different interpretations of the term *privacy*, Posner identifies one as the most deserving of economic attention: concealment. Second, Posner narrows down the scope of fruitful economic analysis of privacy to the study of *concealment of information*—and, more specifically, *negative information*: to the extent that an individual is deficient in some characteristics (in Posner's example, an employee may be deficient in terms of diligence, loyalty, or mental health), she will have an incentive "to conceal these deficiencies" (405) and to "invoke a 'right of privacy.'" If privacy is the concealment (first point) of information, and specifically of negative information (second point), the third point logically follows: "[b]y reducing the amount of information available to the 'buyer'" (in Posner's labor market example, an employer), privacy "reduces the efficiency of that market" (405). Posner's fourth point concerns consumer privacy behavior, which he deems consistent with theories of rational choice: "the literature on the economics of nonmarket behavior suggests that people are rational even in nonmarket transactions [. . .] [t]herefore, there seems to be no solid basis for questioning the competence of individuals to attach appropriate (which will often be slight) weight to private information—at least if 'appropriate' is equated with 'efficient'" (406).

I am not going to claim that Posner's construction of privacy as the concealment of *negative* information (his second point) still influences today's economic scholarship around privacy.[3] The notion of privacy being about something to hide has been repeatedly debunked (Solove 2007), and nowadays most economists, I venture, would reject the reasoning behind that claim. I am interested, instead, in discussing how Posner's other claims have influenced economic research in this area (including, for full disclosure, my own), and how they compare to the theories and findings of some prominent privacy scholars outside the economic domain. I am also not going to claim that the entirety of the economic discipline still endorses in lockstep all of Posner's other three points. Below, I attempt to highlight both cases where the field evolved and diversified, and cases in which Posner's conception of privacy still profoundly permeates our writings—including the research questions we tackle and the implications we draw.

A first difference between the mainstream economic approach to privacy and that of privacy scholars in other social sciences pertains to the very definition of privacy. Posner proposed that *concealment* (of information) was privacy's most interesting meaning from an economic standpoint. Since then, explicit or implied references to privacy as concealment, restriction, or protection of information have remained common in both analytical economic perspectives on privacy and in empirical economic works. As Lin (2022, 665) recently notes, "Economists often think of privacy preference as generated from the need to *protect one's private information* in market exchanges" (emphasis added). To be clear, in some cases the field has evolved from the Posnerian view. For instance, Noam (1997) referred to privacy as "an interaction, in which the rights of different parties collide" (51). And Jin and Stivers (2017) drew the key distinction between privacy processes and privacy outcomes, noting that consumers "want [. . .] to have a certain amount of *control* over the flow [of individual information]" (emphasis added). But the focus on information restriction still trickles up in our economic writings. For instance, Jin and Stivers also define "an individual's privacy outcome" as "the realized *restriction* on the flow and use of information" (1, emphasis added); "[a]n entity has more privacy as the flow and use

3. Although it still sporadically shows up in the public debate around privacy. In a 2013 interview, Eric Schmidt (then Google's CEO) famously answered a question concerning Google's privacy controversies by stating, "If you have something that you don't want anyone to know, maybe you shouldn't be doing it in the first place." See https://www.cnbc.com/inside-the-mind-of-google/.

of information about it is more restricted" (5).[4] And in a remarkable study of the use of electronic medical records to prevent AIDS deaths by enabling patient tracing, presented at the first NBER Workshop on the Economics of Privacy, Derksen, McGahan, and Pongeluppe (2022) construe privacy in terms of patients' refusal to be traced for medical purposes (hence the title: "Privacy at What Cost? Saving the Lives of HIV Patients With Electronic Medical Records").

For most privacy scholars (by which I refer to scholars whose research focuses predominantly on privacy across disciplines as diverse as sociology, psychology, behavioral research, communication, or philosophy), privacy may *include* concealment or protection as one means, but both its means and its ends are broader, more nuanced, and ultimately different from concealment. Across other social sciences, privacy is not just about concealment or exclusion. Privacy has been linked to (and defined in terms of) control, boundary regulation, contextual intregrity, and more (see Altman 1976 for a comparison of privacy theories; see taxonomies and references in Solove 2006 and Acquisti, Brandimarte, and Loewenstein 2015). Even when narrowly applied to information, "control" is construed as more than protection; it implies the ability both to protect and to share about oneself (Westin 1967). In essence, within much social science research, privacy is not a static condition of hiding but rather—as the American social psychologist Irwin Altman (1976) put it—a process of *boundary regulation*. Under this perspective, privacy is a dynamic and dialectic process through which individuals contextually manage the boundaries between the self and others. It is dynamic because the process changes and evolves according to context. It is dialectic because both sharing and protecting (for instance, personal information) can be privacy management behaviors. When a person chooses to share a secret with a friend to get her advice, that person is engaging in boundary regulation, as they selectively opted to share this information only with her. If the friend later betrays the person's trust (for instance, she gossips about that secret), that is the moment the boundary has been broken and the person's privacy violated.

The difference between concealment and control (or regulation) may appear too abstract and ambiguous. As economists, we may feel queasy about studying concepts seemingly as intangible as the "regulation of boundaries," and uncomfortable with the multitude of dimensions of privacy enumerated across the privacy literature. That multidimensionality may appear to lack the precision and rigor we need for analytical research. And yet the distinction is highly consequential in terms of how consumer

4. Dr. Stivers however notes, in reference to his 2017 manuscript, "Privacy, in our view, was a particular kind of outcome that we were in part trying to point out was too limited [. . .] Posner defines privacy as concealment, and throws out the rest, but we make the distinction precisely to point out that concealment isn't the issue, its control and the opening and closing, as appropriate" (personal communication with the author).

behavior around privacy is (mis)interpreted within economics. Through the lens of privacy scholarship, for instance, HIV patients being alarmed about medical tracing and rejecting electronic medical records (as in the findings by Derksen, McGahan, and Pongeluppe 2022 cited above) is not a failure of too much privacy but too little: when patients cannot trust how their data will be used, they avert sharing; if they could trust that their data would be protected and only used for the intended medical treatments, they would be more likely to share it with doctors and benefit from doing so.[5] By missing those nuances, as economists we risk self-selecting into an overly constrained analysis of the phenomenon we purport to study, or, worse, we risk ascribing to privacy merits or faults that may not be its own.[6]

A second notable difference between economic and privacy scholarship follows as a corollary of the definitional difference I have just highlighted. It pertains to the *scope* of the investigable privacy domain. Consistent with Posner's focus on privacy as concealment of information, most of the economic scholarship has concentrated on the study of *protection of data*. While the specific application areas have expanded through the years (to include medical privacy, technological innovation, algorithmic bias, online advertising, and so forth), the modeling literature has tended to focus on the collection of consumer preferences, traits, or reservation prices across various application domains and, with some exceptions (see Section 2.2.2.1), the empirical literature has focused on the economic ramifications of curtailing access to those data through regulation, self-regulation, or technology.

Privacy economic research has good reasons to focus on information and data. Information assets have become central to the economic calculus of people and organizations, and the novel privacy concerns that have arisen in recent decades are, at least on first analysis, informational concerns. However, in doing so, privacy economic scholarship deviates from the rest of social science privacy research and (I argue in Section 2.2.2.2) misses the bulk of harm individuals and society can suffer when privacy is mismanaged. Privacy scholars do not identify privacy with data, and Altman's theory of boundary regulation does not merely apply to informational boundaries. Multiple boundaries exist between the self and others, including spatial, bodily, and decisional. Those boundaries can take different embodiments depending on context; what they have in common is the alternating of the opening and closing of the self to others. This is why privacy, for privacy

5. In a study of state genetic privacy laws, Miller and Tucker (2018) find that approaches that give users control over redisclosure *encourage* individuals to obtain genetic testing, while notifications deter them.

6. With some exceptions (for instance, Laudon 1996 citing Westin 1967, or Bleier, Goldfarb, and Tucker 2020 citing Nissenbaum 2004), it is telling—and alarming—that references to the writings of some of the most influential scholars and theorists of privacy, such as Westin, Altman, Petronio, or Nissenbaum—to mention a few—are rare in economic writings. I too came to appreciate the significance of Altman's writings for economic research only following the completion of my doctoral studies.

scholars, is tied to—and sometimes a necessary antecedent for—other concepts such as freedom (including bodily freedom), dignity, liberty, autonomy (including decisional autonomy), and so forth. These other dimensions of privacy are hard to quantify and, if not entirely ignored, are thus to a great extent sidestepped in the economic debate around privacy.[7] And yet, sidestepping that definitional richness, I argue in Section 2.2.2, is why economic analysis fails to fully grasp the role and impact of privacy in society.

A third difference pertains to the divide between some economists' interpretation of consumer privacy behavior (and decision-making) and that of behaviorally focused privacy scholars, and their differing estimations of consumer demand for privacy. Posner and Stigler looked at consumers' disclosure decisions as economically rational processes, where individuals strategically signal positive traits but hide negative ones. The belief that consumers can make *economically* rational privacy decisions is still reflected today in the interest some economists have demonstrated toward data markets or toward privacy policy-making that favors informational interventions to assist consumers in navigating privacy trade-offs in the market. Even economists who acknowledge the challenge raised by informational asymmetries (for instance, Jin and Stivers 2017) highlight the role of informational interventions in ameliorating consumer privacy choice in the marketplace. That belief is also reflected in empirical research that attempts to demonstrate the stability of privacy preferences and the economic rationality of privacy decision-making (Lee and Weber 2021). That belief, in turn, informs how the results of empirical consumer research are interpreted in terms of consumer demand for privacy. As economists, we are trained in the concept of *revealed preferences*. If privacy is narrowly construed as *protection* of personal information, and if privacy behavior is (assumed to be) economically rational, then a revealed preferences perspective would lead us to interpret the abundant evidence of widespread public disclosures (facilitated by social media and embraced by a significant portion of the world population) as realizations of market equilibria that reflect consumers' "true" underlying preferences for privacy. In turn, such evidence could then be interpreted as proof that individuals do not care for privacy that much, and that (regulatory) interventions in this domain are therefore not advisable or required. Results from experiments where participants willingly departed with their personal information in exchange for tiny rewards (Athey, Catalini, and Tucker 2017; Grossklags and Acquisti 2007) may be interpreted as ultimately supporting these conclusions.

On the other hand, behavioral privacy research presents evidence in contrast with a Posnerian interpretation of purely strategic privacy decision-

7. Prudent and perhaps intentional as such sidestepping may sound from an economist's perspective, it raises one of the key issues this manuscript attempts to tackle: when we use economics to study privacy, are we aware that we may be missing the forest for the trees?

making and challenges the conclusion that experimental participants' willingness to share data for small rewards betrays lack of demand for privacy tout court. First, an extensive body of work has uncovered numerous hurdles—not just asymmetric information, but also bounded rationality and an array of cognitive heuristics and behavioral biases—that influence (and to some degree impair) strategic privacy decision-making in the marketplace (Acquisti, Brandimarte, and Loewenstein 2015; Acquisti, Brandimarte, and Loewenstein 2020). We will go back to that literature in Section 2.2.2.3. Second, behavioral research has actually provided clear evidence of extensive privacy-seeking behavior, both online and offline. Writing two decades before the Internet, Altman (1975, 1976) noted that privacy-regulating behaviors are common and sometimes instinctual. Boundary regulation implies a "continual adjustment and readjustment as new situations emerge" (1976, 23), with people implementing "desired levels of privacy by behavioral mechanisms such as verbal and paraverbal behavior, nonverbal use of the body, environmental behaviors and cultural norms and customs" (17). Those behaviors may be invisible to us economists merely because they escape our definitions of privacy. Ordinary examples from our daily lives abound offline (we lower our voice or change topic when a third party approaches as we are engaged in an intimate conversation with someone; we step aside from a group of friends when we get the call from the doctor's office with the results of a test), but also online (we alternate between different email accounts or online personae to separate personal from professional spheres; we pick privacy settings to manage the visibility of our social media posts). (See Acquisti, Brandimarte, and Loewenstein 2020, from which these examples are taken.) Actual studies (including self-report surveys, observational field works, and experiments) complement the anecdotal observations. For instance: a majority (58 percent) of social network site users surveyed by Madden (2012) had restricted access to their profiles; only 22 percent of CMU Facebook users publicly shared their date of birth in 2009 (down from 86 percent in 2005; Stutzman, Gross, and Acquisti 2013); 50 percent of participants in an experiment were unwilling to exchange a $10 anonymous gift card for a $12 trackable one (Acquisti, John, and Loewenstein 2013); following Apple's transition to the App Tracking Transparency framework (ATT) in 2021, which imposed an opt-in tracking framework for apps on the Apple ecosystem, an overwhelming share of iOS users opted *not* to be tracked;[8] and a substantial proportion of Internet users worldwide use ad blockers as tools to block unwanted ads from popping up on their browsers (the proportion varies from study to study, from 27 percent to close to 50 percent).[9] In fact, a recent study of the "reverse" privacy para-

8. See https://www.macrumors.com/2021/05/07/most-iphone-users-app-tracking-opt-out/.

9. See https://www.insiderintelligence.com/content/ad-blocking-growth-is-slowing-down-but-not-going-away.

dox (the investigation of privacy-seeking behavior among individuals who claim privacy to be of little importance to them) found that engagement in a broad array of privacy behaviors was very common in a US-based online sample of 255 participants. The vast majority of participants reported having engaged in most of the privacy behaviors randomly picked from a list and presented to them. In fact, even a majority of those participants who had claimed privacy not to be particularly important to them had engaged in those privacy-protective behaviors (Colnago, Cranor, and Acquisti 2023).

The empirical behavioral evidence may thus suggest that, contra the notion of digital denizens doing little to protect their privacy, consumers engage in privacy management all the time—that is, they continuously, and often without noticing, make decisions to regulate their degree of openness with others. This does not mean that they want to *protect* their data *every time* (Acquisti, Brandimarte, and Loewenstein 2020). Of course they do not: privacy, from an Altmanian perspective, is about dynamically seeking both openness and closeness, depending on context. In fact, and contrary to the notion of privacy as a modern invention, substantial multidisciplinary research (from history, anthropology, and ethnography, as well as ethology) provides evidence that privacy-regulating behaviors may be a universal trait of human societies across space and time. Such historical universality may be explained by an intriguing conjecture: there may be evolutionary roots to modern privacy concerns (Acquisti, Brandimarte, and Hancock 2022). The ability to detect through our senses the presence of others in our physical space and to recognize friend from stranger or foe and react accordingly provides a clear evolutionary advantage. Over time, as human cognition evolved, so did human ability to negotiate the boundaries between self and others for self-interest: to avoid threats and leverage opportunities. Thus, an evolutionary account of privacy can explain the remarkable diversity of dimensions (and definitions) of privacy across time and cultures (as Altman 1977 noted, privacy is simultaneously culturally universal and culturally specific) and can highlight the deep link, now as in our distant past, between the need for security and the drive toward privacy—or, to go back to economic terminology, our *demand for* privacy.

A fourth difference I want to highlight derives from the prior three and pertains to contrasting stances over privacy regulation. By and large, in other social sciences and in computer science, the value of privacy is often normatively (for economists, perhaps, paternalistically) assumed; strengths and weaknesses of different forms of protection are discussed; and among them, regulation is commonly accepted as a legitimate tool for policy intervention. In contrast, mainstream economic analysis has often been skeptical of or outright averse to privacy regulation (again, exceptions exist: see, for instance, Becker 1980, or Arrieta-Ibarra et al. 2018). At the very outset of the field of research, Posner (1981) lamented "the rash of recent privacy legislation and the high level of public as well as scholarly concern with privacy" (408). A little less than two decades later, Varian (1996) warned that as privacy was becoming a very contentious public policy issue, Congress may "rush into legislation without due consideration of the options. In particular, a poorly thought-out legislative solution would likely result in a very rigid framework that assigns individuals additional rights with respect to information about themselves but does not allow for ways to sell such property rights in exchange for other considerations" (108 of the 2009 edition). Roughly another 20 years later, in an exceptionally balanced piece, Jin and Stivers (2017) considered several tools and interventions available to policy makers interested in privacy, such as educating consumers, voluntary or mandatory disclosures, and minimum quality standards determining how firms should collect, store, use and share consumer data. Although they did not endorse or dismiss any of them, they contrasted interventions that focus on privacy processes, which ensure that "consumers and sellers have the tools to exercise appropriate control on the process" and "should help bolster a *healthy market to facilitate and honor their choice of privacy*" (emphasis added, as later in this manuscript I will get to the issue of whether policy interventions such as informational or educational campaigns can in fact assist consumer privacy choice), to "a more paternalistic approach that attempts to determine consumer preferences on privacy outcomes and directly impose that determination on the market." They also observed that a policy-making body would have such a variety of tools to apply "[o]nce it has decided that a market failure exists and it is likely to cause *net harm* to consumers" (21)—that is, only once economic damage has been established (emphasis added, again as I will go back to the concept of net harm, and whether it can be calculated, in Section 2.2.2.2). These analytical concerns are reflected in the empirical literature. Echoing Posner's skepticism toward regulatory interventions, a large share of empirical economic research on privacy has focused on documenting the costs and inefficiencies caused by protection of personal information and privacy regulation (see Section 2.2.2.1).

Different training and ideological differences can explain in part the gap between economists' and other scholars' stances on the merits of privacy regulation. Yet surely that gap is also driven by differences in how economists and privacy scholars *construe* privacy. The four differences I highlighted in this section are logically interrelated. If privacy is construed mainly in terms of concealment and in terms of individual, locally optimized, decision-making, then the abundant evidence of online disclosures will be taken as proof of weak individual preferences for privacy; and if rational behavior in the marketplace accurately captures those preferences, it will follow that privacy regulation is unnecessary at best and deleterious at worst. If, instead, privacy is more than concealment and pertains to more than information, then evidence of public disclosures will not be taken as proof that individuals do not care for privacy; in fact, under this alternative view they do, but behavioral hurdles and economic barriers make it hard for them to achieve the privacy they desire in the digital marketplace; hence regulation will be needed to allow individuals to manage their privacy in a world of endemic information asymmetry and systemic power imbalances. I expand on this in Section 2.2.2.3.

2.2.2 Unintended Consequences

The success of the economics of privacy as a research field was built in part on a narrow but analytically rigorous focus which pioneers such as Posner and Stigler proposed. That approach deviates from much of other social sciences' theorizing on privacy. In this section I discuss the unintended consequences of that deviation. Because as economists we sidestep the richness of the multiform dimensions of privacy in the literature outside economics, we end up spending more time focusing on the trees (informational costs) than the forest (the profound ramifications of the evolution of privacy boundaries in our digital societies). In doing so, we insulate ourselves from an array of empirical research questions that go beyond the study of the impact of data protection (Section 2.2.2.1), from the evidence of widespread consumer privacy harm (Section 2.2.2.2), and from the implications of privacy behavioral research (Section 2.2.2.3).

2.2.2.1 The Disconnect Between Empirical and Theoretical Economic Privacy Research

A first consequence of the narrow economic view of privacy is the disproportionate attention that empirical works have paid to one particular research question. While several exceptions exist (I offer examples below), a common focus of empirical research in this field has been the quantification of economic inefficiencies and costs arising from privacy regulation: from reducing the impact of online ads on hypothetical purchase intentions (Goldfarb and Tucker 2011) to decreasing the speed of adoption of electronic medical records and technologies that can save infants' lives (Miller and Tucker 2011) to reducing ecommerce spending (Goldberg, Johnson, and Shriver 2023)—just to name a few. Individually, these and many other studies are rigorous. In the aggregate, they highlight a disconnect between the dominant empirical analysis and the theoretical privacy economics literature.

The theoretical privacy literature has repeatedly reported highly nuanced economic effects of both information protection and information sharing. It has demonstrated over and over again (see a review in Acquisti, Taylor, and Wagman 2016) that both at the individual level (that is, in terms of individual welfare) and at the societal level (aggregate welfare), privacy protection can be either welfare-decreasing or welfare-enhancing, depending on context. The nuanced effects in terms of individual welfare are the easiest to illustrate intuitively using simple economic theory: Varian (1996) had already pointed out that *not* sharing personal data could both benefit the consumer (when that data was her reservation price) and harm her (when that data was her product preferences). Further, as Noam (1997) observed (and as we noted in Section 2.1), privacy is a domain where the interests and rights of different parties collide. Thus, there is no reason to expect ex ante that the interests of both data subjects and data holders will align, nor that the degree of privacy in the market will be optimal for both parties. There is no way (aside, perhaps and sometimes, through the use of privacy-enhancing technologies; see Section 2.3) to avoid certain trade-offs between data subjects and data holders. If privacy is redistributive, as Posner (1981) proposed, so is the *lack* of privacy (Acquisti, Brandimarte, and Loewenstein 2020).

The theoretical argument that illustrates how the effects of privacy on aggregate welfare may be similarly nuanced is less intuitive, because it can take multiple forms. Several theoretical analyses show, for instance, that *lack* of privacy protection can *decrease* aggregate welfare. They range from Hirshleifer's (1971) classic argument about private (not necessarily personal) information (the private benefits of information acquisition may outweigh its social benefit; in a pure exchange setting, information may have no social value as it merely results in a redistribution of wealth; thus, economic agents may overinvest in private information acquisition), to Hermalin and Katz's (2006) ex ante vs. ex post trade efficiency argument (under which the provision of privacy can create welfare-increasing equilibria that otherwise would be destroyed). One illustration of Hermalin and Katz's argument appears prescient today: "[f]or example, absent the ability to keep information confidential, people may not collect information about themselves (e.g., individuals might forgo AIDS testing if disclosure were mandatory), resulting in unintended adverse consequences" (212). Compare this example to the results in Derksen, McGahan, and Pongeluppe (2022): HIV patients may dodge tracing precisely because of their (often justified) fear that medical conditions will not be kept confidential. Credible assurances of privacy protection may induce patients to consent to tracing, thereby improving both individual and societal well-being.

With—again—important exceptions (such as Marthews and Tucker 2017; Neumann, Tucker, and Whitfield 2019; Buckman, Adjerid, and Tucker 2022), these theoretical nuances rarely surface in empirical works. Even when they do, the economist's skeptical stance toward regulation percolates all the way up to how we frame our results for the public; for instance, the careful study by Buckman, Adjerid, and Tucker (2022) I just cited—which found that privacy protection can *increase* demand for COVID-19 vaccines—was titled "Privacy Regulation and *Barriers* to Public Health" (emphasis added).

One possible explanation for the divide between empirical vs theoretical privacy economic literatures is simple: the empirical literature has tested all sorts of theoretical predictions but found support only for those which highlight the costs of data protection; the costs *are* there, and those results get published. An alternative explanation is self-selection in how we pick research questions and dependent variables (metrics) to investigate. For various reasons, we tend to pick questions that focus on the costs of regulation—and, often, we find evidence for those costs, since we rely on short-term metrics most likely to capture them. Those reasons may include training, mindset, exogenous events (the enactment of privacy regulations creating favorable conditions for field experiments), as well as researchers' cost-benefit analysis, based on data availability, accessibility, and publishability: it is hard to conduct rigorous empirical investigations of the impact of privacy regulation even on relatively available short-term market metrics (for instance: venture capital investments following the enactment of the *General Data Protection Regulation* (GDPR): Jia, Jin, and Wagman 2021; or app developers' monetization strategies following the introduction of Apple ATT: Kesler 2022; and so forth); it is even *harder* to look at the long-term ramifications of those regulations on more diverse metrics, including possibly beneficial effects—not because the latter ramifications do not exist but because they are much more difficult to quantify (they may be less tangible; the needed variables may not be readily available from corporate databases) and to causally link to the regulation itself (as those ramifications may manifest progressively in the longer term; I delve deeper into these challenges in Section 2.2.2.2.) Ultimately, our scholarly drive toward robust identification (which these papers often address with cleverness and rigor) shrinks the space of admissible research questions that can be addressed with sufficient precision to withstand the exacting peer-reviewing process. And given that economic journals are not usually averse to results exposing the unintended effects of regulation, the researcher's cost-benefit calculus can ultimately steer our choice of research questions. The result is a body of works individually rigorous but collectively incomplete.

2.2.2.2 The Economic Paradox of Privacy Harm and the Aggregation Problem

A corollary of empirical economic research's focus on the costs of privacy protection—and a second consequence of the narrow economic theorizing of privacy—is the sidestepping of evidence of an extensive amount of consumer and societal privacy harm.

As noted in Section 2.2.1, the economics of privacy has predominantly focused on informational issues. Accordingly, the literature has concentrated on a limited subset of harms associated with personal *data* and its regulation. For instance, the modeling literature has tended to associate consumer privacy harm with price or product discrimination arising from the tracking of consumer preferences (as in Taylor 2004 or Acquisti and Varian 2005), or with an abstract individual "taste for" privacy, which typically captures an individual's preferences concerning the amount of her personal information available to others (Farrell 2012). As noted, the empirical literature too—

with notable exceptions—has tended to focus on measuring data-related harms such as identity theft or the economic impact of regulatory protection of personal information. Because of this, many typologies of consumer privacy harm have been sidestepped by economic research. In fact, the very existence of consumer concerns over privacy has been sometimes a source of explicit bewilderment in our field. Consider Posner (1978): "[T]he privacy legislation movement remains a puzzle from the economic standpoint." Consider, again, Posner (1981): "[W]hy people should want to suppress such facts is mysterious from an economic standpoint" (referring to publicizing facts that have no possible value to potential transacting partners).[10] And consider, more recently, Wickelgren (2015): "While concerns about privacy and the collection of consumer information are becoming ubiquitous, they are raised in a fashion that is puzzling to an economist. That is, they typically do not explain what potential market failures may exist that would lead the market not to provide the optimal amount of privacy when consumers use Internet services such as search engines or shopping platforms." To be fair, theoretical work (e.g., Becker 1980; Hermalin and Katz 2006; Farrell 2012) did acknowledge the existence of distinct consumer preferences for privacy as an "intermediate" good (whose value is instrumental—e.g., protecting privacy to avoid identity theft) and as a "final" good (whose value is intrinsic—e.g., protecting privacy because of personal taste). But empirical estimates of the vast array and diversity of harm discussed at length in the legal privacy scholarship (Calo 2011; Citron and Solove 2022) are lacking within economics. Empirical evidence in adjacent fields such as communication research or human-computer interaction *has* repeatedly highlighted consumer privacy concerns with several commercial data practices (McDonald and Cranor 2010) and systemic gaps between their privacy expectations and those practices (Rao et al. 2016; Turow, Hennessy and Draper 2018). But those concerns and those gaps are rarely recognized as economic harm. In the US, courts have increasingly expressed skepticism toward the notion that individuals who merely felt that their privacy was violated—but only suffered injuries which were difficult to quantify—should be able to sue (Strahilevitz and Liu 2022).

Once we look at privacy research outside economics, we realize that the paradox of privacy harms is that their measurement is hard not because of their rarity but for the opposite reason: privacy harms are ubiquitous, but diverse in form, heterogeneous in likelihood, and varying in magnitude

10. Professor Strahilevitz alerted me of a 2004 decision signed by Posner, as circuit judge, in *Northwestern Memorial Hospital V. Ashcroft*, written over 20 years after his seminal economic analysis of privacy. The decision highlights the value of (medical) privacy: "Even if there were no possibility that a patient's identity might be learned from a redacted medical record, there would be an invasion of privacy." Professor Strahilevitz, however, added, "Some Posner scholarship after his Northwestern Hospital decision returns to his privacy-skepticism" (personal communication with the author).

and length. These disparate and context-dependent embodiments of harm make it hard to quantify or even just conceptualize privacy damages into a single intuitive metric. We have referred to this as the *aggregation problem* (Acquisti, Brandimarte, and Loewenstein 2020). Harms associated with misuses of personal data include both those immediately recognizable as economic costs and those with less directly quantifiable (yet no less important) repercussions, such as physical harm, reputational harm, psychological harm, autonomy harm, discrimination harm, and relationship harm (Citron and Solove 2022). Under each of these categories, numerous distinct subinstances of harm can be defined: from identity theft to price discrimination, from attention and time waste to chilling effects, from hiring discrimination to filter bubbles narrowing individual choice, from stigma and psychological harm to rare but catastrophic physical consequences, and more. Commercial surveillance (Zuboff 2015) practices that increase the amount of consumer data collected and shared with third parties—often without individuals' knowledge and consent—ultimately increase the stochastic risk that any one of those myriad possible harms may occur. Therefore, while the likelihood of any individual type of harm occurring may be low, the typologies of possible harms are so many that surveillance practices ultimately elevate the statistical expected cost of commercial surveillance for each consumer and for the aggregate of consumers. And yet that expected cost remains hard to quantify (for scholars, policy makers, and the consumer herself) because of the aggregation problem.

Consider the following examples out of the myriad scenarios in which the collection of consumer data has tangible, significant, and far-reaching ramifications which remain challenging to capture in economic analysis.

Scenario 1: every time a person visits a web site, the time it takes for its content to load is extended by the plethora of trackers that collect information about the visitor and pass it to other third parties for the purpose of online advertising. This happens on the vast majority of web sites. This transaction cost is small at the individual visit level.[11] Aggregated across multiple visits conducted by an individual over time, and across multiple individuals, the aggregated opportunity cost of time lost to trackers is however significant. This scenario is an example of a widely common (high likelihood) cost that is minimal at the event-level but remarkable in the aggregate.

Scenario 2: in a handful of cases, American prosecutors "have used text

11. But not negligible. Borgolte and Feamster (2020) tested how privacy-focused browser extensions for Google Chrome and Mozilla Firefox affect browser performance. In their tests, while using those extensions came at some cost, those costs were offset by performance improvements due to blocking tracking. They write, "Contrary to Google's claims that extensions which inspect and block requests negatively affect browser performance, we find that a browser with privacy-focused request-modifying extensions performs similar or better on our metrics compared to a browser without extensions" (2275). For instance, they report that extensions that merely block online trackers, such as Disconnect, can reduce actual page-load time by as much as 244ms (median)—nearly a quarter of a second per visited page, per user.

messages and online research as evidence against women facing criminal charges related to the end of their pregnancies." For instance, in 2017, a Mississippi woman, Latice Fisher, "was charged with second-degree murder after a failed pregnancy [. . .] Prosecutors drew heavily on Fisher's search history. Notably, local reporting claims the police found record of these searches from Fisher's own phone rather than through Google itself."[12] Following the US Supreme Court's overturn of *Roe v. Wade* with its 2022 *Dobbs v. Jackson Women's Health Organization* decision, concerns have grown over the way police agencies may use search, browsing, or app data against women who merely tried to learn about abortion (Ms. Fisher's case was later dismissed, but only after she had spent time in jail).[13] This is an example of an event with low probability of occurrence but major individual consequences.

Scenario 3: in September 2018, a UN report highlighted the role of social media in fomenting hatred and ultimately genocidal violence (including mass killings, rapes, and destruction) in Myanmar.[14] The report called out Facebook as "a useful instrument for those seeking to spread hate" (14): the Myanmar military had used Facebook systematically to engage in propaganda against the Rohingya people. Facebook itself, through an independent report it commissioned to the BSR (Business for Social Responsibility), admitted its role in not "doing enough to help prevent our platform from being used to foment division and incite offline violence."[15] It is important to point out the central role the tracking of personal data by social media platforms plays in these and similar societal dynamics. That role is central not merely because social media relies on the monetization of personal information for its sustainment (for instance, via targeted advertising) but also because personal information is critical to foster engagement. Algorithms use personal data to select which information to show to which users to increase the amount of time they spend using the services and get exposed to ads. And those algorithms may be blind to whether they are encouraging a visitor to watch one more video about their favorite football team—or they are riling her up with rage against the purported misdeeds of another group of people. This is an example of a very common occurrence (algorithmic targeting) contributing to (among other things) exceedingly rare events with catastrophic individual and societal consequences (genocidal violence).

Scenario 4: Bradshaw and Howard (2018) found evidence of organized social media manipulation campaigns in 48 countries, with at least one party or government agency in each of the analyzed countries using social media

12. See https://www.theverge.com/23185081/abortion-data-privacy-roe-v-wade-dobbs-surveillance-period-tracking.

13. See https://www.pregnancyjusticeus.org/victory-for-latice-fisher-in-mississippi/.

14. See https://www.ohchr.org/Documents/HRBodies/HRCouncil/FFM-Myanmar/A_HRC_39_64.pdf.

15. A. Warofka, "An Independent Assessment of the Human Rights Impact of Facebook in Myanmar," Facebook (2018; revised 2020); see https://about.fb.com/news/2018/11/myanmar-hria/.

to manipulate domestic public opinion domestically including through disinformation campaigns. As in the Myanmar case, personal data play a central role in these operations, especially via misinformation designed to target and appeal to specific groups. And yet, while social media *may* sway small but ultimately key portions of voters in very close elections (Aral and Eckles 2019), it may be impossible to conclude definitively whether and when an election was won or lost due to how unknowing voters' data was used to target them.[16] In fact, the very ability of so-called filter bubbles to significantly affect downstream societal dynamics has been a subject of debate (Bruns 2021). Considering the far-reaching ramifications (both social and economic) of a nation voting in one leader over the others (or social media platforms amplifying already occurring dynamics of polarization), researchers and policy makers thus face a paradox and a challenge. The paradox is that data-driven online campaigns may have downstream effects on the citizenry that are potentially staggering, yet for which it is impossible to rigorously demonstrate and precisely estimate a causal relationship. The challenge is that the more we attempt to decrease the probability of a Type I error in investigating those relationships and in guiding policy, the more we risk making a Type II error: dismissing the potentially far-reaching social ramifications of the loss of privacy.[17]

To emphasize complexity and heterogeneity, the four selected scenarios vary in likelihood, magnitude, and typology of privacy harm. And yet they are mere examples from a broader and potentially unbounded set. Countless other scenarios and alternative downstream harms may exist, because, once collected, the boundaries of usage of personal information are undefinable and unpredictable.

Lin (2022) has estimated and compared instrumental and intrinsic preferences (valuations) for privacy—a distinction similar to Farrell's analysis of privacy as an intermediate and as a final good. It is important to note that the distinction between instrumental and intrinsic preferences for privacy is different from the measurement of different typologies of realized consumer

16. At least in the case of the 2016 EU referendum campaign in the UK and the Cambridge Analytica scandal, the letter by the UK Information Commissioner on the investigation into use of personal information and political influence ultimately found that Cambridge Analytica was "not involved in the EU referendum campaign in the UK" (2). The Commission however also confirmed the existence of "systemic vulnerabilities in our democratic systems" associated with new tracking and targeting technologies (see https://ico.org.uk/media/action-weve-taken/2618383/20201002_ico-o-ed-l-rtl-0181_to-julian-knight-mp.pdf).

17. This challenge is underscored by recent and seemingly contrasting results of studies investigating the impact of social media (and Facebook specifically) on variables such as political polarization or subjective well-being. Contrast Nyhan et al. (2023) and Guess et al. (2023), who find an amplifying but not polarizing effect of exposure to like-minded sources or reshares on Facebook, to Allcott et al. (2020), who find that deactivating Facebook for the four weeks before the 2018 US midterm election did reduce political polarization. Or contrast Vuorre and Przybylski (2023), who do not find an association between Facebook use and measures of subjective well-being (using observational data) to, again, Allcott et al. (2020), who find a negative association (using a field experiment).

privacy harm we are considering here. Such harm is stochastically realized and unpredictable ex ante. Thus, it is independent of both a consumer's intrinsic preference for privacy and—due to information asymmetries—of her expected economic trade-offs from sharing or protecting data as well. For example, a consumer may bear high material costs from identity theft regardless of how privacy sensitive she is, and independently of whether she expects her identity to be stolen.

While the ex post realization of consumption utility from any economic good may deviate greatly from its ex ante anticipation and consumer expectation (the costly car the consumer purchases could turn out to be a lemon), the case of privacy is unique. Data, unlike physical goods, can be nonrival (Jones and Tonetti 2020) and nonexclusive, and once revealed is subject to repeated, potentially unending secondary use. Varian (1996) first observed that widespread secondary use of digital data could give rise to externalities. Individuals rarely know or predict the many possible secondary uses of their data or their consequences. Examples in the literature abound: now and again, new ways to collect and use personal information are discovered, and users' expectations regarding the privacy of their data are often distant from reality (for instance, see Liu et al. 2011). Information asymmetries are systemic and endemic in the privacy domain. And since the value of data—and thus of privacy—can often be determined only ex post (that is, based on the context in which information is used),[18] even a consumer who knowingly engages in a data transaction with another party will ultimately face trade-offs she is not able to predict, account for, or control as a rational economic agent.

Those data externalities may be both negative and positive. But the peculiar (among other economic goods) combination of lack of consumer awareness regarding data uses and lack of control over those uses is precisely what makes it impossible for consumers to make optimizing decisions, reducing the risk of negative externalities while increasing the probability of positive ones (choosing consumption levels of privacy, so to say, to match its marginal costs to its marginal benefits). One cannot optimize for something they neither know nor control.

The context-dependent nature of privacy harm and its ex-post-determined trade-offs also raise serious questions over the ability of data markets to fairly capture the value of privacy. At worst, they may make it hopeless to attempt to aggregate privacy net harm into a single economic estimate. Like the consumer, the regulator thus faces the challenge of comparing the social marginal costs to the social marginal benefits of personal data. But the empirical privacy literature stops short of helping the regulator. None of the hurdles we discussed—the aggregation problem, the unbounded set

18. Leakages of jogging patterns from your exercise app may alternately lead to your learning new tips and techniques, receiving undesired advertising, or—if you are a military officer in a war zone—getting killed (see https://meduza.io/en/news/2023/07/11/killed-former-submarine-commander-in-krasnodar-could-have-been-tracked-by-running-app).

of data usages and consequences, and the entanglement of positive and negative data externalities—can reasonably support the conclusion that consumer privacy losses have no harmful effects on consumer welfare aside from subjective concerns. The economics of privacy has to a great extent sidestepped the evidence of consumer privacy harm. Because of that, we measure the tip of the iceberg and remain unfamiliar with its mass underwater; in Hirshleifer's terms, we focus on a peninsula and miss the continent of privacy damages.

2.2.2.3 Implications Arising from the Behavioral Literature

A third consequence of the narrow economic theorizing of privacy is a misapprehension of the implications of several decades of behavioral privacy research.

As we noted earlier in this section, mainstream economics and behaviorally focused research have interpreted differently the results of empirical studies of consumer demand for privacy. Mainstream research, following Posner's mold, tends to believe in a process of rational decision-making. Under this account, consumers' online behaviors adequately capture their demand for privacy. The hurdles consumers face in making privacy choices (especially asymmetric information) are at times acknowledged by careful scholars (see, for instance, Jin and Stivers 2017), but informational and educational interventions are presented as viable strategies to assist privacy-conscious consumers.

Conversely, behaviorally focused research tends to highlight how those hurdles distort revealed preferences for privacy in the marketplace. According to this account, informational, behavioral, and economic hurdles, far from being sidenotes or exceptions, are ubiquitous, systemic, and central in consumer choice. Hence, they make consumers' desired degrees of privacy unattainable through market interactions. Ultimately, no amount of informational or educational intervention may remedy those systemic barriers.

To understand why, let us consider those hurdles. Purely information hurdles (such as asymmetric information) have been considered near the end of Section 2.2.2.2. From a behavioral perspective, educational and informational interventions do not necessarily ameliorate those informational hurdles and thus consumer privacy decision-making. First, the behavioral literature suggests that education and transparency, by themselves, are ineffective—they may be necessary but not sufficient tools for privacy management. Notice and consent regimes do not even resolve the basic problem of information asymmetry: they are exorbitantly costly for end users (McDonald and Cranor 2008), unhelpfully ambiguous and therefore unactionable (Reidenberg et al. 2015),[19] and crash under the weight of both

19. In fact, even when consumers do read privacy notices, their interpretation of what actual data policies those notices entail seems to "depend more on their preexisting expectations" than on the terms of the notices themselves (Strahilevitz and Kugler 2016, S71).

the myriad privacy notifications, options, and requests consumers are inundated with daily[20] and our innate bounded rationality. Second, educational and informational interventions crash against a second set of hurdles: a vast array of cognitive and behavioral factors that can affect and impair privacy decision-making (Acquisti, Brandimarte, and Loewenstein 2015, 2020), and which in fact can be exploited by platforms and services providers via so-called dark patterns (Acquisti et al. 2017): whoever controls the user interface controls the architecture of choice.

Drawing attention to those behavioral factors is far from suggesting that consumer privacy behavior is irrational, or that privacy choices are erratic and unaffected by preferences, incentives, and calculus. Rather, it means emphasizing that privacy decision-making deviates in systematic ways from the theoretical prediction of rational choice models, which assume complete information, stable preferences, and procedural invariance—all assumptions the empirical privacy literature has shown untenable (Rao et al. 2016; Acquisti, John, and Loewenstein 2013; Tomaino, Wertenbroch, and Walters 2021). As we noted elsewhere (Acquisti, Brandimarte, and Loewenstein 2015, 2020), privacy decision-making (as decision-making in general) is rather the result of both deliberative (utility-maximizing) and behavioral factors.

In fact, the evolutionary account of privacy concerns we have presented in Section 2.2.1 offers a unifying explanation for the various informational and behavioral hurdles we have chronicled here. In the offline world, privacy management is often instinctual, almost natural (which does not imply, however, that one can always achieve the privacy they desire). Online, privacy management is more arduous because of an evolutionary *mismatch* (Pani 2000): we lack the cues humans have evolved to rely on to manage the boundaries of public and private, to detect the presence of others and react accordingly. As we travel on a crowded train, we quickly sense another person's peeking at the documents open on our screen; as we walk in a street, we notice the steps of someone following us too closely. On the Internet, we do not *see* or *hear* Facebook or Google tracking us across all sorts of digital domains. Notice and consent mechanisms—as well as educational or informational interventions—fail because they do not account for the underlying nature of consumer privacy decision-making. Worse, they amount to exercises in consumer *responsibilization*—that is, asking consumers to take charge of a problem they did not create and cannot really control. And they do little to solve the worsening problem of user interfaces designed to nudge consumers toward more engagement and self-disclosure.

Other hurdles arise from the "supply side" of privacy (we have considered

20. Skiera, Miller, and Jin (2022) find that if a user were to make all possible decisions regarding the provision of permission for data processing under the GDPR for each new publisher she visits in a day, she would spend 79.13 minutes per day in "decision time." See also Cooper (2023).

them extensively in Acquisti, Taylor, and Wagman 2016). Economic barriers make it overly costly for consumers to comprehensively manage their digital privacy, and they often render privacy options entirely inaccessible. These include lack of viable market alternatives (or alternatives being exceedingly onerous), switching costs, adoption costs, privacy externalities, and so forth.

Informational, behavioral, and economic hurdles combine to cripple consumers' ability to manage online privacy. In Altman's terms, they render *achieved* privacy outcomes different from *desired* ones, thus justifying calls for policy makers' intervention.

Related to this discussion is a specific and contentious stream of behavioral work that has been the object of particular misapprehensions and thus confusion about the implications of empirical research: the privacy "paradox." The paradox is the purported gap or dichotomy between privacy mental states (such as preferences, attitudes, or even intentions, often reflecting a claimed desire for privacy) and actual behaviors (seemingly reflecting a carelessness toward privacy). Few other areas of privacy research have attracted as much attention and caused as much disagreement as the privacy paradox: Is it real, or is it a myth (Solove 2021)? In recent works outside the economic domain (Colnago, Cranor, and Acquisti 2023; Acquisti, Brandimarte, and Loewenstein 2020), we have argued that much of the disagreement over the paradox of privacy has been caused by conceptual confusions. I summarize here a few key points that may be of relevance to the economic debate. A first source of confusion is that the very term *paradox* is interpreted differently by different scholars in the field.[21] This leads to disagreements over the *paradoxical* (or not) nature of a possible mental states/behaviors gap that are entirely lexicological—if a paradox has an explanation, is it still paradoxical? Opinions vary—and thus have little bearing on the actual empirical comparison of those mental states and behaviors. A second and more consequential source of confusion is the seemingly implicit assumption in much of the work in this field that the question, Do privacy mental states match behaviors? can be answered broadly and conclusively in

21. As noted in Acquisti, Brandimarte, and Loewenstein (2020), the term *paradox* has two similar but subtly contrasting meanings: a "self-contradictory statement that at first seems true" (Merriam-Webster), but also a "seemingly contradictory" statement that is "perhaps true." The dichotomy between stated mental states (such as preferences or intentions) and behaviors is the (apparent) contradiction. Some scholars appear to look at the dichotomy through the lens of the first definition: they search for explanations of that dichotomy, and when they find them, they conclude that there is no self-contradiction, and thus also no paradox (see, for instance, Solove 2021). Other scholars appear to look at the dichotomy through the lens of the second definition, which puts the emphasis on the fact that statements that are seemingly in contradiction could in fact be simultaneously correct. For the latter scholars, it's the dichotomy that is paradoxical, even though it can be explained; for them, the fact that dichotomies between privacy attitudes and behaviors can be explained does not imply that the underlying dichotomies do not in fact exist. Ultimately, focusing on the "paradoxical" nature of the gap (that is, focusing on whether the gap is paradoxical, or is a myth) no longer seems productive, because the disagreement over this point is more driven by grammar than empirical evidence. It would be more fruitful to focus on when, whether, and how, behaviors match vs. deviate from mental states.

static, binary terms: yes or no. This, of course, is folly: answering that question in such terms would require believing that attitudes must either always match behaviors or never do. Whereas everything about privacy (including decision-making) is dynamic and contextual. Thus, it is more plausible to expect that privacy attitudes, preferences, and mental states will sometimes predict and match behaviors (Dienlin and Trepte 2015) and sometimes will not (Norberg, Horne, and Horne 2007). The gap between privacy mental states and behaviors is therefore neither a myth, nor is it always guaranteed.

This brings us back to the issue of what policy implications to draw from the evidence that sometimes (but not always) a gap will exist between mental states and behaviors, and what implications to draw from the behavioral privacy literature at large. The privacy paradox has acted as a Rorschach test, to which people assign the most diverse interpretations based on their own assumptions and from which they thus draw the most diverse policy conclusions. One conclusion (with which I disagree) is that the privacy paradox literature demonstrates that people do not really care about privacy or do not really know what they want, and therefore no public intervention is needed, other than perhaps some informational intervention. A different conclusion (with which I agree) is that the existence of a gap between mental states and market choices reflects precisely those economic and behavioral hurdles that we have identified in this section, which justify or may even require public policy intervention.

2.2.3 The Inversion of the Overton Window of Privacy Debate

I have highlighted both successes and unintended consequences of the narrow theorizing of privacy embraced by much contemporary economic research. In concluding this section, I consider the ultimate (if potential) repercussion that embrace may produce: economic arguments progressively crowding out non-economic arguments in the public policy debate around privacy. If this risk were to materialize (and, I argue, there are signs of that happening), it would represent a remarkable inversion of the "Overton window" of legitimate policy discourse around privacy.

In the 1990s, Joseph Overton—a political scientist at the Mackinac Center for Public Policy—argued that politicians are constrained in their support of policies by a "window" of acceptability, which includes the policies that, at any given time, a society accepts as legitimate options.[22] That window can shrink or expand based on how societal values evolve. A radical or even unthinkable idea can, over time, become popular and thus acceptable and ultimately be embedded in policy. Through a reverse process, a once legitimate and acceptable idea can, over time, become radical and eventually unacceptable.

How does the concept of an Overton window apply to privacy? In Section

22. See https://www.mackinac.org/7504.

2.2.1, I pointed to scholarly research indicating that the *drive* for privacy is not a modern phenomenon. Evidence suggests it is a universal (albeit ever fluctuating) construct in human cultures across history and geography. The same, however, cannot be said of the notion of privacy as a fundamental human *right*. Construing privacy as a right is a modern development, a process that has panned out progressively and unevenly over time across different cultures (Hixson 1987). Through that process, in the second half of the 20th century the notion of privacy as a fundamental right reached sufficient legitimacy to be ingrained in the principles of an economic organization such as the OECD. In its 1980 *Guidelines on the Protection of Privacy and Transborder Flows of Personal Data*, the OECD remarked that privacy protection laws had been introduced in several member countries "to prevent what are considered to be violations of *fundamental human rights*, such as the unlawful storage of personal data, the storage of inaccurate personal data, or the abuse or unauthorised disclosure of such data" (Preface; emphasis added).[23] The *Guidelines* added, "Member countries have a common interest in protecting privacy and individual liberties, and in reconciling fundamental but competing values such as privacy and the free flow of information."

That process—which saw even economic organizations legitimize privacy as a fundamental human right—may have started reversing in the 21st century. The rise of the economics of privacy has not merely provided a useful analytical complement to values-grounded views of privacy but may also have diminished the currency of notions of privacy as a right by framing data (and privacy) as tradable assets. When Posner (1977, 1978, 1981) outright dismissed attempts to link privacy to broader values such as freedom and autonomy, his contemporaries (Baker 1977; Bloustein 1977; Hirshleifer 1980) recoiled. They balked at the reductionist viewpoint Posner had espoused. Bloustein (1977) wrote: "Posner's theory is simplistic, not simple, because it accomplishes its objective by avoiding, rather than confronting, complexity. He seduces by reduction, rather than convincing by explanation. The simple analytical elements of the scheme do not add up to the complex whole. His Truth about Privacy turns out to be some truth about one aspect of privacy" (429). Yet Posner's framework flourished within economics and over time may have influenced public policy. When the OECD in 2013 revisited its 1980 *Guidelines*, the term *fundamental value* had replaced the original "fundamental right."[24] In fact, the term *fundamental human right* was no longer to be found in the revised *Guidelines*. The recognition of a "fundamental right" was no longer explicitly linked to privacy—even though it was explicitly used in reference to *other* rights, such as freedom of speech, freedom of the press, and an open and transparent government, which

23. See https://www.oecd.org/sti/ieconomy/oecdguidelinesontheprotectionofprivacyandtransborderflowsofpersonaldata.htm.

24. See https://www.oecd.org/sti/ieconomy/oecd_privacy_framework.pdf.

"[p]rivacy rules should also consider" (35). The 2013 revision also replaced the term *danger* (to privacy and individual liberties) with the term *risk* (35), reflecting an increased emphasis on risk assessment. What else had changed? The terms *right* and *economic* appeared 32 and 7 times, respectively, in the 1980 *Guidelines*. They appeared 61 times and 48 times, respectively, in the 2013 revision, reflecting both the phenomenal growth of the data economy and the evolution of our priorities in discussing it.

The encroachment of economic considerations in matters of privacy policy was not limited to OECD documents. As the number of lobbyists for the data industry kept growing in Brussels and DC in recent decades, industry-funded think tanks increasingly promoted data-economics arguments against the enactment of privacy regulation. Not coincidentally, references to economic considerations (such as consumers' right to opt out of sale of their data or businesses' legitimate interest to process data) and economic factors appeared in regulations such as the *California Consumer Privacy Act* (CPPA) in the US and the GDPR in the European Union. Even the historical 2022 *Rulemaking on Commercial Surveillance* by the Federal Trade Commission included numerous questions aimed at quantifying or estimating the economic dimensions of privacy.

Economist colleagues may disagree with my interpretation of the trends of the privacy debate and may spot an opposite trend. They may lament—much like Posner four decades ago—regulators' archaic reliance on values-based normative arguments and their blindness to the soundness and objectivity of economic arguments. Some may even consider what I detect as an emergent unintended consequence to be a very much intended and well-needed progression in the policy discussion around privacy. Yet if values-grounded arguments had remained so powerful and persuasive among policy makers, US regulators would eventually have implemented the OECD principles from the 1980s—which stipulate mandatory standards of protection for all personal data—rather than the patchwork of notice and consent approaches still dominant today (and which we have critiqued in prior sections). On the contrary, the influence of economic considerations and industry interests has been evident even in the evolution of drafts of comprehensive European policy interventions such as the *GDPR* (Atikcan and Chalmers 2019; Christou and Rashid 2021). Considering the vast network of organizations lobbying against privacy regulation—as well as the inherent power asymmetry between the concentrated economic interests of large industry players and the diffuse, atomistic interests of uncoordinated individual citizens (Olson 1965; Acquisti, Brandimarte, and Loewenstein 2020)—a once unthinkable scenario now seems possible: the Overton window of acceptable discourse around privacy may be inverting. After a centuries-long evolution in the direction of construing privacy as a fundamental right, the very act of valuing privacy independently of economic evidence may be deemed naïve, and eventually radical in some circles. An emerging policy mindset would be that, if there is no easily quantifiable economic harm, then there is no privacy concern worth worrying about. Under such a mindset, policy-making would narrow its focus on what our field has been able to quantify in economic terms—at the risk of discounting harder-to-quantify evidence of privacy harm.

Even nowadays, at economic conferences, I have observed scholars anticipating and preemptively shutting down (in the mold of Posner's 1981 article) references to freedom or autonomy, policing the contours of acceptable economic discourse around privacy. Delimiting the contours of the debate is, of course, laudable when our goal is to safeguard rigor in analysis, and when we use the results of our precise but narrow economic observations as complements to the findings of other fields. Delimiting the contours of the debate is instead problematic if we do not exercise similar restraint in also delimiting, carefully and publicly, the *scope* of our contributions—that is, when we use economics as a substitute for other findings to influence public policy and public discourse. Yet such restraint is rarely exercised in our writings. The custom began with Posner. In 1978, he commenced his piece "Economic Theory of Privacy" by stating, "I will sidestep the definitional problem by simply noting that *one aspect of* privacy is the withholding or concealment of information" (19; emphasis added). After focusing his analysis on that one aspect, Posner ended the piece on much broader terms: "In the perspective offered by economics and by the common law, the recent legislative emphasis on favoring individual and denigrating corporate and organizational privacy stands revealed as still another example of perverse government regulation of social and economic life" (26). Contemporary economic literature on privacy is not as acerbic, but often follows a similar rhetorical template: the benefits of modern data analytics are espoused at the onset of our articles; the (typically negative) effects of regulation that protects personal information may have on those benefits are then analyzed; performative and typically perfunctory references to privacy's other dimensions are interjected, sometimes; but then broad, encompassing warnings to regulators (with pleas to consider carefully the unintended consequences of their interventions) are offered as conclusions.

As economists, we are certainly permitted to articulate the implications of our research.[25] What we should be wary of is the risk of an intellectual sleight of hand: studying a part (the effects on a subset of directly measurable, hand-picked metrics) but making conclusions for a whole (broad warnings to regulators) that our analyses have barely grazed.

25. I too have done so. When it comes to drawing implications from privacy research, I have found it worth distinguishing two related but distinct questions: Should digital privacy be better protected? If so, how? I find the former question harder to resolve in purely economic terms (see Section 2.3) but have been more sanguine about the latter and thus about articulating the policy implications of available research that addresses it.

2.3 Turning the Tables: The Economic Argument for Privacy

A rhetorical template originated with the 1980s economics of privacy literature: limiting the scope of analysis to a particular dimension of privacy but broadening the implications of that analysis to encompass privacy at large. That template exemplifies a particular way of framing the public debate around privacy. Figure 2.1 crudely captures key features of that framing. The rest of this section critiques it.

Under the framing that economics has popularized within the public discourse around privacy, a metaphorical scale is weighing two possible outcomes. One outcome is "more" privacy (for instance, regulatory interventions enforce minimum data protection guidelines, privacy-enhancing technologies are deployed, and so forth). The other outcome is "less" privacy and more liberal flows of personal data. The scale measures and compares the benefits to humanity of those two outcomes. Inherent to that framing is the assumption that interventions such as regulation aimed at protecting privacy may increase abstract benefits such as freedom or autonomy (which are measured on the right-side pan) but may threaten the more tangible economic benefits from data, such as more free content and services, more innovation, more efficiency, and so forth (which are measured on the left-side pan). Vice versa, refraining from regulating privacy may harm intangibles like freedom and autonomy but may allow more concrete economic benefits to be extracted from data.

The rest of this section argues why this scale—and in fact this way of implicitly or explicitly framing the debate around privacy—is flawed. It is flawed not on abstract moral grounds but on objective economic grounds. The section argues that uncritically (or unknowingly) internalizing this framing of the debate—as a contest or trade-off between benefits of more data versus the value of more autonomy, dignity, or control—is an errone-

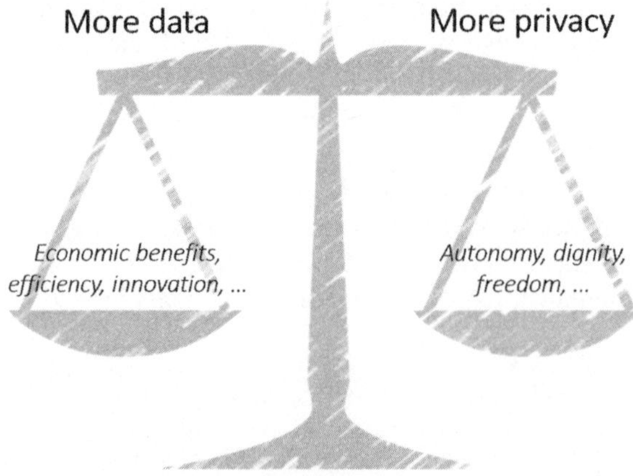

Figure 2.1 A popular framing of the public debate around privacy

ous reading of the available scholarly evidence around privacy. Section 2.3.1 focuses on the left pan. It questions how much we actually know about the allocation of benefits from consumer data and concludes that we assume a lot but know little. Section 2.3.2 focuses on the "beam"—the assumption that privacy protection is inherently and inevitably antithetical to the extraction of societal value from data. It rebuffs that assumption and challenges the notion that data protection is inherently welfare-decreasing. Section 2.3.3 focuses on the right pan. It highlights how little we know about the economic ramifications of privacy invasions. Finally, Section 2.3.4 proposes alternative ways of framing economic research around privacy, suggesting research questions that are complementary to the current focus on the costs of privacy regulation and proposing a reframing of the economic debate around privacy.

2.3.1 Missing the Forest for the Trees: What Do We Know about the Allocation of Benefits in the Data Economy?

The left pan of the scale presented in Figure 2.1 measures the economic benefits that arise from consumer data collection. How much do we actually know about those benefits, and their allocation to different stakeholders, including consumers themselves? That societies can extract value from consumer data is undeniable. But can we separate the snake oil of analytics from its demonstrable gains, and identify the allocation of those benefits?

Extant economic research falls short of these goals. I will focus, as a case study, on the online advertising market. It is not the only sector in which consumer data is tracked and analyzed. However, historically, it has played an outsized role in the process through which the Internet became an architecture of commercial surveillance, and in channeling consumer data into a black box of secondary uses and applications.

A quote from an online advertising executive published in *AdExchanger* (an online magazine related to the online advertising industry) in 2011 captures a widespread way of thinking about the benefits of online advertising, and in particular behaviorally targeted advertising—one of the key innovations in advertising made possible by consumer tracking:

> Behavioural targeting is not only good for consumers it's [sic] a rare win for everyone. [. . .] [It] ensures that ad placements display content that you might be interested in rather than ads that are irrelevant and uninteresting. [. . .] Advertisers [. . .] achieve [. . .] a greater chance of selling the product. Publishers also win as being able to offer behavioral targeting increases the value of the ad placements.[26]

The notion of behavioral advertising as an economic win-win for multiple stakeholders is consistent with some of the academic literature more critical of regulatory privacy interventions. Figure 2.2, left side (Frame 1),

26. See https://www.adexchanger.com/online-advertising/why-is-tracking-good/.

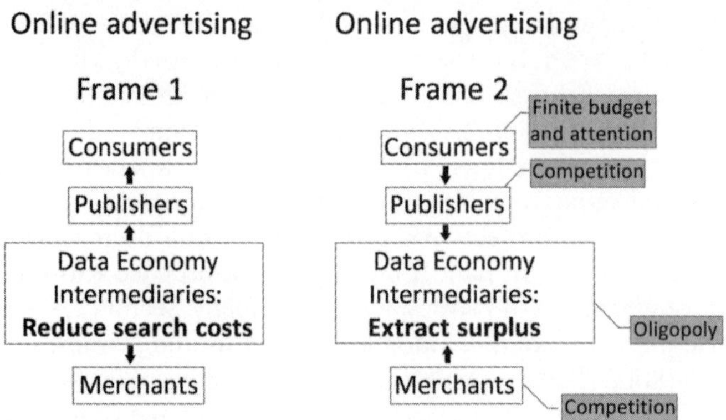

Figure 2.2 Two ways of framing the behavioral advertising market with multiple stakeholders

presents an economic interpretation of that notion. The figure represents online advertising as a two-sided platform market. Consumers (who visit online publishers, by which I refer to outlets producing various contents and services) want to find merchants to buy from. Merchants (who advertise on the publishers' web sites) want to find consumers to sell to. Significant search costs exist on both sides of this market. The data economy intermediaries (companies such as Google, Meta, and other stakeholders in the ecosystem) play the role of matchmakers.[27] They use the vast amount of consumer and merchant or product data they collect to facilitate matching between consumers and merchants, via the publishers. By doing so, they reduce search costs on both sides of the market (in particular, for smaller firms trying to reach niche consumer segments) and increase efficiency. Thus, they create economic utility (value creation is symbolized by the arrows coming out of the intermediaries box in the directions of merchants and publishers/consumers). Under this framing, online (behavioral) advertising does create economic win-win for all stakeholders in the market.

The right side of Figure 2.2 (Frame 2) presents an alternative economic representation of the same market. The stakeholders are the same. The focus, however, changes from search costs to competition, and from the role of intermediaries in reducing search costs to their ability to extract surplus from both sides of the market. This alternative economic interpretation of the market is equally legitimate, on theoretical grounds, to the economic win-win scenario depicted on the left side, but—as we will see—its conclusions regarding the allocation of benefits from data are different.

Central to Frame 2 is the observation that consumers have finite budgets and finite attention; they cannot pay attention to all the ads shown to them

27. The online advertising ecosystem is, of course, more complex than how Figure 2.2 depicts it. There are different types of intermediaries, and some intermediaries may also act as publishers and/or advertisers. I am abstracting from those details to focus on its key trends.

online and cannot purchase all the products advertised to them. Therefore, publishers aggressively compete with each other for that limited consumer attention, and merchants compete aggressively for that limited budget. This has several consequences for those stakeholders.

I will consider publishers first. The rise of online advertising (and then of behavioral advertising specifically)[28] has acted as a double-edged sword for publishers. First, it has supported the creation of new content dissemination channels and supported new content creators; in doing so, it has increased competition faced by both traditional, legacy publishers, and by new content creators. At any moment, an online publisher (for instance, nyt.com) may be competing for a finite amount of consumer attention not just with other traditional publishing outlets but with a myriad of content providers across a vast array of other channels—TikTok, Instagram, YouTube, blogging platforms, Twitter, online games, apps, and so forth—putting downward pressure on revenues per-publisher. Second, the particular form of advertising that consumer data collection has made possible—behavioral targeting via third-party tracking by data intermediaries—has had two opposite effects on publishers' economic returns. On the one hand, behavioral targeting has made online ads generally more valuable *at the impression level* (targeting is correlated with higher ad conversion rates, and therefore more profitable for publishers, many marketers claim; see Boerman, Kruikemeier, and Zuiderveen Borgesius 2017). On the other hand, behavioral targeting has diminished publishers' power to match consumers with advertisers, creating an opposite (downward) pressure on publishers' revenues. Before the rise of behavioral advertising, a merchant selling golf-related products who wanted to advertise to golf-interested consumers may have allocated advertising budget to a specific subset of outlets that counted such consumers among their readers. Online third-party tracking allows advertising intermediaries to target ads to consumers based on the latter's preferences, regardless of the web site, platform, or channel they may be visiting at any given moment (for instance, a visitor to a TikTok video may have been identified as a golf lover and may be presented with a golf-related ad). Worse (for high-quality, high-cost publishers), a high-value consumer (a reader of the *New York Times*, for instance) may be targeted while she is visiting lower-quality sites where it is cheaper to advertise (Srinivasan, 2019). These technological opportunities stretch out the supply of advertising spaces—the set of outlets and channels where merchants can find (and buy ad spaces for) interested consumers—shifting the power to match consumers with advertisers away from publishers and toward third-party data intermediaries. With that shift, the ability to extract surplus from advertising transactions also shifts from publishers to intermediaries[29]—a second source of downward pressure on publishers'

28. I will try, below, to distinguish which arguments specifically pertain to behavioral online advertising, rather than online advertising tout court.

29. In theoretical work, we have shown how an intermediary in a two-sided advertising market can strategically modulate consumer tracking to increase its profit (Marotta et al. 2022).

revenues notwithstanding (or, in fact, precisely because of) the advent of more precise ad targeting techniques.

Under this alternative framing of the advertising market (Frame 2), merchants, too, aggressively compete with each other to reach consumers with their ads. Before the rise of behavioral advertising, a merchant selling golf-related products intent on advertising to golf-interested consumers may have allocated its advertising budget to related publishing outlets. On those outlets, it would have competed for advertising space with merchants in the same or related industries. Online tracking allows data intermediaries to target ads to a given consumer across platforms based on her multidimensional preferences: the same consumer may be interested in golf, but also in Italian shoes, vacations to Mexico, and cooking lessons. Hence the golf-related merchant interested in reaching a golf-interested consumer may, at any point in time, be competing for the purchase of ad space with a larger array of merchants bidding to show ads about shoes, vacations, and cooking classes. In this sense, behavioral advertising can increase competition for ad space between advertisers (increasing their bids). Such increased competition is not lessened by the fact (which we observed above) that the advertising inventory has also increased, because there is a finite upper boundary to how many ads a consumer can pay attention to and how many products she can buy.

Under Frame 2, the economics agents who benefit from tracking and targeting are the intermediaries. The particular features of this technology have increased competition on both sides of the online advertising market, but have favored a concentration of data, and power, in the middle. Under this market structure, control over data translates to control over profits. The large oligopoly intermediaries may be able to extract more surplus from advertising transactions than the aggressively competing stakeholders on either side.

Both Frame 1 and Frame 2 of Figure 2.2 are based on plausible theoretical arguments. In fact, Bergemann and Bonatti (2022) highlight how digital platforms can generate both dynamics I have highlighted: surplus creation from matching, and surplus extraction from market power. One frame focuses on micro-level effects: per-impression reduction in search costs. The other frame focuses on macro-level effects: the aggregate impact on merchants' and publishers' revenues of competition through oligopoly intermediaries. To some extent, both the search cost reduction story and the oligopoly intermediaries' surplus extraction story may in fact be simultaneously occurring. But does either frame have (more) empirical validation? That is, does current research measure how data-driven advertising differentially affects Figure 2.2's stakeholders? And even if we were to disregard issues of redistribution of wealth among those stakeholders, does current research cleanly identify increases in overall surplus due to those technologies?

The answer is not yet. The degree of attention empirical scholarly research has paid to the different stakeholders in Figure 2.2 is uneven, possibly because the entities best positioned to measure the value of online advertising (the intermediaries) may not have incentives to conduct or sponsor research that may be critical of that value. (This raises obvious concerns over the risk of corporate capture of research in the field.) Oligopoly intermediaries' record-high profits are evident, although the evidence tends to come more often from industry reports than from empirical scholarly work. Advertising merchants have received most of the research attention, as a substantial amount of work has examined online advertising effectiveness (Boerman, Kruikemeier, and Zuiderveen Borgesius 2017). Measuring returns on online advertising spending is notoriously difficult (Johnson 2022),[30] and experimental results have shown that online ad spending does not always produce meaningful effects (Blake, Nosko, and Tadelis 2015). That noted, work in this area has supported the notion that *behaviorally* targeted ads can increase consumer conversion rates and expenditures (Farahat and Bailey 2012; Tadelis et al. 2023). And yet, their impact on merchants' *aggregate* welfare is probably more nuanced than conversion rates associated with specific ad campaigns can capture. This becomes apparent when we contrast per-impression metrics to general-equilibrium metrics. As all merchants can easily engage in this form of advertising, they may, collectively, wind up in zero-sum prisoner's dilemma dynamics. Individually (at the per-impression level), each advertiser experiences a high conversion rate from behaviorally targeted ads. However, each advertiser may have to engage in behavioral targeting merely to avoid competitors poaching its consumers. In equilibrium, advertisers may maintain their respective market share but spend more for it than if they had spent on (for instance) contextual ads.[31] Alternatively, rather than generating prisoner's dilemma dynamics, online advertising may benefit all participating merchants by expanding consumer demand and consumer spending (possibly via a reduction in consumers' search costs). There is little causal evidence, however, for or against an *aggregate* demand expansion effect of behaviorally targeted advertising, as opposed to it having a mere *redistribution* effect.[32]

30. For instance: on the one hand, failing to account for endogeneity and selection bias can vastly overestimate the effect of targeted ads, as conversion rates may hide the fact that targeted ads successfully reached those consumers who were, already, highly likely to purchase the product (Aral 2021). On the other hand, merely tracking online conversion rates may miss the effect that online ads may have on offline purchases.

31. This argument is based on the premise that behavioral targeting does work for most merchants. Because of its black box opacity, which allows rampant ad fraud (Hwang 2020) and makes attribution challenging, its aggregate effect remains murky. Anecdotal evidence suggests, for instance, that after large and small brands alike curtailed their digital spending, they observed no measurable negative impact on downstream business outcomes (see Fou 2021 and Rowe 2021).

32. Lefrere et al. (2022) fail to detect a differential effect of the GDPR on the quantity and quality of content generated by EU-based publishers relative to US-based publishers. The result is robust across all but one metric investigated by the authors. The metrics include both

Publishers—and the impact online advertising and behavioral advertising in particular have on their revenues—are a distant second in terms of scholarly attention. On theoretical grounds, antipodal dynamics are plausible (Chen and Stallaert 2014): behavioral advertising can increase publishers' revenues because merchants are willing to bid more for ads with a higher likelihood of conversion; behavioral advertising can also *reduce* publishers' revenues by creating hyper-targeted subsets of consumers and shrinking competition across merchants to target those consumers, reducing their bids and ultimately publishers' revenues (Levin and Milgrom 2010). Various experiments have shown that behaviorally targeted ads do increase per-impression revenues for publishers relative to non-behaviorally targeted ones. The amount revenues increase, however, varies across studies: from over 50 percent in a study by Google (Ravichandran and Korula 2019), to about a third of that (18 percent) in an independent study (Laub, Miller, and Skiera 2022), to even less in a study using an empirical approach similar to Laub, Miller, and Skiera but drawing data from a single large and arguably sophisticated media company (Marotta, Abhishek, and Acquisti 2019).[33] As in the case of empirical studies of privacy regulation, however, these studies individually offer useful data points but are collectively uninformative about the aggregate effect of behavioral advertising (or regulatory restrictions on it) on publishers. Again, we miss the forest for the trees.

First, these studies compare the revenues of targeted and untargeted ads but do not capture the effect of the rising competition publishers face for visitors' attention from an ever-increasing set of advertising channels (and advertising spaces) made possible by behavioral advertising. Therefore, these studies estimate the marginal revenue-increasing effect of targeting advertising space to visitors who actually reached the publisher's site (per-impression returns: Frame 1) but are mute on the *overall* revenue-decreasing effect of competition and the infinite inventory problem (Frame 2). Behavioral advertising giveth, and behavioral advertising taketh away. And yet, to our knowledge, no study has quantified and compared the two contrasting effects. Second, studies on the impact of regulations or self-regulatory restrictions on tracking and targeting are similarly uninformative about the *aggregate* impact of those interventions, as they only capture the *local*, redistribu-

variables whose data collection processes may, conceivably, have themselves been affected by the GDPR (such as data collected by third-party services including Alexa), and variables whose data collection practices were not affected. Note that the argument in this paragraph focuses on behavioral targeting. If we look at the impact of online advertising tout court, we have some indirect evidence: Todri (2022) finds that ad blockers decrease a consumer's online spending by 1.45 percent on average. And yet even this evidence is agnostic regarding aggregate demand effects: it is not known whether the decrease in digital spending implies an overall decrease in demand or, again, a redistribution from online to offline demand, or an increase in other digital spending not captured by the data set.

33. Wang, Jiang, and Yang (2023), mentioned above, found that GDPR compliance for a large publisher led to a modest 5.7 percent decrease in revenue per click.

tive effects of particular interventions (Ding, Wu, and Acquisti 2022). By local, we refer to the fact that even the more far-reaching privacy interventions limit tracking and targeting for only some specific subsets of Internet users; for instance, Apple ATT affects users of iOS devices, while the GDPR applies to EU residents who did not consent to tracking or who are visiting web sites that invoke the legitimate business interest clause to dispense with visitor consent altogether, and so forth. Those interventions therefore do not impair the tracking of many other categories of users, who thus remain targetable. Hence, those studies are more likely to capture a budget *reallocation* effect of privacy interventions (that is, advertisers reduce ad spending for affected categories and increase it for unaffected categories). They are not designed to study the *aggregate* effects of broadly encompassing regulations and interventions.[34] In short, the current scholarly evidence on publishers' revenues captures a valuable but limited piece of the puzzle. That piece holds as much empirical significance as the anecdotal, correlational evidence, coming from publishers' balance sheets, of continuous declines in revenues associated with the rise of behavioral advertising: the revenues of the largest European publishers stagnated over the past ten years, "while Alphabet (Google) and Meta's revenues increased by more than 500% during the same period" (Armitage et al. 2022, 9). Globally, newspaper revenue dropped from $107 billion in 2000 to roughly $32 billion in 2022 (based on data from GroupM cited in Angwin 2023).[35]

A legitimate counterpoint to the above argument is that the decline in traditional publishers' revenues has coincided with an increase in the supply (or, at least, in the number of *suppliers*) of other online content (from bloggers to influencers; from TikTok creators to Substack writers). The popularity of this content demonstrates a consumer demand for it. Leaving aside counterfactual questions (could contextual ads support this new content?), how the emergence of new vectors of content dissemination and new creators has affected consumer welfare is harder to establish, as that emergence also raises the thorny issue of content *quality*. As economists, we tend to sidestep those questions by observing that a consumer's demand for a good demonstrates the utility the consumer (expects to) derive from it. Prudent as that may be, it is also unsatisfactory in an online economy which is explicitly designed to employ choice architecture to nudge individuals to consume ever-shrinking sound bites of content, and where more and more content is recycled, manipulated, or misleading, if not outright malicious (Swire-Thompson and Lazer, 2020). As challenging as the conversation may be regarding

34. Professor Mayer offers a practical example of this argument: "Advertiser bidding behavior would change in a world without behavioral advertising or where it's a rarity. We don't know what those bids would look like, because advertisers just place behavioral bids now. For example, advertisers might start bidding more often and higher prices for demographically, geographically, or contextually targeted ads" (personal communication with the author).

35. See also https://www.pewresearch.org/journalism/fact-sheet/newspapers/.

the quality of the new content dissemination and communication channels that behavioral advertising is fostering, it seems an important conversation to be had, much like the conversation regarding the hurdles of estimating the value consumers accrue from social media consumption (Brynjolfsson, Collis, and Eggers 2019) versus its negative effects on subjective well-being (Allcott et al. 2020).

Finally, what do we know about consumers? Surprisingly little. Among the stakeholders represented in Figure 2.2, consumers have received the least attention in scholarly work. The argument for consumers benefiting from online advertising in general and behavioral advertising in particular is more often posited on intuitive arguments than validated with data. In principle, the benefits consumers receive from online advertising may be direct or indirect. The purported direct benefit of *behavioral* advertising is captured in the advertising executive's words quoted earlier in this section: consumers benefit from being presented ads that are more relevant and more interesting. This is a plausible search cost argument: online ads decrease consumers' search cost and present them with offers closer to their preferences, thereby increasing utility. This argument has empirical support: as noted, behaviorally targeted ads are more likely to generate conversions. This argument is also limited, however, and ultimately inconclusive. Search costs are but one factor in consumer utility. Other factors that affect consumer utility from purchasing products advertised to them online include the prices consumers end up paying, the quality of the product they end up buying, the quality of the merchant they end up interacting with, and so forth. Absent counterfactual evidence on the differential effects, along those possible factors, of targeted ads-linked purchases relative to other purchases, it is impossible to draw evidence-based conclusions about the direct consumer welfare effect of behavioral advertising. Only recently has some of that counterfactual evidence started emerging. In a recent working paper, we found that purchasing products from targeted ads, rather than from search results, increased the likelihood of purchasing from a lower-quality merchant and increased the expected price of the product (Mustri, Adjerid, and Acquisti 2022). This evidence suggests a potential welfare-decreasing effect of behavioral advertising due to prices and product quality that may countervail the welfare-increasing effect of search cost reduction.

Free access to content and services is often presented as a key *indirect* benefit of the online advertising economy to consumers. To scrutinize the robustness of evidence supporting this claim, it is useful to distinguish between the role of online ads in general and the role of behaviorally targeted ads in particular. The role of online ads in supporting the provision of content and services seems indisputable. Many online services *are* supported via ads. Consumers seem comfortable "paying" for online services with their eyeballs rather than with cash (although a substantial amount of consumers now prefers to block ads altogether[36]). The role of *behaviorally* targeted ads specifically in the provision of free services and content—and thus the role of consumer tracking and consumer data—is harder to tease out on causal rather than mere correlational grounds, due to the double-edged effect that behavioral advertising can have on the revenues of content creators, which we noted above. In attempting to tease out these effects, extant research leaves us with more questions than answers. Virtually all of today's typologies of online free services and free content already existed on the Internet before the rise of behavioral advertising in (roughly) the mid-2000s. At the time, those services and content were supported by contextual or untargeted advertising. To what extent has the dramatic increase in consumer data collection—including the growing ability to identify consumers and link their behaviors across different online and offline contexts—fueled an increase in the provision or quality of free content and services, and to what extent has it fueled an increase in the profit of the matchmakers, that is, the data intermediaries?[37] In fact, to what extent is the degradation of privacy an unavoidable price to pay for more or better content, or in fact a necessary condition for innovation?[38]

Conceptually, these questions amount to a simple economic comparison between the marginal cost of privacy loss and the marginal benefit of data collected. Empirically, answering those questions is anything but simple. We face an array of disparate pieces of anecdotal evidence but lack causal analysis. Anecdotally, the business model of a large number of content or service providers, from online publishers to app developers, does rely on monetizing consumer data. At the same time, a large number of content providers today use hybrid (freemium) models—including online publishers that have been switching to subscription models in both the US and the EU (Lefrere et al. 2022)—perhaps signaling that an insufficient amount of economic value generated from consumer data reaches downstream creators (with the rest, perhaps, being appropriated by data intermediaries). The limited academic research evidence available has produced mixed results. The GDPR may have reduced EU app developers' incentives to create new apps (Janßen et al. 2022); YouTube's removal of personalization for child-directed content following its settlement with the Federal Trade Commission over violations of the Children's Online Privacy Protection Act (COPPA) may have caused

36. Interestingly, ad blocker adoption can have *positive* effects on the quantity and variety of articles users consume. See Yan, Miller, and Skiera (2022).

37. For instance, the number of average ads *per video* has seemingly kept increasing on YouTube over time (Berman 2022); to what degree has that increase led to more or better YouTube videos or services?

38. Or, in fact, a sufficient condition? Over the past two decades, Facebook/Meta has gained access to more consumer data than most other companies in history, making significant financial gains from it. To what degree has this unique degree of accumulation of data and wealth led to societally beneficial innovations? See also Ohm (2012).

child-directed content creators to produce less content (Johnson et al. 2023); and Google's 2019 ban of targeted advertising in Android children's games may have reduced the release of feature updates (Kircher and Foerderer 2023). On the other hand, Apple's introduction of ATT does not appear to have negatively affected the supply of new apps for iOS users (Cheyre et al. 2022) and may have had only a short-term effect on developers' app-monetization strategies (Kesler 2022). Furthermore, the GDPR does not appear to have negatively affected the quantity and quality of EU news and media web sites' content (Lefrere et al. 2022).[39]

The issue considered in this section is not whether economic value can be created from data. That much is clear. The issue is how much we (scholars, regulators, the public) actually and conclusively know about how that value is allocated, and to what extent the claims that new content, services, and even innovation depend on unrestrained data collection (and are damaged by privacy measures) have empirical validation. The analysis presented here suggests that these are unresolved questions. This absence of a definite answer may in and of itself give us pause.

2.3.2 Revisiting Assumptions about the Costs of Protection

The second problem with the scale presented in Figure 2.1 (and with the economic framing of the debate around privacy) lies in the very notion of a beam counterbalancing the value of data and the value of privacy, casting them as opposed rather than parallel policy goals.

The rash of privacy legislation Posner lamented in 1981 and Varian warned us about in 1996 *did* occur. Even though the US still lacks a comprehensive federal privacy law, since the 1980s and the 1990s a myriad of acts, regulations, and enforcement initiatives materialized in the US at both the federal and state levels. And yet, those regulatory efforts did not seem to produce the damages early contributors to the economics of privacy feared. They did not prevent an unprecedented explosion in consumer data collection, the rise of an (estimated: Atikcan and Chalmers 2019) trillion-dollar data economy, the growth of new data-driven products and services, and record profits for several data intermediaries. (They also, one may add, failed to soothe consumers' privacy concerns.) Is there a disproportion between economists' fears about privacy protection and its actual impact? Are privacy and analytics (and the extraction of value from data) inherently antithetical, or could both be simultaneously achieved, at least sometimes, through a combination of technology and targeted policy intervention?

As we noted in Section 2.2, empirical economic research *has* provided evidence of negative implications of privacy regulation. That evidence, how-

39. Note that we are focusing here on the effect on content provision (and benefits allocation) of varying amounts of personal information used in online ads. This is related to, yet distinct from, the discussion of content providers' reliance on online advertising more broadly (see Shiller, Waldfogel, and Ryan 2018).

ever, has to be carefully contextualized. First, there is parallel evidence that, under certain conditions, privacy regulation can have a positive effect on economic variables, for instance, increase in technology adoption (Adjerid et al. 2016) or identity theft reduction (Romanosky, Telang, and Acquisti 2011), as well as other non-economic policy goals (such as COVID vaccination; see Buckman, Adjerid, and Tucker 2022). We noted in prior work (Acquisti, Brandimarte, and Loewenstein 2020) how this mixed evidence is consistent with extant economic research on the nuanced impact of regulation on innovation:[40] the direction of the impact will vary based on how particular interventions are designed, implemented, and enforced (BERR 2008).

Second (and with exceptions, as usual: see, for instance, Janßen et al. 2022), many of the studies showing a negative economic impact of privacy regulation ultimately report effects that are precisely identified but small in magnitude. Even a major regulation such as the GDPR has been shown to have produced a combination of diverse effects (Johnson 2024), including negative but modest (Wang, Jiang, and Yang 2023), and even null. (Several possible explanations exist, including the regulation not being actually enforced or being enforced and adhered to, but the decrease in data availability not causing the downstream damages some economists had predicted: see Lefrere et al. 2022.) The same appears to be happening with Apple ATT (see Section 2.3.1).

Third (and again with exceptions: consider Miller and Tucker 2011), a sizable portion of the literature in this area has focused on regulations' direct impact on business metrics (for instance, reduction in advertising effectiveness, or reduction in the supply of new apps following the GDPR) and has assumed or extrapolated, but not actually measured, downstream welfare effects on consumers (for instance, a reduction in consumer welfare due to less precisely targeted ads or a reduction in their usage of or satisfaction with available apps).

Fourth, some of the literature has focused on local effects rather than general equilibrium effects. We noted above (Section 2.3.1) that much of the work on restrictions on behavioral targeting are uninformative about the general impact of those restrictions because they capture the effect of local interventions that will affect some audiences and not others and will therefore allow advertisers to reallocate budgets from one entity to another.

Fifth, much of this literature focuses on short-term effects of regulation, from a few months to a few years. The reasons are various and valid, such as producing timely results and identifying robust causal links. But the result is an emphasis on the short-term impact of regulatory shocks (which

40. In the context of environmental protection, Porter (1991) proposed that strict regulations may incentivize innovations and produce efficiency gains. Shao et al. (2020) review the body of literature that over the years developed around the "Porter hypothesis" and find that the impacts of environmental regulation on innovation behavior are complex and include the creation of new technologies, products, and systems.

includes costs that businesses incur as they adapt to new technological and legal frameworks, and which often reflects a different problem: market concentration), rather than comprehensive analyses of long-term effects of different privacy regimes. As we noted in Acquisti, Brandimarte, and Loewenstein (2020), the short-term focus is likely to miss the long-term downstream effects of increased consumer protection and of competition and innovation in privacy between firms.

Sixth, the literature has so far by and large ignored the role of privacy-enhancing technologies (Goldberg 2007) and, in particular, privacy-preserving analytics (PPAs), by which I refer to statistical and cryptographic techniques—from homomorphic encryption to differential privacy (Iezzi 2020)—that make it possible to analyze and extract value from data while, to some degree,[41] protecting privacy. Granted, there is no free lunch: as we noted, both privacy and the lack of privacy are redistributive (the interests over data of different stakeholders are not necessarily ex ante aligned), and reducing the granularity of data can be costly, as it can diminish its value. But research suggests that those costs may be minimized by careful interventions (Abowd and Schmutte 2019). In recent work, we considered how the application of differentially private mechanisms to census data affects educational funding calculations (Steed et al. 2022). We found that funding misallocations due to the use of a differentially private mechanism do occur but are marginal compared to much larger misallocations due to existing data error. In addition, we found that a number of simple policy interventions or reforms could reduce the misallocation due to both privacy mechanisms and data errors. Ultimately, the cost (in terms of funding misallocations) due to privacy interventions may be mitigated with proper policy design. One implication of this research is that before worrying about the alleged costs of privacy protections, it may be prudent to consider whether other steps (such as reduction in data error and noise) may improve statistical practice.

41. Privacy-preserving analytics (and, more broadly, privacy-enhancing technologies) can help to some degree but are no panacea, because processes such as anonymization or data aggregation can mask individual identities or even protect some types of personal information without necessarily averting downstream privacy harm. Consider Google Topics, a framework for interest-based advertising that does without third-party cookies and cross-device tracking (see https://blog.google/products/chrome/get-know-new-topics-api-privacy-sandbox/). Professor Cheyre writes, "It can be privacy preserving, but it may not change how targeting ultimately operates in the online advertising ecosystem" (personal communication to the author)—that is, the fact that, even when their identities are nominally protected, individuals may be targeted with offers that may or may not be beneficial to them. Furthermore, doubts have been raised about the extent to which privacy measures (such as Apple ATT or Google Topics) materially enhance or will enhance consumer protection or act as tools for increasing control over a market (Sokol and Zhu 2021). This is a valid concern, but its root cause should not be confused: these dynamics are not inherent to privacy protection per se but to specific measures firms may implement to increase market power under the veil of privacy protection.

2.3.3 Tackling the Aggregation Problem and the Economic Dark Matter

The third and final problem in the economic framing of the debate around privacy consists in the lack of adequate measurements of harms from lost privacy—the right-side pan in Figure 2.1.

In Section 2.2, I argued that the economics of privacy has, with few exceptions, bypassed all but a handful of the harm of privacy invasions and the benefits of privacy protection. This creates a knowledge gap that hampers evidence-based policy-making. Worse, by stacking tangible economic benefits of data against intangible, unmeasured benefits of abstract concepts such as autonomy or freedom, the scale (and thus the economic debate around privacy) is vitiated by an inherent asymmetry between salient and measurable metrics contrasted against no less important but less salient, less direct, and less tangible factors. The framing therefore emphasizes the importance of one side over the other.[42]

The scale presented in Figure 2.1 (and the economic framing of the privacy debate it reflects) is thus flawed not merely on moral grounds (that is, on account of its failure to consider what as economists we may consider "paternalistic" values, such as the moral foundations for privacy protection). The scale is flawed on *economic* grounds, because it misses the "economic dark matter" (Acquisti, Brandimarte, and Loewenstein 2020): the vast evidence of privacy harm we discussed in Section 2.2 and exemplified through four scenarios.

Whether it is prudent or advisable to measure that economic dark matter is a valid question. The wisdom of considering certain values untradeable (and, in our context, of approaching privacy as a human right when considering regulation, and accepting negative changes in some business metrics—when and if they materialize—as the price to pay for those values) lies, precisely, in the knowledge that those values are essential to the functioning of a society even though they may not be (on first analysis) economically measurable or economically efficient. Policy makers (and, more broadly, the public debate around privacy) are therefore stuck in a seemingly unresolvable dilemma. On the one hand, they are expected to calculate the *net* harm of privacy invasions before a market failure is deemed sufficiently alarming to justify policy intervention (Jin and Stivers 2017). On the other hand, economic research is currently failing policy makers, because, by sidestepping privacy harm and not property scrutinizing the allocation of benefits

42. The differential privacy community faces a similar problem: "Because of the way [differential privacy mathematics] frames privacy loss through [privacy loss budgets], disclosure risks can appear abstract and difficult to interpret. By contrast, the effects of setting a [privacy loss budget] on downstream data utility are more easily tracked. This asymmetry can privilege data utility as the driving force behind how [privacy loss budgets] are allocated to different queries. We refer to this problem in this section as "the allocation dilemma" (Seeman and Susser 2022).

from data, it is not measuring net harms. What can policy makers do when quantifying net harm is very difficult? In the next section, I suggest several potential frameworks that could be considered.

2.3.4 Changing the Frame of the Privacy Economic Debate

So far, in Section 2.3, I have used an economic perspective to highlight systemic problems with the current economic framing of the privacy debate. I have remarked on the paucity of evidence on the allocation of benefits from data; I have emphasized the lack of adequate research on the economic harm of privacy loss; and I have questioned the very premise of construing the debate as a contest between value of privacy and value of data. In short, I have questioned the scientific grounding for the framing. Conversely, I have presented other evidence: consumers care for privacy and act to protect it; yet, economic and behavioral hurdles make it infeasible for individuals to adequately manage their privacy in the online marketplace; the costs of regulatory corrections to those hurdles may be overblown in the current debate; in fact, economic research has bypassed a massive amount of privacy harms, and the evidence that current equilibria ensure fair allocation of benefits from data is scant; furthermore, tools are available to allow both data analytics and privacy protection.

If this critique has merit, it may suggest a way forward in the economic debate around privacy that alters its framing and changes the burden of proof of the arguments around it. Rather than uncritically accepting the current way of framing the debate (*Privacy protection is often costly and at worst inefficient; unless one can demonstrate quantifiable privacy harms, what need is there for government intervention and regulation?*), we could ask instead, *What is the evidence that current products and services cannot be provided in more privacy-preserving manners, and that new privacy-preserving systems and processes cannot efficiently replace current ones?* This is, in essence, a call for turning the tables in the economic debate around privacy. To reach that lofty goal, we need to foster those nascent lines of inquiry I have cited throughout the manuscript—those that tackle new, difficult, and less-studied research questions around the complex interplays of privacy and economic value.

We need to better understand the harms of privacy loss: How do we help consumers and policy makers process the current asymmetry between tangible benefits of data and intangible harms of privacy? Can we (and should we) calculate the economic dark matter? If so, how do we tackle the "aggregation" problem of privacy harm?

We need to better understand the relationship between data protection and value extraction: What are the downstream (long-term, less obvious), and non-easily-quantifiable effects of privacy regulation? What are its beneficial effects? What are the economic effects of the deployment of privacy-enhancing technologies and privacy-preserving analytics, and how are they distributed to different stakeholders—firms, consumers, society as a whole?

And, ultimately, we need to understand better the allocation of value from data: How is the value of data allocated? Who truly benefits from the data economy?

2.4 Conclusions

The debate we considered in this manuscript is not new. It started over forty years ago. As Posner (1978) decided to sidestep the "definitional problem" and restrict his analysis of privacy to the withholding or concealment of information, Hirshleifer (1980) responded that such a narrow lens of analysis perhaps explained "why our pioneers' attitude toward privacy is—occasional qualifications aside—on the whole hostile. Their tone suggests that we have more privacy than ever before—probably more than is actually good for us or, at any rate, good for economic efficiency and, furthermore, that any person displaying a special desire for privacy is probably just out to hoodwink the rest of us" (650). And while Hirshleifer argued that "the mainland of 'privacy' is not the idea of secrecy [. . .] what we mean by 'privacy' is, rather, a concept that might be described as autonomy within society" (649), Posner (1981) rebuffed that "[t]o affix the term privacy to human freedom and autonomy [. . .] is simply to relabel an old subject—not to identify a new area for economic research" (405).

The rigorous but narrow Posnerian approach to the economic analysis of privacy proved distinctly successful in terms of scholarly research and impact on public discourse. But that very narrow approach and that success have laid the foundations for a crisis now emerging on the horizon. The economics of privacy has become more relevant in the debate around privacy, while sidestepping the evidence of significant and far-reaching harms and systemic behavioral hurdles imperiling market solutions to privacy problems. It has bypassed critical research questions outside of a narrow set that has received outsized attention. In doing so, I have argued, the economics of privacy ultimately risks crowding out critical dimensions of privacy not merely from its own field of research but also from the debate over privacy at large, brushing aside non-economic considerations.

That concern, too, is not novel. Hirshleifer (1980)'s words appear, today, prophetic:

> Recently a new territory has been discovered by economists, the intellectual continent we call "privacy." The pioneers are our peerless leaders Posner and Stigler whose golden findings have already dazzled the world. It is high time for rattlers and desperadoes—that's the rest of us—to put in an appearance. Of course, I ought to add parenthetically, "new" is relative to one's point of view. Our pioneering economists, like explorers in other places and other times, found aborigines already inhabiting the territory—in this case intellectual primitives, Supreme Court justices and such. Quite properly, our explorers have brushed the natives aside,

> and I shall follow in that honorable tradition [. . .] The first issue I shall address is whether our pioneers have correctly mapped the major features of the "privacy" continent. Have they possibly mistaken a peninsula for the mainland, foothills for a grand sierra, or perhaps even misread their compass so as to reverse north and south? Well, not quite so bad as the last, but I will be contending that the mainland of "privacy" is not the idea of secrecy as our pioneers appear to believe—secrecy is only an outlying peninsula.

Posner won the round, insofar as the economics of privacy adopted a decidedly Posnerian viewpoint. But (to paraphrase the title of a manuscript we cited earlier in this manuscript), at what price? Considering the centrality that information flows have commandeered in our lives and societies over the last four decades, and the extraordinarily far-reaching implications of the control over data and digital boundaries today, the intellectual continent of privacy has become possibly even vaster than Hirshleifer himself may have imagined in 1980. And so when we, as economists, narrow our lens of analysis without correspondingly narrowing the scope of our claims, what dramatic shifts in our societies' economic and social imbalances may we be neglecting? Can we do both—maintain the methodological rigor of our research toolkit, but also expand its narrow horizon of investigation? Will we be able to alter the framing of our research (and the debate around privacy) by accounting for the rich privacy theorizing from other social sciences, and by admitting that a drive for privacy is not inherently antithetical to the extraction of societal benefits from data, since we have technologies and strategies to often allow one and the other?

Posner (1981) wrote that "here as in other areas of nonmarket behavior the economist has a distinctive and valuable contribution to make to social science scholarship" (408). We agree. Used as a complement to the scholarship of other disciplines, the economics of privacy has much to contribute. Used with hubris, mistaking the outlying peninsula for the continent, the economics of privacy risks success at the expense of impoverishing the public debate over privacy; or risks demise by rendering itself decreasingly relevant to it. There is another way, which consists in focusing on a different set of research questions that brave new pioneers in the field may dare to explore, and challenging the way we frame this debate. The economics of privacy is at a crossroads.

References

Abowd, J. M., and Schmutte, I. M. 2019. "An Economic Analysis of Privacy Protection and Statistical Accuracy as Social Choices." *American Economic Review* 109 (1): 171–202.

Acquisti, A., I. Adjerid, R. Balebako, L. Brandimarte, L. F. Cranor, S. Komanduri, P. G. Leon, N. Sadeh, F. Schaub, M. Sleeper, and Y. Wang. 2017. "Nudges for Privacy and Security: Understanding and Assisting Users' Choices Online." *ACM Computing Surveys (CSUR)* 50 (3): 1–41.
Acquisti, A., L. Brandimarte, and J. Hancock. 2022. "How Privacy's Past May Shape Its Future." *Science* 375 (6578): 270–272.
Acquisti, A., L. Brandimarte, and G. Loewenstein. 2015. "Privacy and Human Behavior in the Age of Information." *Science* 347 (6221): 509–514.
Acquisti, A., L. Brandimarte, and G. Loewenstein. 2020. "Secrets and Likes: The Drive for Privacy and the Difficulty of Achieving It in the Digital Age." *Journal of Consumer Psychology* 30 (4): 736–758.
Acquisti, A., L. K. John, and G. Loewenstein. 2013. "What Is Privacy Worth?" *Journal of Legal Studies* 42 (2): 249–274.
Acquisti, A., C. Taylor, and L. Wagman. 2016. "The Economics of Privacy." *Journal of Economic Literature* 54 (2): 442–92.
Acquisti, A., and H. R. Varian. 2005. "Conditioning Prices on Purchase History." *Marketing Science* 24 (3): 367–381.
Adjerid, I., A. Acquisti, R. Telang, R. Padman, and J. Adler-Milstein. 2016. "The Impact of Privacy Regulation and Technology Incentives: The Case of Health Information Exchanges." *Management Science* 62 (4): 1042–1063.
Allcott, H., L. Braghieri, S. Eichmeyer, and M. Gentzkow. 2020. "The Welfare Effects of Social Media." *American Economic Review* 110 (3): 629–676.
Altman, I. 1975. *The Environment and Social Behavior: Privacy, Personal Space, Territory, and Crowding*. Monterey, CA: Brooks/Cole Publishing Company.
Altman, I. 1976. "Privacy: A Conceptual Analysis." *Environment and Behavior* 8 (1): 7–29.
Altman, I. 1977. "Privacy Regulation: Culturally Universal or Culturally Specific?" *Journal of Social Issues* 33 (3): 66–84.
Angwin, J. 2023. "If It's Advertised to You Online, You Probably Shouldn't Buy It. Here's Why." *New York Times*, April 6. https://www.nytimes.com/2023/04/06/opinion/online-advertising-privacy-data-surveillance-consumer-quality.html.
Aral, S. 2021. "What Digital Advertising Gets Wrong." *Harvard Business Review 19*.
Aral, S., and D. Eckles. 2019. "Protecting Elections from Social Media Manipulation." *Science* 365 (6456): 858–861.
Armitage, C., N. Botton, L. Dejeu-Castang, and L. Lemoine. 2022. "Study on the Impact of Recent Developments in Digital Advertising on Privacy, Publishers and Advertisers." *European Commission Final Report. Publications Office of the European Union*.
Arrieta-Ibarra, I., L. Goff, D. Jiménez-Hernández, J. Lanier, and E. G. Weyl. 2018. "Should we treat data as labor? Moving beyond 'free.'" *AEA Papers and Proceedings* 108: 38–42.
Athey, S., C. Catalini, and C. Tucker. 2017. "The Digital Privacy Paradox: Small Money, Small Costs, Small Talk." NBER Working Paper 23488. Cambridge, MA: National Bureau of Economic Research.
Atikcan, E. Ö., and A. W. Chalmers. 2019. "Choosing Lobbying Sides: The General Data Protection Regulation of the European Union." *Journal of Public Policy* 39 (4): 543–564.
Baker, C. E. 1977. "Posner's Privacy Mystery and the Failure of Economic Analysis of Law." *Georgia Law Review* 12: 475.
Bao, T., B. Liang, and Y. E. Riyanto. 2021. "Unpacking the Negative Welfare Effect of Social Media: Evidence from a Large Scale Nationally Representative Time-Use Survey in China." *China Economic Review* 69: 101650.

Becker, G. S. 1980. "Privacy and Malfeasance: A Comment." *The Journal of Legal Studies* 9 (4): 823–826.
Bergemann, D., and A. Bonatti. 2022. "Data, Competition, and Digital Platforms." Working paper.
Berman, M. 2022. "Why Does YouTube Have So Many Ads in 2022?" *Programming Insider*, April 6. https://programminginsider.com/why-does-youtube-have-so-many-ads-in-2022/.
BERR (Department for Business, Enterprise, and Regulatory Reform). 2008. "Regulation and Innovation: Evidence and Policy Implications." BERR Economics Paper no. 4. UK: BERR.
Blake, T., C. Nosko, and S. Tadelis. 2015. "Consumer Heterogeneity and Paid Search Effectiveness: A Large-Scale Field Experiment." *Econometrica* 83 (1): 155–174.
Bleier, A., A. Goldfarb, and C. Tucker. 2020. "Consumer Privacy and the Future of Data-Based Innovation and Marketing." *International Journal of Research in Marketing* 37 (3): 466–480.
Bloustein, E. J. 1977. "Privacy Is Dear At Any Price: A Response to Professor Posner's Economic Theory." *Georgia Law Review* 12: 429.
Boerman, S. C., S. Kruikemeier, and F. J. Zuiderveen Borgesius. 2017. "Online Behavioral Advertising: A Literature Review and Research Agenda." *Journal of Advertising* 46 (3): 363–376.
Borgolte, K., and N. Feamster. 2020. "Understanding the Performance Costs and Benefits of Privacy-Focused Browser Extensions." In *Proceedings of The Web Conference 2020*, 2275–2286. Association for Computing Machinery. https://dl.acm.org/doi/proceedings/10.1145/3366423.
Bradshaw, S., and P. N. Howard. 2018. "Challenging Truth and Trust: A Global Inventory of Organized Social Media Manipulation." *The Computational Propaganda Project* 1: 1–26.
Brynjolfsson, E., A. Collis, and F. Eggers. 2019. "Using Massive Online Choice Experiments to Measure Changes in Well-Being." *Proceedings of the National Academy of Sciences* 116 (15): 7250–7255.
Buckman, J. R., I. Adjerid, and C. Tucker. 2022. "Privacy Regulation and Barriers to Public Health." *Management Science 69 (1)*.
Bruns, A. 2021. "Echo Chambers? Filter Bubbles? The Misleading Metaphors That Obscure the Real Problem." In *Hate Speech and Polarization in Participatory Society*, 33–48. New York: Routledge.
Calo, R. 2011. "The Boundaries of Privacy Harm." *Indiana Law Journal* 86: 1131.
Cecere, G., F. Le Guel, M. Manant, and N. Soulié. 2017. *The Economics of Privacy*. Working paper.
Chen, J., and J. Stallaert. 2014. "An Economic Analysis of Online Advertising Using Behavioral Targeting." *Mis Quarterly* 38 (2): 429–450.
Cheyre, C., B. Leyden, S. Baviskar, and A. Acquisti. 2022. "The Impact of Apple Tracking Transparency Framework on the App Ecosystem." Working Paper presented at WISE.
Christou, G., and I. Rashid. 2021. "Interest Group Lobbying in the European Union: Privacy, Data Protection and the Right to Be Forgotten. *Comparative European Politics* 19 (3): 380–400.
Citron, D. K., and D. J. Solove. 2022. "Privacy Harms." *Boston University Law Review* 102: 793.
Colnago, J., L. F. Cranor, and A. Acquisti. 2023. "Is There a Reverse Privacy Paradox? An Exploratory Analysis of Gaps between Privacy Perspectives and Privacy-Seeking Behaviors." *Proceedings on Privacy Enhancing Technologies* 1: 455–476.

Cooper, J. 2023. "Does Privacy Want To Unravel?" Forthcoming in *Harvard Journal of Law & Technology*.
Derksen, L., A. McGahan, and L. Pongeluppe. 2022. "Privacy at What Cost? Using Electronic Medical Records to Recover Lapsed Patients Into HIV Care." *NBER Workshop on the Economics of Privacy*.
Dienlin, T., and S. Trepte. 2015. "Is the Privacy Paradox a Relic of the Past? An In-Depth Analysis of Privacy Attitudes and Privacy Behaviors." *European Journal of Social Psychology* 45 (3): 285–297.
Ding, Z., Y. Wu, and A. Acquisti. 2022. "Regulation of Targeted Advertising: Profit Implications for Ad Intermediaries and Publishers." Working Paper presented at WISE.
Farahat, A., and M. C. Bailey. 2012. "How Effective Is Targeted Advertising?" In *Proceedings of the 21st international conference on World Wide Web*, 111–120. April.
Farrell, J. 2012. "Can Privacy Be Just Another Good?" *Journal on Telecommunications and High Technology Law* 10: 251.
Fou, A. 2021. "When Big Brands Stopped Spending On Digital Ads, Nothing Happened. Why?" *Forbes*, January 2. https://www.forbes.com/sites/augustinefou/2021/01/02/when-big-brands-stopped-spending-on-digital-ads-nothing-happened-why/?sh=14736b151166.
Goldberg, I. 2007. "Privacy-Enhancing Technologies for the Internet III: Ten Years Later." Chapter 1 in *Digital Privacy: Theory, Technologies, and Practices*. New York: Auerbach Publications.
Goldberg, S., G. Johnson, and S. Shriver. 2023. "Regulating Privacy Online: An Economic Evaluation of the GDPR." Forthcoming in *American Economic Journal: Economic Policy*.
Goldfarb, A., and V. F. Que. 2023. "The Economics of Digital Privacy." *Annual Review of Economics* 15.
Goldfarb, A., and C. E. Tucker. 2011. "Privacy Regulation and Online Advertising." *Management Science* 57 (1): 57–71.
Grossklags, J., and A. Acquisti. 2007. "When 25 Cents Is Too Much: An Experiment on Willingness-to-Sell and Willingness-to-Protect Personal Information." In *WEIS*, June.
Guess, A. M., N. Malhotra, J. Pan, P. Barberá, H. Allcott, T. Brown, A. Crespo-Tenorio, D. Dimmery, D. Freelon, M. Gentzkow, and S. González-Bailón. 2023. "Reshares on Social Media Amplify Political News But Do Not Detectably Affect Beliefs or Opinions." *Science* 381 (6656): 404–408.
Hermalin, B. E., and M. L. Katz. 2006. "Privacy, Property Rights and Efficiency: The Economics of Privacy as Secrecy." *Quantitative Marketing and Economics* 4 (3): 209–239.
Hirshleifer, J. 1971. "The Private and Social Value of Information and the Reward to Inventive Activity." *American Economic Review* 61 (4): 541–556.
Hirshleifer, J. 1980. "Privacy: Its Origin, Function, and Future." *The Journal of Legal Studies* 9 (4): 649–664.
Hixson, R. F. 1987. *Privacy in a Public Society: Human Rights in Conflict*. New York: Oxford University Press.
Hui, K. L., and I. P. L. Png. 2006. "The Economics of Privacy." In *Handbooks in Information Systems*, edited by Terrence Hendershott. Vol. 1. Elsevier.
Hwang, T. 2020. *Subprime Attention Crisis: Advertising and the Time Bomb at the Heart of the Internet*. FSG originals.
Iezzi, M. 2020. "Practical Privacy-Preserving Data Science with Homomorphic

Encryption: An Overview." In *2020 IEEE International Conference on Big Data (Big Data)*, 3979–3988. IEEE. December.
Janßen, R., R. Kesler, M. E. Kummer, and J. Waldfogel. 2022. "GDPR and the Lost Generation of Innovative Apps." NBER Working Paper 30028. Cambridge, MA: National Bureau of Economic Research.
Jia, J., G. Z. Jin, and L. Wagman. 2021. "The Short-Run Effects of the General Data Protection Regulation on Technology Venture Investment." *Marketing Science* 40 (4): 661–684.
Jin, G. Z., and S. Stivers. 2017. "Protecting Consumers in Privacy and Data Security: A Perspective of Information Economics." SSRN 3006172.
Johnson, G. A. 2022. "Inferno: A Guide to Field Experiments in Online Display Advertising." *Journal of Economics & Management Strategy 32 (3)*.
Johnson, G. 2024. "Economic Research on Privacy Regulation: Lessons from the GDPR and Beyond." This volume.
Johnson, G., T. Lin, J. C. Cooper, and L. Zhong. 2023. "COPPAcalypse? The Youtube Settlement's Impact on Kids Content." *The Youtube Settlement's Impact on Kids Content*, April 26.
Jones, C. I., and C. Tonetti. 2020. "Nonrivalry and the Economics of Data." *American Economic Review* 110 (9): 2819–58.
Kesler, R. 2022. "The Impact of Apple's App Tracking Transparency on App Monetization." SSRN 4090786.
Kircher, T., and J. Foerderer. 2023. "Ban Targeted Advertising? An Empirical Investigation of the Consequences for App Development." Forthcoming in *Management Science*.
Laub, R., K. M. Miller, and B. Skiera. 2022. "The Economic Value of User Tracking for Publishers." SSRN 4251233.
Laudon, K. C. 1996. "Markets and Privacy." *Communications of the ACM* 39 (9): 92–104.
Lee, Y. S., and R. Weber. 2021. "Revealed Privacy Preferences: Are Privacy Choices Rational?" Working paper. https://www.dropbox.com/s/w6q5v5dzpsqferw/Revealed%20Privacy%20Preferences%202021-12-10.pdf?dl=0.
Lefrere, V., L. Warberg, C. Cheyre, V. Marotta, and A. Acquisti. 2022. "Does Privacy Regulation Harm Content Providers? A Longitudinal Analysis of the Impact of the GDPR." NBER Workshop on the Economics of Privacy.
Levin, J., and P. Milgrom. 2010. "Online Advertising: Heterogeneity and Conflation in Market Design." *American Economic Review* 100 (2): 603–07.
Lin, T. 2022. "Valuing Intrinsic and Instrumental Preferences for Privacy." *Marketing Science 41 (4)*.
Liu, Y., K. P. Gummadi, B. Krishnamurthy, and A. Mislove. 2011. "Analyzing Facebook Privacy Settings: User Expectations vs. Reality." In *Proceedings of the 2011 ACM SIGCOMM conference on Internet measurement conference*, 61–70.
Madden, M. 2012. "Privacy Management on Social Media Sites." *Pew Internet Report* 24: 1–20.
Marotta, V., V. Abhishek, and A. Acquisti. 2019. "Online Tracking and Publishers' Revenues: An Empirical Analysis." Presented at the *Workshop on the Economics of Information Security*.
Marotta, V., Y. Wu, K. Zhang, and A. Acquisti. 2022. "The Welfare Impact of Targeted Advertising Technologies." *Information Systems Research* 33 (1): 131–151.
Marthews, A., and C. E. Tucker. 2017. "Government Surveillance and Internet Search Behavior." SSRN 2412564.
McDonald, A. M., and L. F. Cranor. 2008. "The Cost of Reading Privacy Policies." *Journal of Law and Policy for the Information Society* 4: 543.

McDonald, A. M., and L. F. Cranor. 2010. "Americans' Attitudes about Internet Behavioral Advertising Practices." In *Proceedings of the 9th annual ACM workshop on Privacy in the electronic society*, 63–72.

Miller, A. R., and C. E. Tucker. 2011. "Can Health Care Information Technology Save Babies?" *Journal of Political Economy* 119 (2): 289–324.

Miller, A. R., and C. Tucker. 2018. "Privacy Protection, Personalized Medicine, and Genetic Testing." *Management Science* 64 (10): 4648–4668.

Mustri, E. A. S., I. Adjerid, and A. Acquisti. 2022. "Behavioral Advertising and Consumer Welfare: An Empirical Investigation." *Federal Trade Commission PrivacyCon*. https://papers.ssrn.com/sol3/papers.cfm?abstract_id=4398428.

Neumann, N., C. E. Tucker, and T. Whitfield. 2019. "Frontiers: How Effective Is Third-Party Consumer Profiling? Evidence from Field Studies." *Marketing Science* 38 (6): 918–926.

Nissenbaum, H. 2004. "Privacy as Contextual Integrity." *Washington Law Review* 79: 119.

Noam, E. M. 1997. "Privacy and Self-Regulation: Markets for Electronic Privacy." Chapter 1, Part B in *Privacy and Self-Regulation in the Information Age*. National Telecommunications and Information Administration. https://www.ntia.gov/page/chapter-1-theory-markets-and-privacy.

Norberg, P. A., D. R. Horne, and D. A. Horne. 2007. "The Privacy Paradox: Personal Information Disclosure Intentions versus Behaviors." *Journal of Consumer Affairs* 41 (1): 100–126.

Nyhan, B., J. Settle, E. Thorson, M. Wojcieszak, P. Barberá, A.Y. Chen, H. Allcott, T. Brown, A. Crespo-Tenorio, D. Dimmery, and D. Freelon. 2023. "Like-Minded Sources on Facebook Are Prevalent But Not Polarizing." *Nature* 620: 137–144. https://doi.org/10.1038/s41586-023-06297-w

Ohm, P. 2012. "The Underwhelming Benefits of Big Data." *University of Pennsylvania Law Review* 161: 339.

Olson, M. L. 1965. *The Logic of Collective Action*. Cambridge, MA: Harvard University Press.

Pani, L. 2000. "Is There an Evolutionary Mismatch between the Normal Physiology of the Human Dopaminergic System and Current Environmental Conditions in Industrialized Countries?" *Molecular Psychiatry* 5 (5): 467–475.

Porter, M. E. 1991. "America's Green Strategy." *Scientific American* 264 (4): 193–246.

Posner, R. A. 1977. "The Right of Privacy." *Georgia Law Review* 12: 393.

Posner, R. A. 1978. "Economic Theory of Privacy." *Regulation* 2: 19.

Posner, R. A. 1981. "The Economics of Privacy." *American Economic Review* 71 (2): 405–409.

Ravichandran, D., and N. Korula. 2019. "Effect of Disabling Third-Party Cookies on Publisher Revenue." Google White Paper. Accessed October 4, 2021. https://services.google.com/fh/files/misc/disabling_third-party_cookies_publisher_revenue.pdf.

Rao, A., F. Schaub, N. Sadeh, A. Acquisti, and R. Kang. 2016. "Expecting the Unexpected: Understanding Mismatched Privacy Expectations Online." In *Twelfth Symposium on Usable Privacy and Security (SOUPS 2016)*, 77–96. Association for Computing Machinery. https://dl.acm.org/doi/10.5555/3235895.3235903.

Reidenberg, J. R., T. Breaux, L. F. Cranor, B. French, A. Grannis, J. T. Graves, F. Liu, A. McDonald, T. B. Norton, and R. Ramanath. 2015. "Disagreeable Privacy Policies: Mismatches between Meaning and Users' Understanding." *Berkeley Technology Law Journal* 30: 39.

Rowe, A. 2021. "How Uber's Ad Fraud Lawsuit Highlights a Billion-Dollar

Brand Problem." Tech.co, January 4. https://tech.co/news/uber-ad-fraud-brand-problem.

Romanosky, S., R. Telang, and A. Acquisti. 2011. "Do Data Breach Disclosure Laws Reduce Identity Theft?" *Journal of Policy Analysis and Management* 30 (2): 256–286.

Seeman, J., and D. Susser. 2022. "Between Privacy and Utility: On Differential Privacy in Theory and Practice." SSRN 4283836.

Shao, S., Z. Hu, J. Cao, L. Yang, and D. Guan. 2020. "Environmental Regulation and Enterprise Innovation: A Review." *Business Strategy and the Environment* 29 (3): 1465–1478.

Shiller, B., J. Waldfogel, and J. Ryan. 2018. "The Effect of Ad Blocking on Website Traffic and Quality." *The RAND Journal of Economics* 49 (1): 43–63.

Skiera, B., K. Miller, and Y. Jin. 2022. *The impact of the General Data Protection Regulation (GDPR) on the online advertising market*. Bernd Skiera. https://gdpr-impact-book.github.io/gdpr_impact/.

Solove, D. J. 2006. "A Taxonomy of Privacy." *University of Pennsylvania Law Review 154 (3)*: 477–564.

Solove, D. J. 2007. "I've Got Nothing to Hide and Other Misunderstandings of Privacy." *San Diego Law Review* 44: 745.

Solove, D. J. 2021. "The Myth of the Privacy Paradox." *George Washington. Law Review* 89: 1.

Sokol, D. D., and F. Zhu. 2021. "Harming Competition and Consumers under the Guise of Protecting Privacy: An Analysis of Apple's iOS 14 Policy Updates." *Cornell Law Review Online* 107: 94.

Spiekermann, S., A. Acquisti, R. Böhme, and K. L. Hui. 2015. "The Challenges of Personal Data Markets and Privacy." *Electronic Markets* 25 (2): 161–167.

Srinivasan, D. 2019. "The Antitrust Case against Facebook: A Monopolist's Journey towards Pervasive Surveillance in Spite of Consumers' Preference for Privacy." *Berkeley Business Law Journal* 16: 39.

Steed, R., T. Liu, Z. S. Wu, and A. Acquisti. 2022. "Policy Impacts of Statistical Uncertainty and Privacy." *Science* 377 (6609): 928–931.

Stigler, G. J. 1980. "An Introduction to Privacy in Economics and Politics." *The Journal of Legal Studies* 9 (4): 623–644.

Stigler, G. J., and G. S. Becker. 1977. "De gustibus non est disputandum." *American Economic Review* 67 (2): 76–90.

Strahilevitz, L. J., and M. B. Kugler. 2016. "Is Privacy Policy Language Irrelevant to Consumers?" *Journal of Legal Studies* 45 (S2): S69–S95.

Strahilevitz, L., and L. Y. Liu. 2022. "Cash Substitution and Deferred Consumption as Data Breach Harms." University of Chicago Coase-Sandor Institute for Law & Economics Research Paper, 963.

Stutzman, F. D., R. Gross, and A. Acquisti. 2013. "Silent Listeners: The Evolution of Privacy and disclosure on Facebook." *Journal of Privacy and Confidentiality* 4 (2): 2.

Swire-Thompson, B., and D. Lazer. 2020. "Public Health and Online Misinformation: Challenges and Recommendations." *Annual Review of Public Health* 41 (1): 433–451.

Tadelis, S., C. Hooton, U. Manjeer, D. Deisenroth, N. Wernerfelt, N. Dadson, and L. Greenbaum. 2023. "Learning, Sophistication, and the Returns to Advertising: Implications for Differences in Firm Performance." NBER Working Paper 31201. Cambridge, MA: National Bureau of Economic Research.

Taylor, C. R. 2004. "Consumer Privacy and the Market for Customer Information." *RAND Journal of Economics* 35 (4): 631–650.

Todri, V. 2022. "The Impact of Ad-Blockers on Online Consumer Behavior." *Marketing Science* 41 (1): 7–18.
Tomaino, G., K. Wertenbroch, and D. J. Walters. 2021. "Intransitivity of Consumer Preferences for Privacy." Working paper.
Turow, J., M. Hennessy, and N. Draper. 2018. "Persistent Misperceptions: Americans' Misplaced Confidence in Privacy Policies, 2003–2015." *Journal of Broadcasting & Electronic Media* 62 (3): 461–478.
Varian, H. R. 1996. "Economic Aspects of Personal Privacy, Privacy and Self-Regulation in the Information Age." *National Telecommunications and Information Administration Report*. Reprinted in *Internet Policy and Economics: Challenges and Perspectives*, edited by W. H. Lehr and L. M. Pupillo. New York: Springer.
Vuorre, M., and A. K. Przybylski. 2023. "Estimating the Association between Facebook Adoption and Well-Being in 72 Countries." *Royal Society Open Science* 10 (8): 221451.
Yan, S., K. M. Miller, and B. Skiera. 2022. "How Does the Adoption of Ad Blockers Affect News Consumption?" *Journal of Marketing Research* 59 (5): 1002–1018.
Wang, P., L. Jiang, and J. Yang. 2023. "The Early Impact of GDPR Compliance on Display Advertising: The Case of an Ad Publisher." *Journal of Marketing Research*. https://doi.org/10.1177/00222437231171848,
Wernerfelt, N., A. Tuchman, B. Shapiro, and R. Moakler. 2022. "Estimating the Value of Offsite Data to Advertisers on Meta." University of Chicago, Becker Friedman Institute for Economics Working Paper 114.
Westin, A. 1967. *Privacy and Freedom*. New York: Atheneum.
Wickelgren, A. L. 2015. An Economic Analysis of Internet Privacy Regulation.
Zuboff, S. 2015. "Big Other: Surveillance Capitalism and the Prospects of an Information Civilization." *Journal of Information Technology* 30 (1): 75–89.

3 The Platform Dimension of Digital Privacy

Alessandro Bonatti

3.1 Introduction

The past two decades have witnessed an unprecedented scale of collection and dissemination of individual-level data. Large digital platforms such as Amazon, Facebook, Google, Alibaba, JD, and Tencent are at the forefront of this data collection, often through ostensibly free services offered to users. These platforms generate revenue by matching users with advertisers, merchants, and content producers, effectively selling access to a qualified consumer audience. The implications of such practices for individual privacy have raised concerns among academics and policy makers, resulting in regulatory interventions like the European Union's General Data Protection Regulation (GDPR) and the California Privacy Rights Act (CPRA).

Taking a closer look, the challenge of protecting individual privacy in today's digital markets reveals a new dimension. The equilibrium level of privacy and its welfare consequences depend on the mechanisms employed by two-sided platforms to mediate the exchange of consumer data. Notably, the presence of network effects stemming from both users (on one side) and advertisers (on the other side), as well as the potential for platform competition, collectively determine the scale and granularity of consumer data intermediation.

In this paper, I review recent advancements in economic theory that

Alessandro Bonatti is the John Norris Maguire (1960) Professor of Applied Economics at the MIT Sloan School of Management.

I acknowledge financial support through NSF Grant SES-1948692. I would like to thank Dirk Bergemann for years of joint work on this topic, as well as Andrew Koh and the participants in the 2022 NBER Privacy Tutorial for helpful comments. For acknowledgments, sources of research support, and disclosure of the author's material financial relationships, if any, please see https://www.nber.org/books-and-chapters/economics-privacy/platform-dimension-digital-privacy.

explore the platform dimension of digital privacy, examine potential sources of market failure, and suggest open areas for future research. The economic theory of privacy is decades old, beginning with the classic work of Stigler (1980) and Posner (1981), and more recently surveyed in the comprehensive work of Acquisti, Taylor, and Wagman (2016). However, the platform dimension of privacy and the dual role of digital platforms as gatekeepers of information and competition (Bergemann and Bonatti 2023) introduce new challenges and require new modeling tools.[1]

Due to its platform dimension, privacy has evolved into a social, competition, and regulation issue. Throughout the paper, I concentrate on three key questions: (1) How do different consumers' privacy choices interact with one another? (2) Is there a trade-off between privacy and competition? In other words, does preserving consumer data privacy also result in limited competition for the consumer? (3) How do regulatory interventions assist, and what are the potential drawbacks?[2]

I argue that data acquisition by platforms is significantly facilitated by data externalities—the impact of other consumers' data on an individual user's decision to share their own data. When consumers' characteristics are positively correlated, I demonstrate conditions under which little stands in the way of a large platform amassing vast amounts of individual data. This holds true even if consumers had full control over their privacy, as the marginal cost of acquiring each user's data is small relative to the overall value of a data set. Additionally, I discuss whether competition among platforms for acquiring user data, given the nature of information goods, is likely to yield substantial welfare gains.

Shifting focus to data monetization, I illustrate how a digital platform with market power can transfer that power downstream to advertisers by offering exclusive access to consumers. The platform leverages its data from past and concurrent transactions to generate surplus through enhanced matching of consumers and sellers. At the same time, the possibility of awarding "de facto monopoly positions" (Cremèr, de Montjoye, and Schweitzer 2019) to advertisers limits the diffusion of consumer data (which may be viewed as privacy protecting) but opens the door to surplus extraction through personalized offers (e.g., price discrimination and product steering).[3] The resolu-

1. Huge amounts of attention have been devoted to privacy in several fields, including law, political science, and computer science. A common theme is that improvements in information and communications technology facilitate individual-level data collection and naturally introduce concerns. These concerns are not limited to big tech data sets and market power but extend to the role, for example, of government tracking and surveillance. The analysis in this chapter is highly specialized and complementary to those perspectives.

2. The regulation dimension of privacy is examined by Johnson (2022), and I refer the reader to that paper for an in-depth analysis of the GDPR.

3. The availability of granular individual-level data can, of course, introduce other concerns, including government surveillance, data leakages, fraud, misinformation campaigns, and addictive social media.

tion of this trade-off by a monopolist seller is then critical to understanding the welfare implications of market power by digital platforms and hence the relationship between privacy and competition for access to consumers.

The welfare implications of data acquisition and data monetization by digital platforms are not straightforward. In particular, the expansion of a platform's database affects its capacity to match products to individual preferences, but it also diminishes each consumer's alternative options. This gives rise to a new form of data externality, where different consumers' privacy choices interact with one another, even in the presence of regulatory interventions like GDPR and CPRA that aim to assign formal control rights over data to individual users. Similarly, the optimal mechanisms for monetizing data create a tension between privacy and competition for the consumer.

The overall scenario that emerges depicts data externalities leading to economies of scale on the data acquisition side, while market power on the monetization side enables the sale of exclusive access to each consumer's attention. Under these circumstances, the welfare effects of privacy ultimately depend on the type of firms that gain access to the consumer—whether they primarily utilize information to generate or extract value.

To address these questions, Section 3.2 introduces a model of a two-sided platform as a monopolist data intermediary and examines the economics of privacy through this lens; Section 3.3 focuses on the data-acquisition side; and Section 3.4 examines the data-monetization side. Section 3.5 concludes and suggests open areas for future research.

3.2 Basic Framework

The basic role of any digital platform is to intermediate large numbers of users and producers. Here, we develop a basic data-intermediation model that captures some of the key dimensions of real-world platforms. First, any information it acquires must be obtained from multiple users. Second, any data it has acquired can be monetized through multiple producers or firms of merchants. Third, consumers and producers may have outside access opportunities or the ability to meet off the platform. As we will see, a critical determinant of the platform's bargaining power is whether it is instrumental for a match between consumers and producers or merely enables this match to occur under better complete information. Figure 3.1 illustrates.

3.2.1 Value of Privacy

We begin this section with a simple framework to think about consumer privacy as private information about preferences. We develop a first model where a single consumer interacts with a representative producer (or "firm"). We later augment the framework by introducing multiple users, multiple

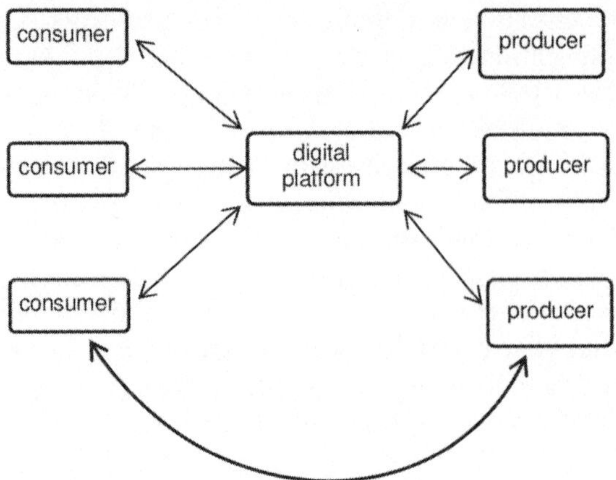

Figure 3.1 Platform interaction with a direct channel

producers, and potentially other agents (e.g., governments or platforms) interested in learning about the consumer.

The consumer has a preference type $\theta \in \mathbb{R}$ that parametrizes their utility function. The firm chooses an action $a \in \mathbb{R}$ (e.g., advertising message, product quality, or price) to maximize profits. When the firm chooses action a, the consumer obtains utility

$$u(\theta, a).$$

Without the need to specify the firm's preferences, we shall assume here that the firm chooses the action a to match the consumer's type:

$$a^* = \mathbb{E}[\theta].$$

Our focus is on the role of information about θ in this market. We assume that the consumer knows their true type θ, while the firm initially knows the prior distribution $F_0(\theta)$ only. In addition, the firm receives an informative signal s. Thus, the firm will be able to segment the market by choosing a different action a after observing each signal s.

It is useful to represent the signals observed by the firm as a *segmentation* (Yang 2022). Here we follow the exposition in Bonatti, Huang, and Villas-Boas (2023). A segmentation

$$\mathcal{S} = \{(\pi_s, F_s)\}_{s \in S}$$

is a mixture distribution with weights π_s over individual distributions F_s. A segmentation $\mathcal{S}$ admits two equivalent interpretations. By definition, π_s denotes probability of the signal realization s and $F_s(\theta)$ denotes the distribution of the firm's posterior beliefs upon observing s. Equivalently, the signal structure induces a partition of the consumer types (i.e., a market segmentation) where the size of each segment is given by π_s and the composition of each segment is given by $F_s(\theta)$.

Any segmentation $\mathcal{S}$ is a mean-preserving spread of the prior distribution F_0. In particular, for each θ, the distributions $F_s(\theta)$ integrate to the prior, i.e.,

$$\int_s F_s(\theta)\pi_s\, ds = F_0(\theta),\ \forall\theta \in \Theta.$$

Furthermore, all consumers in segment s (i.e., conditional on the firm observing signal s) receive the same action, which we denote by

$$a^*(F_s) = \mathbb{E}_{F_s}[\theta] = \int_\theta \theta\, dF_s(\theta).$$

We can then write the average surplus of consumers in segment s as

$$V(F_s) = \int_\theta u(\theta, a^*(F_s))\, dF_s(\theta).$$

Finally, averaging over segments (i.e., taking expectations over signal realizations) yields the expected (ex ante) consumer surplus under segmentation $\mathcal{S}$,

$$U(\mathcal{S}) \triangleq \mathbb{E}_s[V(F_s)] = \int_s V(F_s)\pi_s ds. \tag{1}$$

It is often useful to contrast the consumer's welfare under an informative segmentation $\mathcal{S}$ to the consumer surplus under prior information (i.e., full privacy), which is given by

$$U(\varnothing) \triangleq V(F_0).$$

This formulation for consumer surplus suggests a characterization of utility functions for which consumers unambiguously (i.e., for all segmentations) like or dislike privacy.

Proposition 1 (Value of Privacy)

If $V(\cdot)$ is concave (convex), consumers like (dislike) privacy.

This result (which follows from Jensen's inequality) is spelled out in greater detail in Bonatti, Huang, and Villas-Boas (2023). Under the conditions of Proposition 1, the consumer's ideal segmentation is either $\mathcal{S} = \varnothing$ or $\mathcal{S} = \mathcal{S}^*$, where $\mathcal{S}^*$ is the full information segmentation consisting of a collection of degenerate random variables ($s = \theta$).

In what follows, we shall make repeated use of the comparison between $U(\mathcal{S})$ and $U(\varnothing)$ to denote the equilibrium value of privacy for consumers. We now illustrate the usefulness of this compact representation for the value of privacy through a parametrized example.

3.2.2 Application

This example illustrates our model with a quadratic utility function. The firm's action a can denote either quality or price as in Argenziano and Bonatti (2021). Let the consumer's utility function be given by

$$u(\theta, a) = (\theta + \lambda a)^2.$$

The parameter $\lambda \in [-1, 1]$ intuitively captures the value creation vs. extraction role of the firm's action: when $\lambda < 0$, the firm's action resembles a price, and when $\lambda > 0$ it resembles a quality choice. Indeed, the case of $\lambda = -1$ is outcome-equivalent to the case of linear price discrimination, where a consumer type of θ facing a unit price of p obtains an indirect utility proportional to $(\theta - p)^2$.

To illustrate how this basic model yields sharp predictions on the welfare consequences of linear price discrimination, consider the surplus of segment s

$$V(F_s) = \int_{\theta} (\theta + \lambda \mathbb{E}_{F_s}[\theta])^2 dF_s(\theta),$$

which we can write as

$$V(F_s) = \mathbb{E}_{F_s}[\theta^2] + (2 + \lambda)\lambda(\mathbb{E}_{F_s}[\theta])^2.$$

Notice that the first term (which is an expectation) is linear in probabilities, while the second term (which is a square expectation) is convex. Because $\lambda \in [-1, 1]$, we immediately conclude that $V(\cdot)$ is a concave (convex) function of F_s if and only if $\lambda < (>)0$. Therefore, if $\lambda < (>)0$, any mean-preserving spread hurts (benefits) consumers. In particular, for the fully informative segmentation S^*, we have $U(S^*>>)<(>)U(\varnothing)$.

For the case $\lambda = -1$, we thus recover the classic result (Robinson 1933; Schmalensee 1981) that enabling market segmentation by a monopolist facing a linear demand function (and full market coverage) is detrimental to consumer surplus.

3.2.3 Generalizations

The model presented in this section is stylized along several dimensions. The general effect of market segmentations and the achievable combinations of consumer and producer surplus are analyzed in the seminal work of Bergemann, Brooks, and Morris (2015) and more recently by Haghpanah and Siegel (2022) and Elliott et al. (2022). The consumer's type was assumed one-dimensional, but Ichihashi (2020) and Bonatti, Huang, and Villas-Boas (2023) illustrate how the main logic of Proposition 1 extends to multidimensional environments such as those, for example, where the consumer has both a vertical willingness to pay attribute and a horizontal product match attribute.

Finally, the consumer was assumed entirely passive, whereas a long literature (summarized in Section 3.3.2 below) studied the impact of consumer actions on the equilibrium market segmentations. In the remainder of this chapter, we explore the conditions under which a platform can profitably intermediate the exchange of data in markets where consumers like (or dislike) privacy.

3.3 Data Acquisition

The previous section provided a language to talk about a consumer's preferences over the amount of data that a platform holds about them. We now focus on the key dimensions of the platform dimension of privacy, namely the collection and the monetization of consumer data, beginning with the former.

Why do consumers allow platforms to collect significant amounts of data? One possibility is that consumers benefit from data collection and that data intermediation is socially efficient. Another possibility is that consumers are unaware of the extent of data collection, or that their stated preferences for privacy differ from their actual preferences—the *privacy paradox* (Athey, Catalini, and Tucker 2017). In this section, we specifically ask why platforms are able to intermediate information at little or no cost, why competition does not seem to discipline data acquisition, and whether there are limits to consumer data usage that emerge in a market context—for example, why do we see little or no personalized pricing?

3.3.1 Captive Consumers

Consider a single consumer and a single producer who meet on a monopolist digital platform with no alternative means to contract with each other. Figure 3.2 simplifies Figure 3.1 as follows.

Assume that the consumer makes a onetime participation decision. This decision takes place ex-ante, i.e., before the consumer's type is drawn. If the consumer participates on the platform, which means it uses the platform repeatedly, then it is going to reveal segmentation $\mathcal{S}$ to the platform, which observes a signal realization s and transfers it to the producer. We are going to remain agnostic as to how this transfer occurs—whether the data is effectively sold to the producer, or the producer is merely able to learn something about the consumer when it interacts with them on the digital platform. At this level of abstraction, data intermediation is equivalent to buying a database as informative as $\mathcal{S}$ from the consumer and reselling it to the producer. With one platform and one producer, it is also immediate to show that the platform will charge the producer their entire willingness to pay to access the consumer's information. Therefore, we now focus on implications for consumers.

The consumer's ex-ante surplus, aggregating across both signals and types, is going to be given by $U(\mathcal{S})$ as in the previous section, if participat-

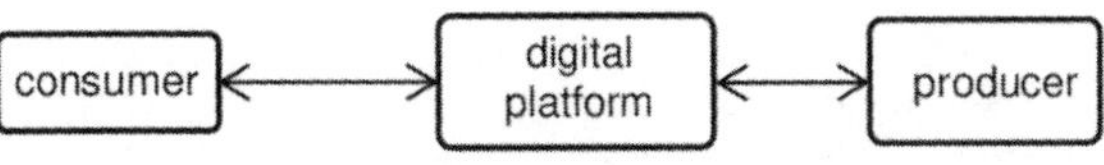

Figure 3.2 "Captive" consumer and producer

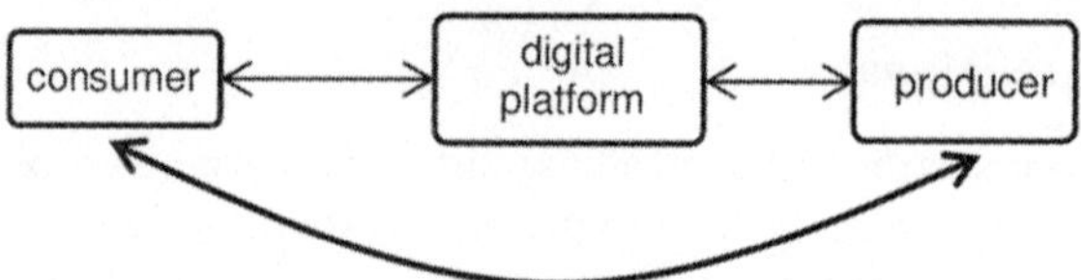

Figure 3.3 Consumer and producer with an alternative channel

ing, and zero otherwise.[4] Why is the consumer surplus nil if they do not participate? Because in this setting the platform is necessary for the consumer. For example, the platform lowers search costs, offers valuable independent services and matches of higher quality. At this stage if

$$U(S) \geq 0,$$

the consumer participates. In addition, if

$$U(S) \geq \max\{0, U(\varnothing)\}, \tag{2}$$

data intermediation yields a Pareto improvement: the consumer gains from interacting with the platform, and so does the producer. However, the more challenging case is one in which

$$U(\varnothing) > U(S) > 0. \tag{3}$$

The consumer finds it profitable to join the platform but loses relative to the case of anonymous transactions. This observation has prompted many scholars to refer to privacy loss as an unobserved price of accessing a digital platform. This occurs when the platform's services are nominally free, but consumers pay with their data.

Under these conditions, it was extremely easy for a platform to acquire the consumer's data. Let us now make the platform's problem more realistic (and a little harder) by allowing consumers and producers to meet off-platform.

3.3.2 Consumer Consent

Suppose now, as in Figure 3.3, that the consumer can choose whether to grant consent and reveal information to the platform, or deny consent and remain anonymous. If they do not reveal information, the consumer can still interact with the producer in an anonymous transaction (for example, because they can visit the producer's own web site). This is akin to consent requirements in recent legislative efforts aimed at protecting consumer privacy, e.g., CPRA.

In this model, absent any form of compensation, the consumer agrees to reveal their information if and only if they dislike privacy. When consumers

4. The use of the indirect utility function $U(\cdot)$ here underscores that the value of privacy to the consumer depends on the nature of the producer's actions a and on the underlying interaction $u(\theta, a)$. This is an important departure from philosophy and legal approaches to privacy. Unlike in Zuboff (2019), data collection makes no first-order difference to a consumer unless of course privacy enters utility function (which may well be the correct behavioral assumption).

have a positive value of privacy, as in (3), the platform must compensate consumers to reveal their information. While direct monetary payments are quite rare, compensation can occur through better-quality services and matches.

To quantify those payments, let us maintain the assumption that the platform is a monopolist facing a single producer. Thus, the platform can extract the producer's entire value of information downstream. This is the setting that has prompted many scholars to appeal to the Coase Theorem (Coase 1960) and argue that the simple assignment of property rights over data is going to yield the efficient level of information intermediation. The idea is simple and appealing: say the consumer owns the rights to their data and can sell them to the platform. In turn, the platform sells the consumer data to the producer. The three parties will be able to agree on the terms of trade—a price paid by the platform to the consumer and a price paid by the producer to the platform—if and only if the transfer of data from consumer to producer increases total surplus. In other words, if the loss in consumer privacy is worth more than the value of the information for the producer, then the platform will not be able to profitably intermediate this transaction.[5] This suggests that under well-specified property rights, the only trades of data that take place are those that satisfy condition (2).

In practice, however, there are at least two problems with the efficiency of the market for consumer information. The first problem is moral hazard: consumers do not reveal their information directly, e.g., by uploading spreadsheets with all their purchase data to an online retail platform. Instead, consumers reveal information through their online (and sometimes offline) behavior. The nature of data usage is critical for the trade of information in this setting. For instance, if consumers know their data will be used to set prices or steer their searches toward more expensive products, they have an incentive to distort their behavior. Such manipulation incentives may both bias and confound the information collected by the platform, thereby reducing its value to the producers.

These forces were first uncovered in the literature on behavior-based price discrimination and ratchet effects. The classic papers by Taylor (2004), Villas-Boas (2004), Acquisti and Varian (2005), and Calzolari and Pavan (2006) allow consumers to take actions (e.g., the level of purchases) at two different times in order to manipulate the second-period firm behavior. More recently, Bonatti and Cisternas (2020) show that the applicability of these models goes beyond business to consumer relationships. For example it can be used to shed light on B2B price discrimination.[6] While business privacy is

5. The 2020 California Privacy Rights Act also implicitly appeals to the Coase Theorem: consumers who opt out of data sharing have a *right to equal service and price*, but firms can "offer a different price, rate, level, or quality of goods or services to the consumer if that price or difference is reasonably related to the value provided to the business by the consumer's data."

6. For example, "Google induced advertisers to bid their true value, only to override pre-set AdX floors and [. . .] generate unique and custom per-buyer floors depending on what a buyer had bid in the past." (*Texas vs. Google*).

not typically an object of study, many of the same trade-offs face businesses and consumers who are aware of data collection. Argenziano and Bonatti (2021) study how consent regulation and other forms of property rights over data impact the level of trade and welfare in a signaling model.

The second problem is due to externalities, which we explore at length below.

3.3.3 Social Data

Unlike in the single-agent model discussed so far, many consumers make the decision as to whether to participate in the platform simultaneously. A central dimension of information intermediation is then its social aspect. The social aspect of information refers to the correlation in the underlying traits of consumers who join the same platform. Their decisions interact with one another, not directly but indirectly through the correlation structure of their types. This may lead to a market failure, because the social nature of data generates a data externality—the phenomenon that some consumers' data reveal information about other consumers. Data externalities do not have an a priori sign like carbon emissions or vaccinations. For example, if my data is used to offer better products to others, then I impose a positive externality on them; but if others' data is used to steer me toward expensive products instead, others impose a negative externality on me.

A recent and growing literature has shown how data externalities can reduce the cost of acquiring information from consumers—see for example Choi, Jeon, and Kim (2019), Acemoglu et al. (2022), Ichihashi (2021b), and Bergemann, Bonatti, and Gan (2022). The core idea is the following: when there are many consumers, even if the aggregate effect of revealing all their data might be large and negative for the surplus of any individual, the marginal impact of a single consumer's decision to participate on a digital platform is small. In the language of our basic framework, even if consumer i chooses not to participate on the platform, the producer will now have access to a potentially very informative segmentation $\mathcal{S}_{-i}$. Figure 3.4 illustrates this scenario.

To formalize this intuition, we follow Bergemann, Bonatti, and Gan (2022), who develop a model of monopolistic data intermediation with $i = 1, \ldots, N$ consumers. In their setting, as in the previous section, a platform can compensate each consumer for their own data, which it then resells to a single producer.

Suppose platform offers t_i to each consumer i for access to (data leading to) a segmentation $\mathcal{S}_i$ of i's type. Denote by $\mathcal{S} = (\mathcal{S}_1, \ldots, \mathcal{S}_N)$ the segmentation induced by every consumer's data. Consumer i makes a participation decision prior to learning their type. This consumer participates if and only if

$$t_i + U_i(\mathcal{S}) \geq U_i(\mathcal{S}_{-i}). \tag{4}$$

The interpretation of this participation constraint is that the transfer t_i must induce the consumer to prefer segmentation $\mathcal{S}$ to the alternative of withhold-

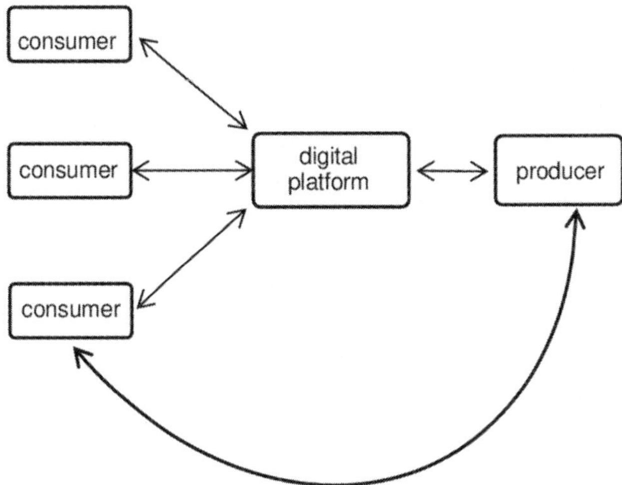

Figure 3.4 Many consumers with competing channel

ing their data, in which case the platform collects and transmits segmentation $\mathcal{S}_{-i}$. We can then formally define a data externality as follows.

Definition 1 (Data Externality)

The data externality imposed by consumers $-i$ on consumer i is given by

$$DE_i(\mathcal{S}) \triangleq U_i(\mathcal{S}_{-i}) - U_i(\varnothing).$$

The data externality DE_i captures the welfare effect for consumer i of all consumers $j \neq i$ revealing their data while i withholds theirs. We can then immediately put the data externality to work and obtain a characterization of profitable intermediation. Let $W_i(\mathcal{S})$ denote the total surplus (consumer welfare plus producer profits) generated by consumer i when the producer is endowed with segmentation $\mathcal{S}$, and define

$$\Delta W_i(\mathcal{S}) \triangleq W_i(\mathcal{S}) - W_i(\varnothing).$$

Bergemann, Bonatti, and Gan (2022) then show the following result.

Proposition 2 (Profitability of Intermediation)

Intermediation of data $\mathcal{S}$ is profitable if and only if, for all i,

$$\Delta W_i(\mathcal{S}) - DE_i(\mathcal{S}) \geq 0.$$

Intuitively, there are two channels through which a platform can potentially profit from data intermediation. A classic channel is that of surplus creation, which operates when revealing information to the producer helps (or does not excessively hurt) consumers. In particular, the transmission

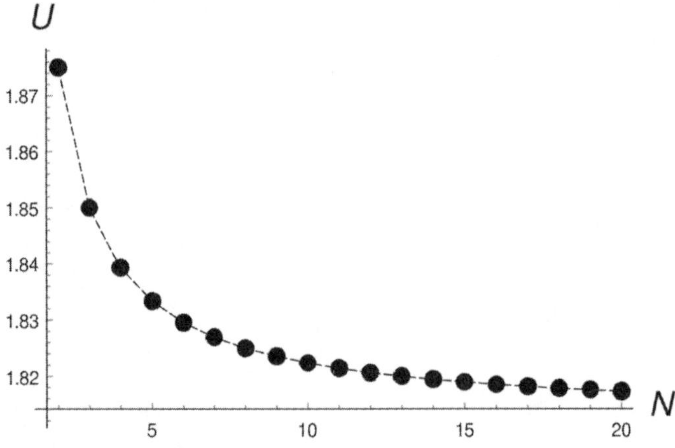

Figure 3.5 Consumer surplus $U(\mathcal{S}^*(N))$

of information may increase total surplus ($\Delta W_i > 0$), in which case data intermediation is both profitable for the platform and socially efficient. A more novel channel operates through the social dimension of the data: if individual consumers' decisions impose negative data externalities on other consumers ($DE_i < 0$), the platform can enlist additional consumers at lower marginal cost, thereby directly increasing its profits.

The latter scenario is more likely as the number of consumers increases. It is not hard to find conditions as in Figure 3.5 below, where consumer surplus decreases in the number of signals the platform procures, but it does so at a decreasing rate. Thus, a negative data externality combined with a diminishing marginal impact of each consumer's signal allow data intermediation to be both profitable and socially inefficient.

At this point, it may seem like this model predicts complete and unhinged data sharing. This is not always the case. Indeed, Bergemann, Bonatti, and Gan (2022) also show that the platform-optimal data sharing policy does not necessarily involve complete data sharing. In this sense, the nature of information qualifies the externality effect above and extends insights from the literature on contracting with externalities (Segal 1999) to the case of social data. In particular, the platform finds it optimal to intermediate individual-level information when the data increases total surplus (e.g., in the case of customized product recommendations). Conversely, when this information is used for *socially inefficient* price discrimination, the platform aggregates the consumers' signals and intermediates market-level information.

To summarize, the platform-optimal data sharing policy involves socially efficient data-anonymization decisions. Nonetheless, there are very few guarantees, if any, that the allocation of data is going to be socially efficient. After all, consumers are compensated for the individual harm that they receive, but not for the social harm that they create. Finally, as the markets grow large, which is a reasonable approximation for digital platforms, thc cost of acquiring the information from consumer vanishes, while the gains persist.

The social aspect of the data relates to the digital privacy paradox, whereby consumers require negligible compensation to reveal their data, in contrast with their stated preferences.[7] These results have prompted several scholars, most notably in psychology, philosophy, and law, to refer to privacy as a collective issue or public good, because the effectiveness of the tools used to monetize and leverage our information depends on our collective choices. Most notably, Zuboff (2019) argues,

> Privacy is not private, because the effectiveness of these and other private or public surveillance and control systems depends upon the pieces of ourselves that we give up.

3.3.4 Regulation and Competition

The potential market failures highlighted in this section naturally pose the question of the effectiveness of regulation. The discussion of data externalities above strongly suggests that individual-level regulation is unlikely to restore efficient outcomes in data collection.[8] A market structure that might achieve a more efficient outcome, without the aid of regulatory interventions, would be one where multiple platforms compete as in Rochet and Tirole (2003) for the (ideally exclusive) engagement of every consumer.

However, several recent papers have shown that the effect of competition is not at all straightforward, and that it is not hard to imagine realistic settings where platform competition does not lead to gains in consumer surplus. Most notably, Ichihashi (2021a) develops a model of competing data intermediaries that can acquire one or more "units" of data from a single consumer. The key property of data is that it can be sold to any number of intermediaries at zero cost by the consumer. Furthermore, all copies of the data must be identical—there is no room for selling differentiated data products as in Admati and Pfleiderer (1986). Therefore, if multiple intermediaries hold the consumer's data, they compete away all profits. In this model, when revealing their data has a negative impact on consumer surplus, a single platform is able to make an offer to the consumer that leaves them exactly

7. This result appears in the randomized control trial of Athey, Catalini, and Tucker (2017), and it was also true in a recent paper on the effects of the GDPR (Aridor, Che, and Salz 2020). In that paper, a large number of users paid no attention whatsoever to cookies and privacy-enhancing techniques even prior to the regulation. This is consistent with, even though not causally related to, the privacy paradox.

8. Viljoen (2021) emphasizes the relational aspect of digital markets whereby data creates value by enabling people to connect and the difficulties in regulating the nexus of links created by online data.

indifferent. In equilibrium, no other platform can then offer a positive price to the consumer for the data. Hence, the monopoly outcome obtains.

In complementary work, Casadesus-Masanell and Hervas-Drane (2015) offer an explanation for the shortcomings of competition, based on service quality; Loertscher and Marx (2020) provide an explanation for the emergence monopoly platforms based on data aggregation; and Prüfer and Schottmüller (2021) develop a dynamic model of "tipping" in data-rich industries that also supports the near-natural-monopoly theory.

Finally, even if competitive forces were strong, "privacy fixing" has emerged as a new anticompetitive concern. The idea is that, instead of fixing prices (because they are constrained to be zero), competing platforms might agree to not preserve their users' privacy. For example, the 2022 *Texas v. Google* complaint claims,

> Effective competition is concerned about both price and quality, and the fact that Google coordinates with its competitors on the quality metric of privacy—one might call it privacy fixing—underscores Google's selective promotion of privacy concerns only when doing so facilitates its efforts to exclude competition.

Similarly, the United States 2010 Horizontal Merger Guidelines require that

> [w]hen the Agencies investigate whether a merger may lead to a substantial lessening of non-price competition, they employ an approach analogous to that used to evaluate price competition.

3.4 Data Monetization

The mechanisms by which data is monetized are critical to understand the privacy implications of data intermediation. In this section, we consider a model where a platform has freely collected a single consumer's information, with the understanding that this is a metaphor for the equilibrium effect of data externalities. We also imagine that the platform can monetize this data by allowing any number of producers in a given industry to access the consumers' attention and target them with personalized offers.

Before turning to the privacy implications of such a market structure, let us think for a moment about potentially less profitable ways in which data might be sold.

3.4.1 Direct Sale of Information

In practice, digital platforms very rarely sell consumer data directly to advertisers and other parties. For one, the reputation backlash and the risk of leakages would be significant, but it is equally important to understand why this would be a suboptimal strategy even absent these concerns.

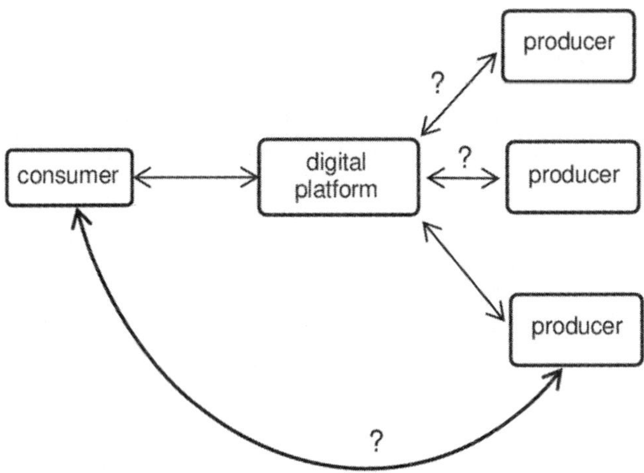

Figure 3.6 (Potentially) competing producers

Indeed, there are at least five reasons why platforms would not want to sell data directly.

1. The first problem a platform would face when selling data directly would be that information about consumers' willingness to pay is likely to create negative externalities downstream: if two or more competitors are informed about the correct product or price level to offer, each one is forced to lower prices. In this world, relative to physical goods, exclusive sales tend to be more profitable as shown in the classic contribution by Admati and Pfleiderer (1986).

2. The second problem relates to data pricing under exclusive sales. Let us entertain the possibility that a digital platform sells individual-level data to a single merchant only. The value of this information is a complicated equilibrium object, which depends on the complex game between one informed firm and its uninformed competitors (Bonatti et al. 2022).

3. The third problem is a classic difficulty with selling information. "Selling wine without bottles" is a famous metaphor (Barlow 1994) that refers to the zero marginal cost of data reproduction, which might easily lead to a profitable resale market for data (Shapiro and Varian 1999; Jones and Tonetti 2020). In other words, any data-selling platform creates its own competition by simply letting the data flow out of its own hands.

4. The fourth problem is that data about an individual consumer becomes obsolete over time, but not very quickly. Therefore a data seller is able to charge for the incremental information that they provide over and above the data buyer's initial information (Bergemann, Bonatti, and Smolin 2018). In

other words the platform can charge for the innovation component in the data, and not for the entire value of the data set.

5. The fifth and fundamental problem relates to how to measure the causal impact of data sales. In practice, it is difficult to prove how much a data product is worth without giving away the information contained in the data itself. This is the famous *information paradox* pointed out by Arrow (1962).

3.4.2 Indirect Sale of Information

While direct sales of information are problematic, targeted advertising is a superior, more profitable means to monetizing consumer information. Consider for example Google or Amazon search ads (or paid placement on Taobao.com). Advertisers buy a slot on a keyword-results page, which means they can tailor their message, the link they want to show, to the consumer's search query, which is informative of their underlying preferences. Of course, the search engine could sell data about those searches directly, but prefers to leverage the data to sell access to qualified eyeballs instead. Indirect sales of information are far more prevalent than direct sales, which is entirely consistent with what economic theory would have predicted (Admati and Pfleiderer 1990; Bergemann and Bonatti 2019).

Indeed, selling access to consumers directly solves all five problems we mentioned above. It solves the data exclusivity problem by offering a scarce number of slots. It solves the problem of competition under asymmetric information structures because only a few informed parties access the consumer at one time. It solves the resale and rental problem by never really giving out the data. Finally, it solves the quality measurement problem because advertisers have a number of conversion metrics available to them. Thus, it is only by bundling qualified eyeballs and advertising space that a large digital platform is able to monetize the troves of data at its disposal.[9] With these foundations in mind, we want to understand the implications of selling exclusive access to consumers through targeted advertising space.

3.4.3 Mechanisms for Digital Advertising

We now consider a large digital platform that matches heterogeneous buyers and sellers, running individual-level auctions for targeted advertising. A first treatment of this topic is in de Cornière and de Nijs (2016), who focus on bidding and unit pricing, and derive conditions under which the platform prefers targeting vs. a random allocation of slots. In what follows, we follow the more recent contribution of Bergemann and Bonatti (2023),

9. Indirect sales of information in digital markets are not limited to search advertising platforms: the same advantages relative to direct sales apply to large display advertising networks such as Google, Meta, Criteo, and Microsoft, as well.

who introduce the notion of a "managed campaign." Relative to that paper, we simplify the exposition by considering single-product sellers only.[10]

There are J sellers who offer horizontally differentiated products at no cost and a unit mass of consumers. Each consumer has a multidimensional type denoted by

$$\theta = (\theta_1,\ldots,\theta_j,\ldots,\theta_J) \in \mathbb{R}^J.$$

Each type component θ_j denotes the consumer's value for the product of firm j.

Independent of their type, a fraction $\lambda \in 0,1]$ of these consumers use a platform that runs ads in order to find a seller. The remaining $1 - \lambda$ consumers buy directly from sellers and face unit search costs $\sigma > 0$ after the first free search as in Diamond (1971).

The platform observes all types θ while consumers have arbitrarily precise beliefs m about their valuations. The platform offers a single "sponsored" advertising slot per consumer. In allocating the slot, the consumer's type serves as a *targeting category*: the firms' ads can condition on the entire vector θ.

More formally, the platform offers a *managed campaign* mechanism, which consists of the following. The platform charges a fixed fee t to participating sellers. (This can be viewed as a minimum mandatory campaign budget.) The platform specifies which seller j (among those who pay the fee) obtains the slot for which consumers θ. By releasing additional information, the platform then reveals to the consumer their value θ_j for the advertised product j. Finally, the platform enables each selected seller j to advertise a personalized price $p_j(\theta)$ to the consumer.

Simultaneously to making their participation and personalized pricing decisions on the platform, the sellers also set posted prices $\hat{p}_j$ intended for the (anonymous) off-platform consumers. The two sales channels (on- and off-platform) interact because on-platform consumers can also search, and (if they find a lower price or better product) they may buy off-platform. This introduces a "showrooming constraint" as in Wang and Wright (2020) and Teh and Wright (2022) whereby each seller j must provide weakly greater utility to their on-platform consumers than their off-platform consumers. Figure 3.7 illustrates the model.

In the Varian (1980) model of sales, consumers can be distinguished into shoppers and loyal and derive their surplus from price competition for shopping consumers. In the present model, the off-platform sales channel provides the consumer's outside option. In equilibrium, consumers obtain surplus because they can act anonymously and leverage their own right to

10. See also Bergemann, Bonatti, and Wu (2023) for a comparison between the managed campaign model and data-augmented auctions for digital advertising with manual bidding.

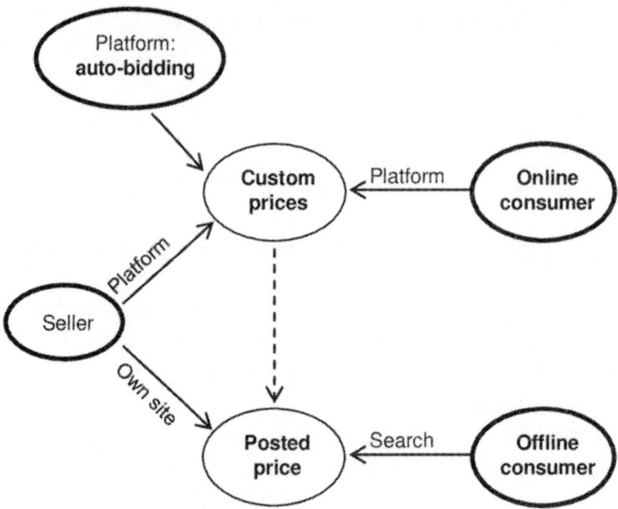

Figure 3.7 Model summary (Bergemann and Bonatti 2023)

privacy, so to speak, in order to acquire a good from the seller's direct channel. More generally, the on-platform consumer's search behavior depends on the criteria by which the platform assigns a sponsored link. Bergemann and Bonatti (2023) establish the following intuitive result, which has immediate implications for the equilibrium search patterns.

Proposition 3 (Optimal Matching Mechanism)

The platform maximizes revenues by matching each consumer θ *to most their favorite seller* $j^* = \text{argmax}_j \theta_j$ *among those who participate in the managed campaign mechanism.*

Under this matching mechanism, the platform fully exploits its informational advantage: the λ on-platform consumers infer that the displayed seller is *seller* $j^* = \text{argmax}_j \theta_j$, and they cannot detect any deviations by nonparticipating sellers. Furthermore, by showrooming, these consumers expect symmetric prices off the platform. Consequently, Bergemann and Bonatti (2023) show that these consumers only consider offers by the advertised seller.

Proposition 4 (Consideration Sets)

Every online consumer θ *only compares the displayed seller* j^**'s personalized (on – platform) and posted (off – platform) prices,* $|I|\, p_{j^*}(\theta)$ *and* $\hat{p}_{j^*}$.

Off the platform, consumers act as in the Diamond (1971) model. These $1 - \lambda$ consumers with beliefs m face search costs $\sigma > 0$ after the first search; they expect symmetric prices and hence visit $\hat{\jmath} = \text{argmax}_j m_j$ only. Figure 3.8

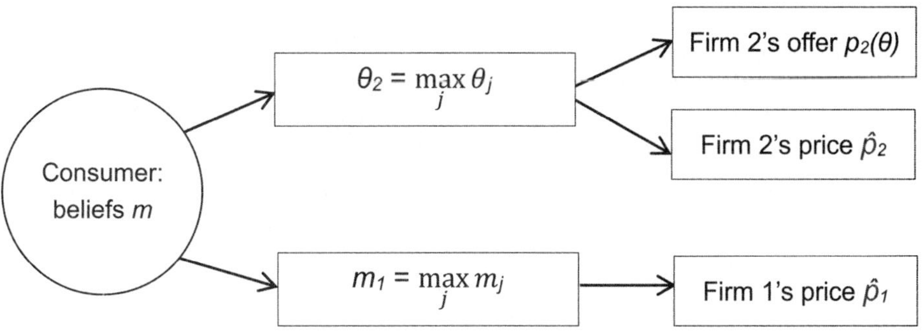

Figure 3.8 Search patterns (Bergemann and Bonatti 2023)

illustrates the search patterns of a consumer with beliefs m and true type θ both off platform and on platform.

The key result is that the platform is able to completely shield the most efficient producer from competition. After a link by the highest-value firm is shown to the consumer, the consumer infers that is indeed the highest-value firm. If this consumer were to showroom, they would only visit that firm's web site. Indeed, the model admits an equivalent interpretation wherein each brand has an identical fraction $(1 - \lambda)/J$ of loyal, imperfectly informed consumers who are already shopping off of the platform. The remaining λ consumers are not currently shopping, but they can be alerted to the existence of a brand. Once they are alerted by an ad, they contemplate shopping either on or off the platform. The equivalence with this behavioral model requires arbitrarily small amounts of search costs and informational advantages by the platform: without an informational advantage, the platform will not be able to control the consumers' outside options because the consumer's own beliefs will determine where they search first off the platform.

Finally, let us look at the results from a welfare perspective. The platform sells prominence to the highest bidder. This enables trade under symmetric information and induces higher total surplus. In this sense it has a positive social effect.[11] The platform, however, also sells market power. Indeed, the firms never compete in price, which leads to higher prices both on and off the platform. This is mostly due to the platform's informational advantage, which narrows the consumers' search options. The growth of a platform's database (through more consumers λ) reduces outside options and leads to higher prices—a different kind of data externality as pointed out in Kirpalani and Philippon (2020).

11. Trading through the platform is inherently more efficient even if consumers know their types. This is because under symmetric information, the platform eliminates any distortions from uniform monopoly pricing—with personalized pricing, all consumers buy. See Hidir and Vellodi (2021) on the price discrimination vs. product matching trade-off.

If, in addition, firms were heterogeneous in their cost function or in the number of on- versus off-platform consumers, the platform would introduce a further source of inefficiency. In particular, lower-quality brands with a smaller off-platform presence might be able to generate higher bids (or be willing to invest larger budgets), and their products might generate lower value for consumers. This scenario is qualitatively consistent with the evidence in Mustri, Adjerid, and Acquisti (2022).

3.4.4 Privacy and Competition

The results in the managed campaign model make apparent the privacy vs. competition trade-off. With any indirect sale of data (such as digital advertising auctions and managed campaigns), advertisers learn relatively little about consumers. The key to the success of this intermediation mechanism is that advertisers are able to use the information exactly as if they owned the data. But in practice, they only learn summary statistics on the return on their investment. With automated bidding, advertisers might not even know how much they bid for each consumer category, because the platform does so for them. Furthermore, only the platform ever holds the consumer data, which reduces the risk of leakages.[12]

However, because only a few firms (in the model, just one) are allowed to use the information at any time, the additional privacy gains can come at the cost of worse terms of trade for the consumer. This is consistent with the concern in Cremèr, de Montjoye, and Schweitzer (2019) that

> [o]ne cannot exclude the possibility that a dominant platform could have incentives to sell "*monopoly positions*" to sellers by showing buyers alternatives which do not meet their needs.

In this sense, the optimal managed campaign mechanism is successful precisely because it restricts competition. Privacy protection sounds anticompetitive in the context of this model, but this is not yet a general conclusion—a lot more work is warranted on this topic, especially as it relates to data-driven mergers (Chen et al. 2022). I outline further critical areas for research below.

3.5 Conclusions

We have focused on the data that large digital platforms collect from individual users, and on the mechanisms by which they monetize the information so-gained with advertisers. Various characteristics of digital markets suggest the emergence of a novel "two-sided" dimension of user privacy,

12. See Fainmesser, Galeotti, and Momot (2022); Jullien, Lefouli, and Riordan (2020); and Tucker (2019) for a discussion of exogenous and endogenous (equilibrium) risks of data leakages.

where the actions of all participants on both sides of the platform (users and advertisers) shape the level of privacy for each individual consumer.

Let us summarize the key findings. Firstly, a platform's ability to profitably collect an individual's data is not solely dependent on that individual's actions or legal rights. The social aspect of data, where others' information provides insights into my preferences, introduces a data externality that creates a gap between the profitable and efficient allocation of information, even when property rights are well defined.

Secondly, the profitability of selling targeted advertising rises as more firms compete for exclusive access to a consumer's attention. This amplifies the incentives for data collection and potentially enhances the quality of matching between consumers and producers through stronger selection effects. However, higher-quality matches may also result in a (smaller) more homogeneous consumer population for each advertiser, enabling surplus extraction through market prices without the need for first-degree price discrimination.

Lastly, the activities of data collection and data monetization by digital platforms interact with each other. The expansion of a platform's database through increased consumer participation facilitates data acquisition while simultaneously increasing advertisers' willingness to pay for premium placement. This, in turn, diminishes the value of their private sales channels as well as the value of each consumer's outside option.

A lot of work remains to be done in this area. For example, the question of competing data platforms and data sellers is conspicuously understudied, with only recent promising initial treatments (de Cornière and Taylor 2023; Ichihashi 2021a). Data combination, federated learning, and other privacy-preserving initiatives are also worth further study (Bergemann, Bonatti, Demirer, and Vilfort 2023), as is the evaluation, both theoretical and empirical, of recent regulatory interventions (Ali, Lewis, and Vasserman 2023; Argenziano and Bonatti 2021; Chen 2022). Finally, the information-design approach can apply to equally, if not more, important dimensions of consumer privacy, such as the political economy implications of government surveillance. Questions of algorithmic fairness, differential privacy, the trade-off between the efficacy of industrial policy and individual liberties (Beraja et al. 2022), as well as the special status of health data (Miller 2022), are all areas deserving of further treatment.

References

Acemoglu, D., A. Makhdoumi, A. Malekian, and A. Ozdaglar. 2022. "Too Much Data: Prices and Inefficiencies in Data Markets." Forthcoming in *American Economic Journal: Microeconomics*.

Acquisti, Alessandro, Curtis R. Taylor, and Liad Wagman. 2016. "The Economics of Privacy." *Journal of Economic Literature* 54 (2): 442–92.

Acquisti, Alessandro, and Hal R. Varian. 2005. "Conditioning Prices on Purchase History." *Marketing Science* 24 (3): 367–381.

Admati, Anat R., and Paul Pfleiderer. 1986. "A Monopolistic Market for Information." *Journal of Economic Theory* 39 (2): 400–438.

Admati, Anat R., and Paul Pfleiderer. 1990. "Direct and Indirect Sale of Information." *Econometrica* 58 (4): 901–928.

Ali, S. Nageeb, Gregory Lewis, and Shoshana Vasserman. 2023. "Voluntary Disclosure and Personalized Pricing." *Review of Economic Studies* 90 (2): 538–571.

Argenziano, Rossella, and Alessandro Bonatti. 2021. "Data Linkages and Privacy Regulation." Discussion paper, Essex and MIT.

Aridor, Guy, Yeon-Koo Che, and Tobias Salz. 2020. "The Economic Consequences of Data Privacy Regulation: Empirical Evidence from GDPR." Discussion paper 26900, National Bureau of Economic Research.

Arrow, Kenneth. 1962. "Economic Welfare and the Allocation of Resources for Invention." In *The Rate and Direction of Inventive Activity: Economic and Social Factors*, edited by Richard R. Nelson. Universities-National Bureau Committee for Economic Research & Committee on Economic Growth of the Social Science Research Council, 609–626. Princeton, NJ: Princeton University Press.

Athey, Susan, Christian Catalini, and Catherine Tucker. 2017. "The Digital Privacy Paradox: Small Money, Small Costs, Small Talk." NBER Working Paper 23488. Cambridge, MA: National Bureau of Economic Research.

Barlow, John Perry. 1994. "The Economy of Ideas." *Wired Magazine, March 1, 1994.*

Beraja, Martin, Andrew Kao, David Y. Yang, and Noam Yuchtman. 2022. "AI-tocracy." Forthcoming in the *Review of Economic Studies*.

Bergemann, D., and A. Bonatti. 2023. "Data, Competition, and Digital Platforms." 2023. Discussion paper 2343R, Cowles Foundation for Research in Economics.

Bergemann, Dirk, and A. Bonatti. 2019. "Markets for Information: An Introduction." *Annual Review of Economics* 11: 85–107.

Bergemann, Dirk, A. Bonatti, M. Demirer, and V. Vilfort. 2023. "Privacy, Federated Learning, and the Value of Data." Discussion paper, Yale University and MIT.

Bergemann, Dirk, A. Bonatti, and T. Gan. 2022. "The Economics of Social Data." *RAND Journal of Economics* 53 (2): 263–296.

Bergemann, Dirk, Alessandro Bonatti, and Alex Smolin. 2018. "The Design and Price of Information." *American Economic Review* 108 (1): 1–48.

Bergemann, Dirk, Alessandro Bonatti, and Nick Wu. 2023. "Managed Campaigns and Data-Augmented Auctions for Digital Advertising." Discussion paper 2359, Cowles Foundation for Research in Economics.

Bergemann, Dirk, Benjamin Brooks, and Stephen Morris. 2015. "The Limits of Price Discrimination." *American Economic Review* 105: 921–957.

Bonatti, A., M. Dahleh, T. Horel, and A. Nouripour. 2022. "Selling Information in Competitive Environments." Discussion paper, MIT.

Bonatti, Alessandro, and Gonzalo Cisternas. 2020. "Consumer Scores and Price Discrimination." *Review of Economic Studies* 87: 750–791.

Bonatti, Alessandro, Yunhao Huang, and J. Miguel Villas-Boas. 2023. "A Theory of the Effects of Privacy." Discussion paper, MIT and UC Berkeley.

Calzolari, Giacomo, and Alessandro Pavan. 2006. "On the Optimality of Privacy in Sequential Contracting." *Journal of Economic Theory* 130 (1): 168–204.

Casadesus-Masanell, Ramon, and Andres Hervas-Drane. 2015. "Competing with Privacy." *Management Science* 61 (1): 229–246.

Chen, Zhijun. 2022. "Privacy Costs and Consumer Data Acquisition: An Economic Analysis of Data Privacy Regulation." Discussion paper, Monash University.

Chen, Zhijun, Chongwoo Choe, Jiajia Cong, and Noriaki Matsushima. 2022. "Data-Driven Mergers and Personalization." *RAND Journal of Economics* 53 (1): 3–31.

Choi, J., D. Jeon, and B. Kim. 2019. "Privacy and Personal Data Collection with Information Externalities." *Journal of Public Economics* 173: 113–124.

Coase, R. H. 1960. "The Problem of Social Cost." *Journal of Law and Economics* 3: 1–44.

Cremèr, J., Y.-A. de Montjoye, and H. Schweitzer. 2019. "Competition Policy for the Digital Era." Discussion paper, European Commission.

de Cornière, Alexandre, and Romain de Nijs. 2016. "Online Advertising and Privacy." *RAND Journal of Economics* 47 (1): 48–72.

de Cornière, Alexandre, and Greg Taylor. 2023. "Data and Competition: A Simple Framework." Discussion paper 1404, Toulouse School of Economics.

Diamond, Peter A. 1971. "A Model of Price Adjustment." *Journal of Economic Theory* 3 (2): 156–168.

Elliott, Matthew, Andrea Galeotti, Andrew Koh, and Wenhao Li. 2022. "Market Segmentation through Information." Discussion paper, Cambridge University.

Fainmesser, Itay P., Andrea Galeotti, and Ruslan Momot. 2022. "Digital Privacy." Forthcoming in *Management Science*.

Haghpanah, Nima, and Ron Siegel. 2022. "The Limits of Multiproduct Price Discrimination." *American Economic Review: Insights* 4 (4): 443–58.

Hidir, Sinem, and Nikhil Vellodi. 2021. "Privacy, Personalization, and Price Discrimination." *Journal of the European Economic Association* 19 (2): 1342–1363.

Ichihashi, Shota. 2020. "Online Privacy and Information Disclosure by Consumers." *American Economic Review* 110 (2): 569–595.

Ichihashi, Shota. 2021a. "Competing Data Intermediaries." *RAND Journal of Economics* 52 (3): 515–537.

Ichihashi, Shota. 2021b. "The Economics of Data Externalities." *Journal of Economic Theory* 196: 105316.

Johnson, Garrett. 2022. "Economic Research on Privacy Regulation: Lessons from the GDPR and Beyond." NBER Working Paper 30705. Cambridge, MA: National Bureau of Economic Research.

Jones, Charles I., and Christopher Tonetti. 2020. "Nonrivalry and the Economics of Data." *American Economic Review* 110 (9): 2819–58.

Jullien, B., Y. Lefouli, and M. H. Riordan. 2020. "Privacy Protection, Security, and Consumer Retention." Discussion paper, Columbia University and TSE.

Kirpalani, R., and T. Philippon. 2020. "Data Sharing and Market Power with Two-Sided Platforms." NBER Working Paper 28023. Cambridge, MA: National Bureau of Economic Research.

Loertscher, Simon, and Leslie M. Marx. 2020. "Digital Monopolies: Privacy Protection or Price Regulation?" *International Journal of Industrial Organization* 71: 1–13.

Miller, Amalia. 2022. "Privacy of Digital Health Information." Discussion paper, National Bureau of Economic Research.

Mustri, Eduardo Abraham Schnadower, Idris Adjerid, and Alessandro Acquisti. 2022. "Behavioral Advertising and Consumer Welfare: An Empirical Investigation." Discussion paper, Carnegie Mellon University, 2022.

Posner, Richard A. 1981. "The Economics of Privacy." *American Economic Review* 71 (2): 405–409.

Prüfer, Jens, and Christoph Schottmüller. 2021. "Competing with Big Data." *Journal of Industrial Economics* 69 (4): 967–1008.

Robinson, J. 1933. *The Economics of Imperfect Competition*. London: Macmillan.

Rochet, Jean-Charles, and Jean Tirole. 2003. "Platform Competition in Two-Sided Markets." *Journal of the European Economic Association* 1 (4): 990–1029.

Schmalensee, Richard. 1981. "Output and Welfare Implications of Monopolistic Third-Degree Price Discrimination." *American Economic Review* 71 (1): 242–247.

Segal, Ilya. 1999. "Contracting with Externalities." *Quarterly Journal of Economics* 114: 337–388.

Shapiro, Carl, and Hal R. Varian. 1999. *Information Rules: A Strategic Guide to the Network Economy*. Harvard Business Press.

Stigler, George J. 1980. "An Introduction to Privacy in Economics and Politics." *Journal of Legal Studies* 9 (4): 623–644.

Taylor, Curtis R. 2004. "Consumer Privacy and the Market for Customer Information." *RAND Journal of Economics* 35 (4): 631–650.

Teh, Tat-How, and Julian Wright. 2022. "Intermediation and Steering: Competition in Prices and Commissions." *American Economic Journal: Microeconomics* 14 (2): 281–321.

Tucker, Catherine. 2019. "Privacy, Algorithms, and Artificial Intelligence." In *The Economics of Artificial Intelligence: An Agenda*, edited by Ajay Agrawal, Joshua Gans, and Avi Goldfarb, 423–437. Chicago, IL: University of Chicago Press.

Varian, Hal. 1980. "A Model of Sales." *American Economic Review* 70 (4): 651–659.

Viljoen, Salome. 2021. "A Relational Theory of Data Governance." *Yale Law Journal* 131.

Villas-Boas, J. Miguel. 2004. "Consumer Learning, Brand Loyalty, and Competition." *Marketing Science* 23 (1): 134–145.

Wang, Chengsi, and Julian Wright. 2020. "Search Platforms: Showrooming and Price Parity Clauses." *RAND Journal of Economics* 51 (1): 32–58.

Yang, Kai Hao. 2022. "Selling Consumer Data for Profit: Optimal Market-Segmentation Design and Its Consequences." *American Economic Review* 112 (4): 1364–93.

Zuboff, Shoshanna. 2019. *The Age of Surveillance Capitalism*. New York: Public Affairs.

4

Economic Research on Privacy Regulation Lessons from the GDPR and Beyond

Garrett A. Johnson

4.1 Introduction

Privacy is a conundrum. Privacy and the data economy are two sides of the same coin. Viewed from each side, progress on the respective dimension can seem obvious. Nevertheless, the two are often at cross-purposes.[1] Economic researchers can illuminate our understanding of privacy, the data economy, and the trade-offs involved. Policy makers and regulators worldwide wrestle with crafting and enforcing privacy regulation. Economic research can inform their difficult task.

The European Union's General Data Protection Regulation (GDPR) is a landmark privacy regulation that elevated the tension between privacy and the data economy. The European Union (EU) passed the GDPR in April 2016, but delayed enforcement until May 25, 2018. In many ways, the GDPR set the privacy regulation agenda globally. Dozens of countries have since passed privacy regulation, including Brazil, China, India, and New Zealand (Greenleaf 2023). At its heart, the GDPR defines personal data expansively to include all data relating to an individual. The regulation provides EU residents with multiple data rights, like the right to access and delete their

Garrett A. Johnson is an assistant professor of marketing at the Questrom School of Business at Boston University.

I thank Samuel Goldberg, Matthew Schneider, Scott Shriver, the book editors, and an anonymous referee as well as seminar participants at the NBER's 2022 Privacy Tutorial, the European Commission's Joint Research Centre Digital Economy Unit, the Federal Communications Commission, and Université Paris Dauphine for providing helpful comments. I thank the NBER for providing funding for this work. I dedicate this work to Luke. For acknowledgments, sources of research support, and disclosure of the author's material financial relationships, if any, please see https://www.nber.org/books-and-chapters/economics-privacy/economic-research-privacy-regulation-lessons-gdpr-and-beyond.

1. The World Bank devoted its 2021 World Development Report to exploring this tension.

data. The GDPR imposes responsibilities on firms like data auditing and data-breach notification. The regulation also lays out multiple legal bases—including consent—for processing personal data. The GDPR's maximum fines of 4 percent of a firm's annual revenue ensured it caught the attention of firms and the wider public. As a landmark and influential regulation, the GDPR is of great interest to economists.

However, the GDPR poses three key challenges for empirical research. First, economists often examine the GDPR as an event study but may lack a suitable control group in certain settings. In particular, the GDPR covers most of Europe and also has substantial global spillovers that contaminate candidate control group members. Second, GDPR compliance and enforcement vary by industry, compliance requirement, firm size, country, and over time. This creates gaps between the regulation as written and the regulation in practice which, in turn, complicates the conclusions we can draw from GDPR research. Third, the GDPR may directly restrict the availability—and selection into—individual-level data that economists can use to understand the impact of the regulation. As we will see, economists have proposed various solutions to and workarounds for these challenges.

Five years after the GDPR's enforcement deadline, economic research on the GDPR is maturing. To date, much economic research examines the GDPR's impact on firms. The GDPR hurt firm performance by imposing costs, decreasing revenue, and thereby hurting profitability. Venture funding for technology firms fell—particularly for more data-related ventures. The GDPR limited economic dynamism by accelerating market exit and slowing entry. At the same time, the GDPR created an opportunity to test hypotheses about the consequences of privacy regulation for firm competition and innovation (see, e.g., Goldfarb and Tucker 2012). Research shows that the GDPR hurt competition by creating greater harms for smaller firms and by increasing market concentration in the data vendor market. The evidence for innovation is more mixed, though several studies suggest that the GDPR constrained data-related innovation. Research shows that the GDPR reduces the share of individual-level data available to firms. When firms rely on consent to process data, consumer data becomes self-selected though consenting consumers tend to be favorably selected. On the web, studies show a decrease in EU traffic to web sites after the GDPR, a modest drop in ad revenue, as well as a short-lived reduction in sites' use of third-party vendors. However, the GDPR had no apparent effect at the Internet's connectivity layer or on web site content provision. Finally, the GDPR seemed to constrain firms' marketing activities for personalized channels like email and online display advertising.

Fewer studies examine the GDPR's consequences for consumers, though this gap largely reflects the inherent measurement challenge. Survey evidence quantifies consumer valuations for their data rights as well as consumer's awareness of privacy and perceived control over their personal data. Empirical research shows post-GDPR reductions in data collection and use that suggest objective improvements in consumer privacy. Structural modeling suggests consumer harm from the GDPR's adverse impact on innovative product development. Theory evidence suggests varying consequences of certain elements of the GDPR for both firms and consumers.

The economics literature also illuminates the consequences of the GDPR's design decisions. The literature documents important spillovers of the GDPR outside of the EU. In particular, research shows that foreign firms that serve EU consumers sometimes exhibit greater compliance than EU firms. This may reflect the GDPR's penalty design: foreign firms that fall under the GDPR's extraterritoriality component may be especially leery of GDPR fines that are based on global revenue rather than EU revenue alone. Research also shows indirect spillovers like global firms implementing their compliance efforts worldwide, so that non-EU consumers benefit. Though the GDPR intended to harmonize regulation within the EU, several scholars document differences in regulatory impact by the perceived strictness of EU country-level regulators.

This review is far from the last word on the GDPR, as the literature and the practical application of the regulation are both still evolving. I focus on the economic literature and the empirical economic literature in particular. However, the study of the GDPR is inherently interdisciplinary, so I occasionally draw on research from law and computer science. This review was commissioned for the NBER Privacy Tutorial in October 2022. As such, my emphasis on research challenges and future research opportunities in part stems from that tutorial's doctoral student audience. Nonetheless, I think that this emphasis is helpful for understanding the literature and the shape it has taken so far. For future research, I indicate more privacy-related changes—whether through regulation or platform policies—that provide possible event studies for empiricists. I also suggest that economists should study privacy-enhancing technologies that are beginning to be commercialized, as these technologies improve the trade-off between privacy and economic uses of data.

This review builds on previous review articles on the economics of privacy and complements other work by great scholars in this volume. For instance, Acquisti, Taylor, and Wagman (2016) provide a general introduction to the economics of privacy. In this volume, the chapter by Miller (2024) on health information privacy describes important antecedents to GDPR research that often exploit changes in health privacy regulation. Carrière-Swallow and Haksar (2019) and the World Bank (2021) examine data policy from an economic perspective. Goldfarb and Tucker (2012) discuss the economics of privacy and innovation. Notably, Prasad and Perez (2020) provide an early review of the economic literature on the GDPR.

The rest of this guide is organized as follows. Section 4.2 provides a background on the GDPR. Section 4.3 discusses key challenges that the GDPR poses for empirical research. Section 4.4 reviews the economic literature to date on the GDPR. Section 4.5 highlights some avenues for future research on the economics of privacy regulation. Section 4.6 concludes.

4.2 GDPR Background

The GDPR is a lengthy and multifaceted regulation, which opens many avenues for economic research. In this section, I share background on the regulation *as written* for economists. The GDPR contains 99 articles and is supported by an additional 173 recitals. Jones and Kaminski (2020) provide a helpful background for those who are more familiar with the American legal context. Jones and Kaminski point out that the GDPR is situated within a broader legal context that includes the EU Charter, complementary EU and national privacy regulations, EU privacy regulator guidance, EU judicial rulings, and the EU's 1995 Data Protection Directive that preceded the GDPR.

I begin by laying out the regulation's essential features. The GDPR takes a broad approach to data protection regulation by defining personal data as all data relating to a person (Article 4(1)). This extends beyond personally identifiable information like a name or address to include pseudonymous identifiers and online identifiers. For brevity, I refer to personal data as simply *data* below. The GDPR refers to the "processing" of data which includes data collection, storage, use, analysis, sharing, and more (Article 4(2)). The GDPR further distinguishes what it refers to as "special category data" as being particularly privacy-sensitive. This includes data on health, genetics, sexual orientation, political opinions, religious beliefs, and more (Article 9(1)). Though this review focuses on firms, the GDPR covers all individuals and institutions (e.g., governments and non-profit organizations) that process personal data.[2]

The GDPR establishes six data rights for EU residents (Articles 12–23). Under this regulation, residents gain the rights to access and correct data that a firm has about them. Residents gain the right to delete their data, which is often referred to as the "right to be forgotten." Residents even receive the right to port their data to another firm. Residents gain the right to object to data processing and even the right to object to decisions made on the basis of automated processing.

The GDPR imposes a number of responsibilities on firms (Articles 24–43). Firms have to fulfill the above rights-related responsibilities in a timely manner. Firms need to audit their data processing activities—also known as a "Data Protection Impact Assessment." Firms need to minimize their data

2. The GDPR distinguishes between data controllers and data processors (Article 4(7–8)). This distinction refers to cases where, e.g., firm X delegates data processing to firm Y, but firm X retains decision rights regarding the data processing. In this example, firm X is the data controller and firm Y is the data processor.

processing activities—i.e., data protection by default—which is also a key principle of the GDPR (Article 5(1c)). Firms must encrypt and pseudonymize the data they process—i.e., data protection by design. In the event of a data breach, firms must notify the regulator and affected consumers within 72 hours. Finally, firms should designate a data protection officer—either an employee or an external consultant—to oversee their data protection-related activities.

Though consent sometimes plays an outsized role in discussions about the GDPR (Jones and Kaminski 2020), consent is only one of the GDPR's six legal bases for processing data (Article 6(1)). These legal bases are consent, contractual obligation, legitimate interest, legal obligation, vital interest of an individual, and public interest. For most firms, the first three bases are most relevant. As an example, an ecommerce web site could use contractual obligation as a legal basis for processing a consumer's name and address information for the purpose of shipping products to the consumer. Legitimate interest is the most flexible of the legal bases, but it is not a *carte blanche* as it should not override an individual's right to privacy (ICO 2021). Legitimate interest carries additional duties like carrying out and documenting a "legitimate interest assessment" that weighs the firm's specific interest against consumers' privacy interest (ICO 2021). Regardless of the legal basis, the firm should provide information to the consumer including the purpose(s) of data processing, the relevant legal basis(es), the contact information of the data protection officer (where applicable), and the identities of all third-party data recipients (Article 13). Note that special category data has additional restrictions (Article 11) as does child's consent (Article 7).

The GDPR sets a high standard for consent (Article 7). Consent should be an unambiguous, affirmative act like ticking a box on a web site: preticked boxes or inactivity do not indicate valid consent (Recital 32). Consumers must be able to withdraw consent at any time, and just as easily as they provided consent. In obtaining consent, firms must inform consumers using plain language. Consent should be granular to the purpose(s) of processing (Recital 32). As mentioned above, this includes listing all third-party data recipients. Consent should be freely given in that the firm should not condition its consumer offerings on consent when these do not require data processing. Finally, firms must be able to show a record of the consumer's consent.

The GDPR also covers data transfer outside of the European Economic Area (i.e., EU plus Iceland, Liechtenstein, and Norway). Article 45 permits the transfer to countries that have adequate data protection, which encourages foreign countries to adopt GDPR-like regulation. As of now, the European Commission deems 14 countries as adequate, including: Argentina, Canada, Israel, Japan, New Zealand, South Korea, Switzerland, the United Kingdom, and Uruguay. Articles 45 to 50 lay out alternative data transfer arrangements including foreign firms' adherence to standard contractual clauses adopted by the European Commission. Data transfers to the US remain a thorny issue, however.[3] The 2016 "EU-US Privacy Shield" permitted data transfers to certified firms but was invalidated by the Court of Justice of the European Union in 2020. In 2022, the European Commission and the US agreed in principle to a new data-transfer arrangement, but this is still being finalized. Despite this, Meta received the largest ever GDPR fine of €1.2 billion in May 2023 for processing EU user data in the US. For the same reason, four EU regulators have ruled that Google's popular web site analytics product (Google Analytics) is illegal.

The GDPR charges Data Protection Authorities (DPAs) in all EU countries with enforcing the regulation (Articles 51–59). DPAs are charged with regulating data processing by firms that are located in their country; that substantially affects their country's residents; or for which they have received a complaint by a resident or organization in their country (Articles 4(22), 57). Though the GDPR was intended to harmonize EU-wide regulation, regulators vary in resources by country (EDPB 2020). For multinational firms, the GDPR's "one-stop shop mechanism" allows firms to select a country as their lead regulator by locating their headquarters in that country (Article 56). The lead regulator mechanism simplifies the firm's dealings with EU regulators, though firms may therefore prefer to locate their headquarters in countries which they believe have weaker DPAs. Nevertheless, other EU DPAs retain considerable rights in multi-national cases (Article 60).[4] The GDPR also establishes an EU-wide European Data Protection Board consisting of the European Data Protection Supervisor and the head of each country's DPA (Article 68). The board issues guidelines, promotes cooperation between DPAs, issues opinions on draft DPA decisions, and resolves disputes between DPAs (Articles 65, 70).

The GDPR stipulates that firms can be fined up to the greater of €20 million or 4 percent of their global annual revenue (Article 83(5)). For lesser infractions, the maximum fines are halved (Article 83(4)). Enforcementtracker.com maintains a list of GDPR fines that are made public.[5] As of September 2022, this site lists 1,279 fines totaling €2 billion and averaging €1.6 million per fine. The majority of these fines are €10,000 or less. The largest seven fines have all been issued to big technology firms: Amazon (the single largest fine until 2022), Meta (3 fines), and Alphabet/Google (3 fines). The countries that have issued the most fines are Spain (496), Italy (181), and Germany

3. Using OECD data from 1995 to 2018, Ferracane et al. (2023) show that the EU adequacy is associated with a 6–14 percent increase in digital trade. This finding is driven by the EU granting adequacy to the US in 2000 and 2016.

4. In practice, impatient regulators have sidestepped the one-stop mechanism by enforcing their national privacy laws. For instance, the French DPA fined both Google and Meta despite those firms having their headquarters in Ireland.

5. Presthus and Sønslien (2021) provide an analysis of the first two years of GDPR fines.

(115). The total value of fines are highest for Luxembourg (€746 million), Ireland (€649 million), then France (€272 million). DPAs can instead handle cases by warning firms or requiring compliance plans, but these instances are usually not documented publicly. Despite this, Koutroumpis, Ravasan, and Tarannum (2022) obtain data on thousands of the British DPA's regulatory actions and show that it used fines sparingly. Beyond administrative fines, the GDPR also includes a private right of action, whereby consumers can seek compensation for privacy-related damage suffered through their country's courts (Article 82).

In sum, the GDPR is a multi-faceted regulation that increases the legal risk and cost associated with data processing. In later sections, we will discuss still more features of the GDPR for researchers to consider. As we will see in Section 4.3.2, the GDPR is further complicated by the sometimes substantial gap between the regulation as written and the reality on the ground.

4.3 Research Challenges

The GDPR represents a tremendous opportunity for economists to study privacy regulation and its impact. Nevertheless, the GDPR poses several challenges for research. Below, I focus on three key challenges and describe solutions devised from the literature.

Most economists study the GDPR as an event study. I begin by recalling a leading approach for analyzing event studies: difference-in-differences (see, e.g., Cameron and Trivedi 2005). Difference-in-differences combines two comparisons. First, we compare a treatment group that is subject to the policy with a control group that is not. These groups should satisfy the stable unit treatment value assumption (SUTVA), meaning that the GDPR does not affect the control group. Second, we compare outcomes before and after the policy. As the name suggests, the difference-in-differences approach estimates the policy's impact by subtracting the before-after means comparison in the control group from that of the treatment group. The identifying assumption is that the treatment and control groups' outcome variable would follow parallel trends after the policy, but for the policy's impact.

The GDPR poses several problems for this analysis framework. Section 4.3.1 discusses the potential challenge of finding a suitable control group that satisfies both SUTVA and the parallel trends assumption. Section 4.3.2 notes that both firm compliance and regulatory enforcement were variable under the GDPR. This poses a problem for generalizing from the real-world estimated impact of the GDPR—or lack thereof—to the regulation as written. Finally, Section 4.3.3 notes the GDPR's confounding impact on data observability. By construction, the GDPR creates a missing-data problem whereby observed individual-level data are selected and the corresponding aggregate statistics are incomplete.

4.3.1 Lack of a Suitable Control Group

Most economists study the GDPR as an event study. Event studies should include (1) a suitable control group, and (2) a clear start date. These criteria are often challenging to address satisfactorily. In the case of the GDPR, both criteria pose problems for research, though the first is unusually challenging.

The GDPR's scale and global scope can make a suitable control group difficult to find in many cases. First, the GDPR's large scale makes it appealing to study, but limits the set of suitable control countries. The GDPR covers 28 EU countries and another 3 European Economic Area countries. To put the problem starkly, a substantial idiosyncratic economic shock to the EU after May 2018 would bias many economic studies. Second, the GDPR has substantial spillovers outside of Europe because the regulation's scope includes not only EU firms but also non-EU firms that target EU residents. For instance, a Canadian ecommerce site that offers shipping to customers in the EU is also subject to the regulation. Third, the GDPR may have indirect spillovers outside of the EU as well. International firms may choose to roll out their GDPR compliance efforts globally due to cost efficiencies in treating their customers and data uniformly. Furthermore, the GDPR raised the attention paid to privacy worldwide and—to some extent—raised global commercial compliance standards to the EU's high standard. Bradford (2020) refers to such phenomena that in effect export EU policy globally as the "Brussels Effect."

GDPR researchers need to also reflect on the appropriate timing to use. The GDPR has two main start dates to consider: its passage in April 2016 and its enforcement deadline in May 2018. The GDPR affects all EU countries simultaneously, unlike past research that benefited from variation in the timing of privacy regulation (e.g., Miller and Tucker 2009). Most studies focus on the latter enforcement date, but some consider both. For instance, firms may have incurred compliance costs before and after the enforcement deadline. If consumer-facing compliance efforts come online after the deadline, the GDPR's effect on revenue may manifest after the deadline. In some cases, anticipatory compliance may attenuate GDPR impact estimates. In other cases, firms may have delayed compliance until the enforcement deadline or even later (see, e.g., Demirer et al. 2023). In sum, researchers should evaluate the relevant timing in their setting as a function of its underlying economics and its institutional realities.

Many GDPR papers use difference-in-differences as their identification strategy and most use non-EU countries (or units therein) as a control. For instance, Aridor, Che, and Salz (2023) examine data from travel web sites and argue that these have "separate, country-specific, versions of their web sites," so that the sites' requirement to comply with the GDPR is clear. Moreover, Aridor, Che, and Salz use non-EU travel web sites in Northern Hemisphere countries as a control group, so that these sites are both exempt from the GDPR and should have similar seasonal demand for travel. Similarly, Jia, Jin, and Wagman (2021) examine the GDPR's effect on EU technology venture investment using the US as their primary control group, and a combination of remaining countries as a secondary control group for robustness. In this case, the free flow of capital between countries may create spillovers to the control group. Jia, Jin, and Wagman (2021) therefore argue that they would overestimate (underestimate) the GDPR's impact if the GDPR decreases (increases) investment outside the EU. Johnson, Shriver, and Goldberg (2023b) instead use a "panel differences" approach in their study of web site traffic. This approach is essentially a difference-in-differences strategy that uses the same web sites in the previous year as a control group. By construction, this approach rules out GDPR spillovers and accounts for firm-specific seasonal differences, but requires parallel trends across years.

Several GDPR papers instead apply identification strategies that do not depend on a control group. Some authors argue that a sudden change in an outcome after the GDPR can be attributed to the regulation. For web sites' use of technology vendors, Peukert et al. (2022) use essentially an interrupted time-series design, whereas Johnson, Shriver, and Goldberg (2023b) use before-after differences. An interrupted time-series design (see, e.g., McDowall, McCleary, and Bartos 2019) assumes that the counterfactual outcome continues its baseline (e.g., linear) time trend, as established pre-GDPR. This approach attributes post-GDPR changes in both the outcome's level and trend to the regulation. Lacking pre-trend data, Johnson, Shriver, and Goldberg instead compare outcome levels after the GDPR with a pre-GDPR baseline. The authors argue that unobserved time trends confound their estimates, so that short-run differences best reflect the causal impact of the GDPR. Other authors exploit variation in the degree of exposure to the GDPR. For example, Yuan and Li (2019) compare the financial performance of EU hospitals by whether the hospitals are more or less data-dependent. Chen, Frey, and Presidente (2022) use variation in industry-level exposure to the EU using trade data to calculate the share of output sold to EU countries. Finally, Godinho de Matos and Adjerid (2022) use a GDPR-related marketing field experiment in order to avoid an event-study style analysis entirely.

4.3.2 Variable Firm Compliance and Regulatory Enforcement

The European Commission (2019) status report on the GDPR acknowledges that the regulation fell short of its potential due to a lack of enforcement. The GDPR literature has shown variation in compliance efforts by industry, by country, by compliance requirement, by firm size, and over time. As a result, economists must critically examine the lessons that can be drawn from the GDPR in the context of variable compliance and enforcement.

In general, regulatory outcomes can be thought of as the product of strategic interactions between firms and regulators. Compliance is costly to firms, and small and medium-sized firms in particular may lack the resources to comply. In surveys, a majority of firms reported that they were not compliant with the GDPR at the enforcement deadline and that their compliance efforts were a work in progress (TrustArc 2018). At the same time, enforcement is costly to the regulator, and country-level DPAs vary in resources (EDPB 2020). GDPR fines to date also show that country DPAs vary in their strictness and tactics. We can therefore expect a gap between the regulation as written and the reality on the ground.

GDPR enforcement and compliance are especially challenging for a number of reasons. Unlike vehicle emissions standards, for instance, GDPR compliance is multidimensional and compliance outcomes can be difficult to observe.[6] Moreover, the GDPR is complex and enumerates many compliance options (e.g., bases for data processing), which make some compliance elements subjective. In this sense, compliance can be described as a "cookbook" with more flexibility and options than a single "checklist" for all firms. Relatedly, compliance norms may arise gradually and evolve over time (see, e.g., Hils, Woods, and Böhme 2020; Lefrere et al. 2022).[7] Since personal data is pervasive, the GDPR can be considered to be a "law of the whole economy." Regulators must therefore set enforcement priorities.[8] Finally, privacy regulators, unlike antitrust regulators for example, lack enforcement experience and established precedent to draw upon.

The compliance literature emphasizes that regulators can ensure compliance using a combination of fines and the probability of receiving a fine (see, e.g., Polinsky and Shavell 2000). The above points may reduce the probability of receiving a fine. Perhaps to offset this, the maximum fines under the GDPR are large.

Nevertheless, the cost of strict GDPR compliance may exceed even the maximum fines in some industries. Web sites and the technology vendors that support them provide plausible examples. Many web sites rely on advertising to generate revenue and some research shows that ad prices double when ad impressions contain a cross-site cookie identifier for users (Johnson, Shriver, and Du 2020; Ravichandran and Korula 2019). Web sites may therefore resist complying on dimensions that jeopardize their revenue model.[9]

6. Of course, the observability of compliance outcomes also poses a problem for empirical research. In practice, data breaches are therefore useful entry points for regulators to select and investigate enforcement targets.

7. This poses a challenge if we treat the GDPR as an event study.

8. These priorities should flow from the regulators' democratic mandate, which may in turn constrain the regulators' enforcement targets. For instance, regulators may hesitate to crack down on domestic firms or firms that provide public goods like content creators.

9. Beyond limiting technology vendors, web site compliance strategies include notifying users of the presence of browser cookies, offering the user some consent choice, discontinuing the use of third-party cookies (at least prior to obtaining consent), and/or blocking EU users (Johnson, Shriver, and Goldberg 2023b; Lefrere et al. 2022; Skiera et al. 2022).

However, regulators are concerned about the privacy harm of this industry's use of online identifiers and have repeatedly criticized this industry's level of compliance (AP 2019; CNIL 2019; DPC 2020; ICO 2019). Regulators complain that the industry loads vendor content and cookies prior to obtaining consent and that the industry's consent practices fall short of the GDPR's opt-in standard. Nevertheless, regulators did not fine this industry until the end of 2020. Several economic studies find that web sites cut the number of vendors and/or third-party cookies in May 2018, but also find that these returned to pre-GDPR levels within a few months (Johnson, Shriver, and Goldberg 2023b; Lefrere et al. 2022; Lukic, Miller, and Skiera 2023; Peukert et al. 2022). These papers wrestle with what policy lessons can be drawn as a result, and most focus on the short-run changes. For instance, Johnson, Shriver, and Goldberg argue that the post-GDPR rebound can not be attributed to the GDPR alone due to some combination of low compliance, shifting compliance norms, lack of enforcement, and the industry's exogenous growth.

Despite these prominent cases of low compliance in data-dependent industries, the GDPR did meaningfully change the compliance and enforcement environment within the EU. The GDPR and its large fines in particular caught the attention of European firms (Martin et al. 2019). Using data from Microsoft's cloud computing platform, Demirer et al. (2023) show that the GDPR had its intended impact of reducing data processing. Even US firms increased their attention to data privacy—as evidenced by mentions in publicly listed firms' annual reports—particularly for those firms with a presence in the EU (Boroomand, Leiponen, and Vasudeva 2022; Maex 2022). Before the GDPR, EU enforcement of some privacy laws on the books was low, so non-compliance was a viable strategy for firms (Martin et al. 2019). I emphasize this, because it again shows that economists should not assume that firms comply with the letter of the law where privacy regulation is concerned. However, the GDPR increased political pressure on data protection authorities to use their new powers to increase enforcement and thereby shifted firm beliefs about the probability of penalties (Martin et al. 2019).

Variable compliance and enforcement can obfuscate the lessons that can be drawn from empirical GDPR research. What is clear is that scholars should not assume uncritically that the GDPR *as written* actually happens *in practice*. Instead, scholars should investigate the reality of the GDPR on the ground. In particular, scholars must grapple with how firms comply with the GDPR in their setting. Cost-benefit analysis can illuminate the economics of a firm's compliance decisions. Scholars should also examine regulators' public statements and regulatory actions to understand the enforcement priorities in the setting of interest. On the consumer side, scholars should not assume, for instance, that consumers make use of their new data rights under the GDPR in economically meaningful quantities (DataGrail 2020; Presthus and Sørum 2021).

The literature grapples with these issues in several ways. Researchers look for domains where compliance activities are stronger or at least quantifiable. Finally, scholars acknowledge the variable nature of both compliance and regulation, and the difficulties this presents for generalizing from the short- and long-run impact of the GDPR.

4.3.3 GDPR's Impact on Data Observability

The GDPR limits personal data processing, which creates problems for empirical researchers. The GDPR may increase the cost of accessing data for researchers or prevent data access altogether (Greene et al. 2019).[10] When consent is the legal basis for collecting data, this introduces self-selection into the data. Consent-based selection is more challenging than data missingness alone, because an unknown quantity of individual data will be altogether absent from the database. These data issues pose a challenge for many applied microeconometricians who use individual-level data to deliver economic insight.

Researchers have navigated this problem with a variety of approaches. To begin, economists can still use non-personal data—like accounting or macroeconomic data—which the GDPR should not affect (Chen, Frey, and Presidente 2022; Jia, Jin, and Wagman 2021). Alternately, Zhao, Yildirim, and Chintagunta (2021) use individual data from a panel of consenting consumers to study the GDPR's impact on online search behavior. Though such panels are themselves selected—e.g., presumably panelists have a lower preference for privacy—the panels at least are complete.

Other researchers embrace the GDPR's impact on consent-based missingness as interesting in its own right. For instance, Aridor, Che, and Salz (2023) investigate the impact of the GDPR on online user data. Aridor, Che, and Salz obtain data from a marketing intermediary that sends offers to users on a large collection of online travel agency web sites around the world. These travel web sites share user-level, travel-related search data with the intermediary, which then makes targeted offers to users based on the user's predicted purchase probability. After the GDPR, the intermediary receives less data, which Aridor, Che, and Salz attribute to a segment of users who refuse consent for data sharing. Aridor, Che, and Salz show that the remaining consenting users are favorably selected in that they have longer search histories. Aridor, Che, and Salz attribute this to two explanations. First, privacy-sensitive users obfuscate their browsing histories (e.g., by clearing cookies), so that they appear as multiple user identifiers with short browsing histories prior to the GDPR. Second, user willingness to consent may be correlated with user's travel web site activity, for instance, because users who like the site may be more willing to both browse the site and provide

10. Relatedly, Yom-Tov and Ofran (2022) document a shift in clinical trials out of the EU and toward countries with weaker data protections after the implementation of the GDPR.

consent. After the GDPR, the intermediary can no longer see or sell to non-consenting users, which hurts its revenue. Aridor, Che, and Salz point out an interesting silver lining: as the consenting user data is longer and higher quality, the intermediary may have an easier time predicting user behavior and making successful offers to consenting users.

Goldberg, Johnson, and Shriver (2024) work with similar data from a large number of web sites globally from Adobe Analytics. Web sites use Adobe Analytics to measure outcomes like site visits, page views, and ecommerce revenue. Goldberg, Johnson, and Shriver show that these outcomes—as recorded by Adobe—fell by about 12 percent after the GDPR. As in Aridor, Che, and Salz (2023), Adobe may see less data because of non-consenting users after the GDPR. However, Adobe would also record less site data if the GDPR actually hurt the real outcomes for these sites. Goldberg, Johnson, and Shriver grapple with this identification problem by constructing bounds on the relative contributions of the consent and real effects of the GDPR to the drop in recorded site outcomes.

4.4 Literature Review

In this section, I review the economics literature on the GDPR. Section 4.4.1 examines the GDPR from the perspective of consumers. Section 4.4.2 turns to the GDPR's impact on firms. This literature is larger, so we first consider the GDPR's impact on firms' economic performance measures before diving deeper into the GDPR's impact on competition, innovation, the web, and marketing. Section 4.4.3 discusses the lessons learned about the GDPR's constituent parts and how they work in practice.

At the outset, I point out that the GDPR literature is still maturing. Five years after the enforcement deadline, a minority of economics papers have appeared in print. As such, many of the papers I discuss below are working papers, and will therefore continue to evolve in the future.

4.4.1 Impact on Consumers

The economics literature has explored the GDPR's consequences for consumers. However, privacy economists generally find that consumer privacy preferences are difficult to ascertain (see, e.g., Athey, Catalini, and Tucker 2017). One approach is to survey consumers and ideally to do so prior to the GDPR for a baseline comparison. For instance, Presthus and Sørum (2021) surveyed a cross-section of Norwegian university students annually from 2018 to 2020. However, this evidence failed to show the GDPR's expected improvements: the surveys show no increase in general awareness of privacy or perceived control over personal data.

Sobolewski and Paliński (2017) implement a stated preference discrete choice experiment prior to the GDPR. By surveying Polish university students, Sobolewski and Paliński obtain willingness-to-pay estimates for four individual data rights under the GDPR.[11] This study reveals a similar average willingness to pay for the right to be forgotten, the right to object to profiling, and the GDPR's extended information obligations. However, the willingness to pay for data portability was negative and statistically insignificant. The authors provide an estimate of the welfare benefit of the GDPR by summing consumer willingness to pay for these four rights. Sobolewski and Paliński thus estimate that the GDPR provides a value of €6.50 per person per month.

Other economic papers speak to the consumer welfare impact of the GDPR or show objective improvements in consumer privacy. Janßen et al. (2022) argue that the GDPR hurts consumer surplus by reducing innovation in consumer products. To show this, they use a structural demand model to examine the consumer consequences of the GDPR to the app market. In theoretical work, Ke and Sudhir (2022) and Wang, Xu, and Zhang (2022) investigate the welfare consequences of the GDPR for both firms and consumers.

The GDPR should improve consumer privacy by improving data security and reducing data processing. These objective improvements in privacy may be difficult to quantify across firms and at large scale. Nevertheless, Demirer et al. (2023) show that EU firms reduce both their data storage and computation activity on Microsoft's cloud service after the GDPR. Moreover, these effects grew over time such that, in the GDPR's second year, data storage in the EU fell by 26 percent and "compute" (i.e., core-hours of cloud computation) fell by 15 percent relative to the US. As we will see in Section 4.4.2.3, several researchers find that web sites reduced data sharing after the GDPR, though these privacy improvements were short-lived. A small segment of consumers appears to be exercising their consent privilege by opting out of data collection online (Aridor, Che, and Salz 2023; Goldberg, Johnson, and Shriver 2024).

By drawing attention to data protection, the GDPR may have influenced how firms measure and report their data-protection activities. For example, the GDPR's data-breach notification requirement should have reduced the number of data breaches.[12] Indeed, GDPR research finds increased firm demand for cybersecurity-related skills for both employees (Koutroumpis, Ravasan, and Tarannum 2022) and board members (Klein, Manini, and Shi 2022). Nevertheless, the impact on data breaches would be challenging to evaluate empirically, as the notification requirement should also increase the number of breaches that firms both notice and report. Similarly, the GDPR's encryption requirement should reduce the privacy risk from data breaches. Despite this, Miller and Tucker (2011) show that (public) data-breach inci-

11. See Presthus and Sørum (2019) for related survey evidence.

12. Romanosky, Telang, and Acquisti (2011) show that state-level breach disclosure laws in the US reduced identity theft caused by data breaches by 6.1 percent.

dents actually increased after the American medical sector adopted data encryption.

4.4.2 Impact on Firms

Several scholars document that the GDPR harmed a variety of firms' outcomes including: profits, revenue, investment, market exit, and entry. I first discuss the evidence for firm performance before turning to the GDPR's impact on competition (Section 4.4.2.1), innovation (Section 4.4.2.2), the web (Section 4.4.2.3), and marketing (Section 4.4.2.4).

Multiple studies examine accounting data and attribute a reduction in firms' profit and/or revenue to the GDPR. For instance, Koski and Valmari (2020) examine nearly 267,000 EU and US firms from 2014 to 2018. The authors use difference-in-differences with US firms as a control and 2018 as the treatment year. Koski and Valmari find a statistically insignificant effect on profit margins in their full sample, but a statistically significant −1.9 percent reduction in profit margins among data-intensive sectors in the EU (i.e., information and communications, banking, and other financial services). Chen, Frey, and Presidente (2022) examine almost 700,000 firms across 61 countries and 34 industries. By comparing firms by their sector's revenue exposure to the EU, they attribute a decline in profits and a reduction in sales by the firm's degree of GDPR exposure. Yuan and Li (2019) use difference-in-differences to compare the financial performance of hospitals in the EU by the importance of information, communication, and telecommunication to their business. They find lower operating revenue (scaled by total assets) for more data-intensive hospitals during the GDPR's transition period from passage to enforcement (2016–2018).

Survey evidence finds that firms incurred and continue to incur significant costs in order to comply with the GDPR. The International Association of Privacy Professionals (IAPP 2017) estimated that Fortune 500 global firms would spend $7.8 billion on compliance.[13] DataGrail (2020) finds that 74 percent of small- and mid-sized organizations spent more than $100,000 on compliance. Five years after the GDPR, IAPP (2023) found that the average European privacy budget was €1.1 million, the annual base salary for EU privacy professionals was €98,893, and the number of privacy technology vendors (368) had grown almost eightfold since 2017.

Recent research on the GDPR illuminates firm's compliance cost. Demirer et al. (2023) estimate that the GDPR was equivalent to a 20 percent tax on the cost of data storage. Koutroumpis, Ravasan, and Tarannum (2022) examine the impact of the GDPR in the United Kingdom by comparing sectors by their share of regulatory enforcement cases. Koutroumpis, Ravasan, and Tarannum find that the demand for cyber-related labor increases

13. The IAPP figure extrapolates from survey evidence in the IAPP and Ernst and Young (2017) report.

by 52 percent in more scrutinized sectors. Accounting research by Maex (2022) finds that the GDPR improved proxies of firms' internal information quality, which indirectly improved firms' operational efficiency (i.e., the efficiency of deploying inputs to generate sales). Still, Maex finds that the regulatory burden of the GDPR exceeded this benefit such that firms' operational efficiency fell on net.

Jia, Jin, and Wagman (2021) show that the GDPR reduced investment for EU technology ventures.[14] Using the difference-in-differences strategy described in Section 4.3.1, they find that the number of EU venture deals fell by 26 percent after the GDPR enforcement deadline. Jia, Jin, and Wagman also document that the most affected firms are: early-stage ventures, data-related ventures, business-to-consumer (versus business-to-business) ventures, and ventures in the healthcare and finance industries. These patterns are consistent with a GDPR effect as we may expect the GDPR to have greater effects for ventures that use data, especially consumer data, health data (i.e., special category data), and in heavily regulated industries. Jia, Jin, and Wagman (2020) build on this research by examining differences between EU and foreign investors. Jia, Jin, and Wagman find an increase in investor home bias post-enforcement: that is, foreign investment in EU technology ventures falls by more than local investment. Jia, Jin, and Wagman argue that this is consistent with foreign investors having greater uncertainty about the financial consequences of the GDPR.

Several papers show that the GDPR harms economic dynamism. Koutroumpis, Ravasan, and Tarannum (2022) find that sectors that receive greater scrutiny from the British data protection authority exhibit a 12 percent relative reduction in market entry and a 13 percent relative increase in market exit. Janßen et al. (2022) show a larger impact on both entry and exit for mobile apps on the Android platform after the enforcement deadline. Janßen et al. examine app data from the Google Play Store using a before-after comparison and supplement their findings by surveying German app developers. Relatedly, Kircher and Foerderer (2021) document a small increase in closures of US app startups post-GDPR as well as a small reduction in venture capital transactions for US app startups relative to US enterprise software startups.

4.4.2.1 *Impact on Competition*

Several observers warned of a potential trade-off between privacy regulation and competition (e.g., Brill 2011; Goldfarb and Tucker 2012; Phillips 2019). Indeed, the GDPR literature repeatedly confirms this hypothesis. In general, regulation can impact competition if firms experience returns to scale in compliance. For privacy regulation, consent requirements may also

14. Note that Lambrecht (2017) also finds a reduction in venture investment in certain sectors after the EU's e-Privacy Directive.

favor large established firms if consumers are more likely to provide consent to such firms (Campbell, Goldfarb, and Tucker 2015) or to consent to smaller lists of third-party data recipients. Gal and Aviv (2020) and Geradin, Karanikioti, and Katsifis (2020) discuss several potential channels through which the GDPR may affect competition.

Many researchers find that the GDPR disproportionately hurts smaller firms (e.g., Bessen et al. 2020; Chen, Frey, and Presidente 2022; Jia, Jin, and Wagman 2020; Koski and Valmari 2020; Maex 2022; Zhao, Yildirim, and Chintagunta 2021). Johnson, Shriver, and Goldberg (2023b) and Peukert et al. (2022) focus on the privacy-competition trade-off question. Both find that the market for technology vendors that serve web sites became more concentrated right after the GDPR's enforcement deadline. This provides evidence for a new anticompetitive mechanism: when privacy regulation restricts business-to-business data transfers, firms may prefer to retain their larger vendors. Contrary to Campbell, Goldfarb, and Tucker (2015), Johnson, Shriver, and Goldberg find no evidence that consent drives this increased concentration. However, the simple explanation is that sites rarely make the list of third-party data firms prominent when requesting consent. On the other hand, Goldberg, Johnson, and Shriver (2024) provide indirect evidence that smaller web sites obtain lower consent rates, which would limit the profitable use of data by these smaller firms.

4.4.2.2 Impact on Innovation

Goldfarb and Tucker (2012) argue that a trade-off exists between privacy and innovation. They support their argument with numerous studies focusing on the online-advertising and healthcare sectors. Supported by interviews of startups and lawyers in 2018, Martin et al. (2019) point out that the GDPR can both support and suppress innovation. For instance, the interviews suggested that the GDPR spurred privacy-related innovation as well as increased demand for "regulation-exploiting innovation"—that is, diffusing compliance management software and encryption capabilities. However, Martin et al. also document claims that the GDPR led startups to abandon products, discouraged entrepreneurs, and limited innovators' access to input data (e.g., for artificial intelligence applications).

The empirical evidence for the GDPR's impact on innovation is somewhat mixed. As we have seen at the top of Section 4.4.2, the GDPR reduced technology venture funding and hurt market dynamism. Bessen et al. (2020) survey artificial intelligence startups. Bessen et al. find that GDPR imposes costs on these firms in terms of adding new position(s), reallocating resources, and deleting data. Despite the GDPR's requirements on firms, Bessen et al. find that the use of various data protection methods does not differ by whether the firm has customers in Europe. Venkatesan, Arunachalam, and Pedada (2022) provide evidence that the GDPR increased the return on assets from acquisitions of AI technology companies—particularly for acquisitions related to customer experience and cybersecurity. Perhaps counter to expectations, Chen, Frey, and Presidente (2022) find that patenting among IT service firms increased 30 percent, though this figure is imprecisely estimated.

Blind, Niebel, and Rammer (2023) examine innovation using an annual survey of German firms from 2011 to 2020. Examining the 2018 survey, Blind, Niebel, and Rammer note that 35.0 percent of firms report that data protection regulation hampers their innovation activities, whereas only 4.7 percent report the opposite. Perhaps in contrast with other GDPR research, the share of firms that report either an innovation-facilitating or innovation-complicating role seems to increase with firm size. Blind, Niebel, and Rammer also find that the GDPR shifts innovation to become more incremental and less radical in nature.

4.4.2.3 Impact on the Web

The web uses personal data to personalize web sites, content, and advertising. At a basic level, the Internet requires IP addresses—which the GDPR considers to be personal data—to function. For researchers, the Internet and web sites therefore provide an opportunity to study an industry that is both targeted by the regulation and provides data for empirical study.

Researchers have examined the GDPR's impact on site traffic, site vendor use, site content creation, Internet infrastructure, and online search. Several researchers find that the GDPR reduced sites' use of vendors and/or data sharing using third-party cookies (Johnson, Shriver, and Goldberg 2023b; Lefrere et al. 2022; Lukic, Miller, and Skiera 2023; Peukert et al. 2022). Several computer science researchers concur with these findings (e.g., Libert, Graves, and Nielsen 2018; Urban et al. 2020). Wang, Jiang, and Yang (2023) show that a large publisher saw a modest reductions in ad revenue, though the authors attribute the small effect size to high user-consent rates. Despite these issues, or perhaps due to the rapid post-GDPR bounce-back, Lefrere et al. (2022) find no impact on news and media web sites' production of new content or social sharing of that content. Using data from Adobe Analytics, Goldberg, Johnson, and Shriver (2024) argue that real web site page views and ecommerce revenue from EU users falls by at least about 0.5 percent post-GDPR due to degraded marketing capabilities. Using third-party site-traffic data, Schmitt, Miller, and Skiera (2021) find a larger (5–10 percent) reduction in site visits, Congiu, Sabatino, and Sapi (2022) find an even larger (15 percent) reduction in 2019, but Lefrere et al. find that EU site traffic measures are relatively stable except for a small decline in page views per user.[15] Finally, Zhao, Yildirim, and Chintagunta (2021) examine the brows-

15. These authors assume that their data fully captures real site outcomes (i.e., the ground truth). Nevertheless, it is unclear how their data sources—SimilarWeb (Congiu, Sabatino, and Sapi 2022; Schmitt, Miller, and Skiera 2021) and Alexa web information services (Lefrere et al. 2022)—address traffic from non-consenting users (see Section 4.3.3). In particular, SimilarWeb explains that it somehow models traffic using a variety of data sources, which include

ing behavior of a panel of online users. Zhao, Yildirim, and Chintagunta find that EU users increase their online search intensity after the GDPR relative to their non-EU counterparts.

The GDPR limits international data transfers—particularly to the majority of countries that do not meet the EU's adequacy requirements. As such, we might expect that the GDPR affected data flows between the EU and the rest of the world. Zhuo et al. (2021) investigate this possibility by obtaining data at the Internet's infrastructure level to monitor physical investments in international data flows. However, Zhuo et al. find no GDPR effect in the EU on the Internet's interconnectivity layer. This finding is further notable because it arises despite the reductions—albeit modest—in site traffic and vendor use documented above. Though the authors lack more granular data on the type of data flows, the authors suggest that growth in, for instance, data-heavy video traffic may mask the observed reduction in other web-related data flows. Relatedly, Demirer et al. (2023) find that the GDPR's impact on cloud storage and computing were modest at first but grew over time. This may explain the perhaps contrasting result in Demirer et al. that firms that used cloud-based web services exhibit much greater reductions in both cloud storage and computing.

4.4.2.4 Impact on Marketing

The GDPR was expected to reduce firms' marketing capabilities and thereby limit matching between firms and consumers. In particular, the GDPR's data processing restrictions were expected to hurt personalized marketing channels like email and online display advertising. Consistent with this, Goldberg, Johnson, and Shriver (2024) find larger reductions in recorded EU site traffic originating from email or display ad clicks relative to visits that directly navigate to the web site. Wang, Jiang, and Yang (2023) find that the GDPR degraded online display ad performance including ad click-through and conversion rates. Aridor, Che, and Salz (2023) highlight that the GDPR can limit personalized marketing opportunities, but favorably selected data from consenting users can improve the firm's individual marketing response predictions.

Godinho de Matos and Adjerid (2022) and D'Assergio et al. (2022) examine email permissioning campaigns. Many marketers sought to bring their marketing consent up to the GDPR standard by running a permissioning campaign to (re-)obtain consent. Godinho de Matos and Adjerid run a marketing field experiment with a large European telecommunications firm. This firm sent out a permissioning email in the treatment group, and sent that email after a delay in the control group. Godinho de Matos and Adjerid show that the permissioning campaign succeeded at increasing the share

site analytics data (which must exclude non-consenting users) shared by web sites as well as a panel of browser extension users.

of consumers to which the firm can market. Moreover, Godinho de Matos and Adjerid show that the firm was able to subsequently both increase the marketing messages it sent to treated consumers and increase revenue from these consumers.

D'Assergio et al. (2022) collect and categorize 1,506 different permissioning emails. They find that 29 percent of these emails tried to persuade users (e.g., with discount offers or discussing benefits of data sharing), 35 percent only used an informative approach, and 20 percent combined both approaches. D'Assergio et al. also partner with a European firm to run an email field experiment. The authors find evidence that persuasive tactics can improve opt-in rates and that combining this with informative tactics can further improve opt-in rates. However, the authors find no significant differences in the amount of personal data shared across conditions.

4.4.3 Elements of the GDPR in Practice

One challenge in studying the GDPR is that the regulation contains so many elements. Since these elements were all applied at once, the event-study nature of most GDPR research limits how much can be learned about the GDPR's constituent parts. Nevertheless, unpacking these elements is useful for evaluating the regulation and designing effective privacy regulation. Several researchers have shown patterns that appear to reveal some consequences of the GDPR's design decisions and features of the regulation in practice.

The GDPR intended to harmonize data regulation within the European Union, and this was thought to be a source of efficiencies for firms that serve multiple EU countries (European Commission 2012). However, we have seen that regulators vary in their resources and enforcement strategies. Several authors have found that the size of the GDPR's impact is correlated with firms' beliefs about regulatory strictness specific to data protection at the country level (Goldberg, Johnson, and Shriver 2024; Jia, Jin, and Wagman 2020, 2021; Johnson, Shriver, and Goldberg 2023b). To establish this, these studies use a European Commission (2008) survey of data processors by EU country that asked whether their local data protection regulator was more or less strict than regulators in the rest of the EU. By this metric, the strictest data regulators are Germany and Sweden, and the laxest regulators are Bulgaria and Greece. Though this regulatory strictness measure is dated, it appears to predict the depth of the GDPR's impact.[16]

Other research examines international spillovers from the GDPR. Peukert et al. (2022) highlight the spillovers to non-EU residents using web site data collected from the vantage point of a US user. Non-EU residents see the largest vendor reductions on web sites located in the EU that serve primarily an EU audience. This suggests that EU-focused firms roll their compliance

16. Though country-level strictness is correlated with per capita income, these papers show that the strictness result is robust to including income as a model covariate.

efforts to all their consumers, which benefits their (limited) foreign audience. Non-EU web sites cut their vendors vis-à-vis US users, though by very little for sites that primarily serve a non-EU audience.

Johnson, Shriver, and Goldberg (2023b) instead scan web sites from the perspective of a French user, using a VPN service. They find that—from the perspective of an EU user—foreign sites with a small share of EU users make deeper cuts to their vendors than sites that primarily serve EU users. Johnson, Shriver, and Goldberg attribute this pattern of results to the design of the GDPR fines, which reach 4 percent of a firm's *global* revenue. In particular, the benefit of exploiting user data is relatively small for sites with a small share of EU users, but otherwise equivalent sites would face the same fine. Perhaps due to these differing incentives, Johnson, Shriver, and Goldberg remark that EU firms here do less to protect EU residents than non-EU firms.[17]

Sørum and Presthus (2020) examine the GDPR's data access and portability rights by initiating personal data access requests from 15 firms. They find that almost all these firms responded quickly and provided personal data, though the data provided fell short of the letter of the law (i.e., all eight items regarding data access under Article 15).

Finally, several researchers show that firms that rely more on consumer data and sensitive data exhibit greater harms from the GDPR (e.g., Jia, Jin, and Wagman 2021; Li, Yu, and He 2019). This may oversimplify the picture for certain industries though, as established firms with experience handling sensitive data may instead have lower adjustment costs. Koski and Valmari (2020) discuss this lower adjustment cost as a potential explanation for their findings.

4.5 Future Opportunities for Research

The GDPR is an important and relatively recent regulation. We will undoubtedly see more related research in the future. In the conclusion, I suggest some directions for future research. Below, I suggest two key opportunities for privacy research. Section 4.5.1 enumerates recent and future privacy-related changes to regulation and technology platforms. Section 4.5.2 introduces privacy-enhancing technologies and discusses opportunities for economists to improve these technologies and study their adoption.

4.5.1 More Privacy Regulations and Changes on the Horizon

Though the GDPR received most of the literature's attention in recent years, several other regulations and interventions have since passed or are

17. Note that Lefrere et al. (2022) complement these two studies by scanning 909 news and media publisher web sites from the vantage point of both EU and US users. Lefrere et al. largely confirm the above results using third-party cookies as their dependent variable.

on the horizon. Nevertheless, compliance and enforcement issues (Section 4.3.2) loom large here: the realized privacy results will vary.

First of all, the GDPR remains a worthwhile subject of research. Future research may extend beyond the GDPR's enforcement deadline. Given the GDPR's compliance and enforcement issues, future crackdowns may present opportunities to study the impact of the GDPR. For instance, potential "mini" GDPR events include regulator enforcement deadlines, regulatory actions (see, e.g., Koutroumpis, Ravasan, and Tarannum 2022), major court decisions, voluntary changes in compliance strategies (e.g. self-regulatory changes), and private actions (e.g., noyb 2022).[18] Also, the United Kingdom is considering whether to revisit the GDPR in light of that country's exit from the EU. This may provide opportunities to study the impact of undoing certain elements of the GDPR.

Second, proposed and enacted regulations worldwide provide additional opportunities for research. Many countries have passed, enforced, and/or updated privacy regulation since the GDPR was passed, including: Bahrain, Brazil, Burkina Faso, China, India, Israel, Japan, Kenya, Mauritius, New Zealand, Nigeria, Qatar, Singapore, South Africa, South Korea, Switzerland, Thailand, Turkey, and Uganda. As of early 2023, Greenleaf (2023) counts 162 countries with data privacy laws, which grew by 42 countries since 2017. The EU passed the Digital Services Act and Digital Markets Act in 2022, which contain relevant provisions. For instance, the Digital Services Act largely bans targeted online ads to children under 18. The EU's proposed ePrivacy Regulation will build on the GDPR by establishing particular privacy regulations for electronic communication in the EU. The ePrivacy Regulation will build on its predecessor—the ePrivacy Directive—which Goldfarb and Tucker (2011) and Lambrecht (2017) study. In the US, Congress has considered several privacy laws while nine states have enacted comprehensive privacy laws as of June 2023: California, Colorado, Connecticut, Indiana, Iowa, Montana, Tennessee, Virginia, and Utah. For instance, Abis et al. (2022) study the California Consumer Privacy Act and its impact on voice-AI firms. Also, the Federal Trade Commission (FTC) has telegraphed its desire to more aggressively protect consumer privacy with its 2022 Advanced Notice of Proposed Rule-making on "Commercial Surveillance and Data Security."

Third, some large technology firms responded to increased privacy-related regulatory scrutiny by instituting related changes on their platforms. These changes can mitigate non-compliance issues by instituting platform rule changes that, to a greater extent, force firms on their platform to comply.

18. For example, Johnson, Shriver, and Goldberg (2023b) examine the French regulators' enforcement deadline for web sites (April 2021) as well as a self-regulatory update to the web vendor industry's consent mechanism (Fall 2020). These results (in an online appendix) show that these GDPR-like events replicated the authors' key findings: the GDPR simultaneously reduces vendor use and increases vendor market concentration.

For instance, Apple's "App Tracking Transparency" forced apps to request user opt-in consent for what Apple terms "tracking" as of April 2021. Some research examines the resulting consequences for apps and advertisers on Apple's platform (Kesler 2022; Li and Tsai 2022). In response to two alleged violations of the US Children's Online Privacy Protection Act, other researchers examine the impact of Google removing personalized ads from children's games on Android (Kircher and Foerderer 2023) and all forms of personalization for child-directed content on YouTube (Johnson et al. 2023a).

4.5.2 Privacy-Enhancing Technologies

Privacy-enhancing technologies (PETs) offer a potential solution for the tension between privacy and the data economy. The United Kingdom defines PETs as "technologies that embody fundamental data protection principles by minimizing personal data use, maximizing data security, and empowering individuals" (ICO 2022). Examples of PETs include: differential privacy, federated learning, on-device computation, zero-knowledge proof, and secure multi-party computation.

In particular, differential privacy (Dwork 2006) is a controversial, but popular, example of a PET in practice. Roughly speaking, related methods inject noise into data statistics or the data itself in order to satisfy the differential privacy criterion that protects individuals in the data. Blanco-Justicia et al. (2022) and Williams and Bowen (2023) provide both an introduction to, and a critical review of, differential privacy. These authors point out several limitations that limit the broad use of differential privacy and note that many real-world applications choose permissive privacy parameters that effectively sacrifice privacy for utility. Moreover, Komarova and Nekipelov (2020) note that differential privacy creates challenges for inference by transforming data sets.

Economists can contribute to research on PETs. More fundamental research is required on how to design PETs. Economists in particular can help map out the privacy versus value-creation frontier of PETs (e.g., Hotz et al. 2022). For instance, in marketing applications, scholars have proposed methods to optimally transform the data (Li et al. 2022) or generate synthetic data (Anand and Lee 2023; Schneider et al. 2018) to provide privacy guarantees while retaining data utility on certain dimensions. Economists also can study the adoption and consequences of PETs just as they study other innovations like artificial intelligence and cloud computing (e.g., Zolas et al. 2020). PETs too can have competitive consequences, for instance, because smaller quantities of data are more likely to reveal an individual's data. In the case of online advertising, Johnson, Runge, and Seufert (2022) predict significant consequences of applying PETs for both practitioners and researchers.

PETs are now gaining practical use. For instance, the US Census will add noise to its data before computing its public statistics (i.e., differential privacy) in order to fulfill its legal obligation to not reveal information about individuals in the census. Some have argued that PETs can aid in GDPR compliance efforts (e.g., Cummings and Desai 2018). As well, Google's Privacy Sandbox proposes PETs as alternatives to browser cookies and mobile ad identifiers (Google 2022). Still, privacy regulations and proposed regulations have largely ignored these developments to date. For instance, the FTC's request for public comment on "Commercial Surveillance and Data Security" only mentions PETs in passing.[19]

4.6 Conclusion

The GDPR represents an opportunity for economists to understand the consequences of an economy-wide privacy regulation. However, the GDPR poses several challenges for economic research. First, the GDPR made a global impact as it covers both EU firms and non-EU firms that target EU residents. The GDPR also created substantial global spillovers, so researchers may struggle to find a suitable control group that is both excluded from the regulation and comparable to the EU. Second, the variability of firm compliance and regulatory enforcement under the GDPR complicates the generalizations that we can draw from the literature. Third, the GDPR sought to limit personal data processing and to allow privacy-sensitive consumers to opt out of data processing. This, in turn, can limit empirical researchers' access to data and can introduce consent-based self-selection into the observed data.

The economic literature on the GDPR examines multiple facets of the regulation and its impact. The GDPR presented a novel opportunity for economists to empirically investigate long-held hypotheses like the consequences of privacy regulation for competition and innovation. Most GDPR research points to the GDPR hurting firm outcomes and disproportionately harming smaller and more data-dependent firms. For consumers, the literature illuminates objective improvements in privacy and surveys consumers for their views on the GDPR. The literature also explores the consequences of the GDPR's design elements including its international spillovers.

Looking back at the GDPR literature, one potential criticism is that the literature has documented the *unintended* consequences, but perhaps neglected the *intended* consequences of the GDPR. In particular, we want to better understand the privacy benefits to consumers and rigorously quantify these benefits. As well, we want to better understand and quantify the gains in data protection. To be fair, these are difficult subjects to evaluate

19. The request for comment contains 95 questions. The final question asks about the "potential obsolescence of any rulemaking" and references the privacy-related innovations in the online ad industry.

convincingly with the data at hand, though Demirer et al. (2023) represents a notable exception.

The GDPR and privacy regulation more generally offer several more directions for research. First, Section 4.2 lists many elements of the GDPR that have received little attention so far. Second, more attention should be paid to understanding the strategic interactions between firms and regulators. We would like to better understand which enforcement strategies—e.g., fines, notices, choice of targets, establishing legal precedent—are effective in ensuring compliance. Third, the GDPR literature has so far neglected the GDPR's anticipated impact assessments like those of the European Commission (2012) as well as industry-funded studies like Christensen et al. (2013) and Deloitte (2013). These predictions identify lingering questions like the GDPR's impact on employment. Finally, we wish to better understand how to design effective privacy regulation and improve upon existing regulation like the GDPR. In particular, continued research can explore how to limit the unintended consequences of privacy regulation.

Policy makers and regulators around the globe continue to wrestle with how to regulate privacy effectively in the modern data economy. Research can continue to illuminate their task. As the GDPR continues to evolve in practice, this will present more opportunities to study the law. New privacy laws worldwide also represent opportunities for research. Recent breakthroughs in commercializing privacy-enhancing technologies promise to limit certain trade-offs between privacy and the data economy. More research is needed to understand the novel trade-offs that these technologies present as well as the economic consequences of adopting these technologies.

References

Abis, S., M. Canayaz, I. Kantorovitch, R. Mihet, and H. Tang. 2022. *Privacy Laws and Value of Personal Data*. Technical report, EPFL.

Acquisti, A., C. Taylor, and L. Wagman. 2016. "The Economics of Privacy." *Journal of Economic Literature* 54 (2): 442–92.

Anand, P. and C. Lee. 2023. "Using Deep Learning to Overcome Privacy and Scalability Issues in Customer Data Transfer." *Marketing Science* 42 (1): 189–207.

Aridor, G., Y.-K. Che, and T. Salz. 2023. "The Effect of Privacy Regulation on the Data Industry: Empirical Evidence from GDPR." *RAND Journal of Economics*. Forthcoming.

Athey, S., C. Catalini, and C. Tucker. 2017. "The Digital Privacy Paradox: Small Money, Small Costs, Small Talk." NBER Working Paper 23488. Cambridge, MA: National Bureau of Economic Research.

Autoriteit Persoonsgegevens. 2019. "AP: veel websites vragen op onjuiste wijze toestemming voor plaatsen tracking cookies." https://autoriteitpersoonsgegevens.nl/nl/nieuws/ap-veelwebsites-vragen-op-onjuiste-wijze-toestemming-voor-plaatsen-tracking-cookies.

Bessen, J. E., S. M. Impink, L. Reichensperger, and R. Seamans. 2020. "GDPR and the Importance of Data to AI Startups." SSRN 3576714.

Blanco-Justicia, A., D. Sánchez, J. Domingo-Ferrer, and K. Muralidhar. 2022. "A Critical Review on the Use (and Misuse) of Differential Privacy in Machine Learning." *ACM Computing Surveys* 55 (8): 1–16.

Blind, K., C. Niebel, and C. Rammer. 2023. "The Impact of the EU General Data Protection Regulation on Innovation in Firms." *Industry and Innovation*. https://doi.org/10.1080/13662716.2023.2271858.

Boroomand, F., A. Leiponen, and G. Vasudeva. 2022. "Does the Market Value Attention to Data Privacy? Evidence from US-listed Firms under the GDPR." Wharton Mack Institute working paper.

Bradford, A. 2020. *The Brussels Effect: How the European Union Rules the World*. New York: Oxford University Press.

Brill, J. 2011. "The Intersection of Consumer Protection and Competition in the New World of Privacy." *Competition Policy International* 7 (1): 7–23.

Cameron, A. C., and P. K. Trivedi. 2005. *Microeconometrics: Methods and Applications*. Cambridge University Press.

Campbell, J., A. Goldfarb, and C. Tucker. 2015. "Privacy Regulation and Market Structure." *Journal of Economics & Management Strategy* 24 (1): 47–73.

Carrière-Swallow, Y., and V. Haksar. 2019. *The Economics and Implications of Data An Integrated Perspective*. Technical report, International Monetary Fund.

Chen, C., C. B. Frey, and G. Presidente. 2022. "Privacy Regulation and Firm Performance: Estimating the GDPR Effect Globally." The Oxford Martin Working Paper Series on Technological and Economic Change.

Christensen, L., A. Colciago, F. Etro, and G. Rafert. 2013. "The Impact of the Data Protection Regulation in the EU." Intertic Policy Paper, Intertic.

Commission Nationale de l'Informatique et des Libertés. 2019. "Online Targeted Advertisement: What Action Plan for the CNIL?" https://www.cnil.fr/en/online-targetedadvertisement-what-action-plan-cnil.

Congiu, R., L. Sabatino, and G. Sapi. 2022. "The Impact of Privacy Regulation on Web Traffic: Evidence from the GDPR." *Information Economics and Policy* 61: 101003.

Cummings, R., and D. Desai. 2018. "The Role of Differential Privacy in GDPR Compliance." In *FAT* '18: Proceedings of the Conference on Fairness, Accountability, and Transparency*. ACM.

D'Assergio, C., P. Manchanda, E. Montaguti, and S. Valentini. 2022. "The Race for Data: Gaming or Being Gamed by the System?" SSRN 4250389.

Data Protection Commission. 2020. *Report By The Data Protection Commission on the Use of Cookies and Other Tracking Technologies*. Technical report, Data Protection Commission.

DataGrail. 2020. *The Age of Privacy: The Cost of Continuous Compliance*. Technical report.

Deloitte. 2013. *Economic Impact Assessment of the Proposed General Data Protection Regulation*. Technical report, December.

Demirer, M., D. J. Hernández, D. Li, and S. Peng. 2023. "Data, Privacy Laws, and Firm Production: Evidence from GDPR." Work in progress.

Dwork, C. 2006. "Differential Privacy." In *Automata, Languages and Programming*, edited by M. Bugliesi, B. Preneel, V. Sassone, and I. Wegener, 1–12. Berlin, Heidelberg: Springer Berlin Heidelberg.

European Commission. 2008. "Flash Eurobarometer 226: Data Protection in the European Union: Data Controllers' Perceptions." https://data.europa.eu.

European Commission. 2012. "Impact Assessment Accompanying the document

Regulation of the European Parliament and of the Council on the protection of individuals with regard to the processing of personal data and on the free movement of such data (General Data Protection Regulation) and Directive of the European Parliament and of the Council on the protection of individuals with regard to the processing of personal data by competent authorities for the purposes of prevention, investigation, detection or prosecution of criminal offences or the execution of criminal penalties, and the free movement of such data." Commission Staff Working Paper. Technical report, European Commission.

European Commission. 2019. "Data Protection Rules as a Trust-Enabler in the EU and Beyond—Taking Stock." Communication from the Commission to the European Parliament and the Council, European Commission.

European Data Protection Board. 2020. "Contribution of the EDPB to the Evaluation of the GDPR under Article 97." Technical report, European Data Protection Board.

Ferracane, M. F., B. M. Hoekman, E. van der Marel, and F. Santi. 2023. "Digital Trade, Data Protection and EU Adequacy Decisions." EUI, RSC, Working Paper, 2023/37, Global Governance Programme-505, European Centre for International Political Economy (ECIPE).

Gal, M. S., and O. Aviv. 2020. "The Competitive Effects of the GDPR." *Journal of Competition Law and Economics* 16 (3): 349–391.

Geradin, D., T. Karanikioti, and D. Katsifis. 2020. "GDPR Myopia: How a Well-Intended Regulation Ended Up Favouring Large Online Platforms—The Case of Ad Tech." *European Competition Journal* 17 (1): 1–46.

Godinho de Matos, M., and I. Adjerid. 2022. "Consumer Consent and Firm Targeting after GDPR: The Case of a Large Telecom Provider." *Management Science* 68 (5): 3330–3378.

Goldberg, S., G. A. Johnson, and S. Shriver. 2024. "Regulating Privacy Online: An Economic Evaluation of fhe GDPR." Forthcoming in *American Economic Journal: Economic Policy*.

Goldfarb, A., and C. Tucker. 2011. "Privacy Regulation and Online Advertising." *Management Science* 57 (1): 57–71.

Goldfarb, A., and C. Tucker. 2012. "Privacy and Innovation." *Innovation Policy and the Economy* 12 (1): 65–90.

Google. 2022. "The Privacy Sandbox: Technology for a More Private Web." https://privacysandbox.com.

Greene, T., G. Shmueli, S. Ray, and J. Fell. 2019. "Adjusting to the GDPR: The Impact on Data Scientists and Behavioral Researchers." *Big Data* 7 (3): 140–162.

Greenleaf, G. 2023. "Global Data Privacy Laws 2023: 162 National Laws and 20 Bills." *Privacy Laws and Business International Report* 181 (1): 2–4.

Hils, M., D. W. Woods, and R. Böhme. 2020. "Measuring the Emergence of Consent Management on the Web." In *Proceedings of the ACM Internet Measurement Conference, IMC '20*, 317–332. New York, NY: Association for Computing Machinery.

Hotz, V. J., C. R. Bollinger, T. Komarova, C. F. Manski, R. A. Moffitt, D. Nekipelov, A. Sojourner, and B. D. Spencer. 2022. "Balancing Data Privacy and Usability in the Federal Statistical System." *Proceedings of the National Academy of Sciences* 119 (31): e2104906119.

Information Commissioner's Office. 2019. "Update Report into Adtech and Real Time Bidding." Technical report.

Information Commissioner's Office. 2021. "Guide to the General Data Protection Regulation (GDPR)." Technical report, Information Commissioner's Office.

Information Commissioner's Office. 2022. "Privacy-Enhancing Technologies (PETs)." Chapter 5 in *Draft Anonymisation, Pseudonymisation and Privacy-Enhancing Technologies Guidance*. Information Commissioner's Office.

International Association of Privacy Professionals. 2017. "Global 500 Companies To Spend $7.8b on GDPR Compliance." https://iapp.org.

International Association of Privacy Professionals. 2023. "GDPR at Five." https://iapp.org/media/pdf/resource_center/gdpr_at_five.pdf.

International Association of Privacy Professionals and Ernst & Young. 2017. "IAPP-EY Annual Privacy Governance Report 2017." Technical report.

Janßen, R., R. Kesler, M. E. Kummer, and J. Waldfogel. 2022. "GDPR and the Lost Generation of Innovative Apps." NBER Working Paper 30028. Cambridge, MA: National Bureau of Economic Research.

Jia, J., G. Z. Jin, and L. Wagman. 2020. "GDPR and the Localness of Venture Investment." SSRN 3436535.

Jia, J., G. Z. Jin, and L.Wagman 2021. "The Short-Run Effects of the General Data Protection Regulation on Technology Venture Investment." *Marketing Science* 40 (4): 661–684.

Johnson, G. A., T. Lin, J. Cooper, and L. Zhong. 2023a. "COPPAcalypse? The YouTube Settlement's Impact on Kids Content." SSRN 4430334.

Johnson, G. A., J. Runge, and E. Seufert. 2022. "Privacy-Centric Digital Advertising: Implications for Research." *Customer Needs and Solutions* 9 (1): 49–54.

Johnson, G. A., S. Shriver, and S. Goldberg. 2023b. "Privacy and Market Concentration: Intended and Unintended Consequences of the GDPR." *Management Science* 69 (10).

Johnson, G. A., S. K. Shriver, and S. Du. 2020. "Consumer Privacy Choice in Online Advertising: Who Opts Out and At What Cost to Industry?" *Marketing Science* 39 (1): 33–51.

Jones, M. L., and M. E. Kaminski. 2020. "An American's Guide to the GDPR." *Denver Law Review* 98(1).

Ke, T. T., and K. Sudhir. 2022. "Privacy Rights and Data Security: GDPR and Personal Data Markets." *Management Science* 69 (8).

Kesler, R. 2022. "The Impact of Apple's App Tracking Transparency on App Monetization." SSRN 4090786.

Kircher, T., and J. Foerderer. 2021. "Does EU-Consumer Privacy Harm Financing of US-App-Startups? Within-US Evidence of Cross-EU-Effects." In *Proceedings of the 42nd International Conference on Information Systems (ICIS)*, 12–15. Association for Information Systems (AIS).

Kircher, T., and J. Foerderer. 2023. "Ban Targeted Advertising in Apps? An Empirical Investigation of the Consequences for App Development." *Management Science*. Forthcoming.

Klein, A., R. Manini, and Y. Shi. 2022. "Across the Pond: How US Firms' Boards of Directors Adapted to the Passage of the General Data Protection Regulation." *Contemporary Accounting Research* 39 (1): 199–233.

Komarova, T., and D. Nekipelov. 2020. "Identification and Formal Privacy Guarantees." arXiv preprint arXiv:2006.14732.

Koski, H., and N. Valmari. 2020. "Short-Term Impacts of the GDPR on Firm Performance." ETLA Working Papers.

Koutroumpis, P., F. Ravasan, and T. Tarannum. (2022). "(Under) investment in Cyber Skills and Data Protection Enforcement: Evidence from Activity Logs of the UK Information Commissioner's Office." SSRN 4179601.

Lambrecht, A. 2017. "E-privacy Provisions and Venture Capital Investments in the EU." Working paper.

Lefrere, V., L. Warberg, C. Cheyre, V. Marotta, and A. Acquisti. 2022. "The Impact of the GDPR on Content Providers: A Longitudinal Analysis." SSRN.
Li, D., and H.-T. Tsai. 2022. "Mobile Apps and Targeted Advertising: Competitive Effects of Data Exchange." SSRN 4088166.
Li, H., L. Yu, and W. He. 2019. "The Impact of GDPR on Global Technology Development." *Journal of Global Information Technology Management* 22 (1): 1–6.
Li, S., M. J. Schneider, Y. Yu, and S. Gupta. 2022. "Reidentification Risk in Panel Data: Protecting for k-anonymity." *Information Systems Research* 34 (3):1066–1088.
Libert, T., L. Graves, and R. K. Nielsen. 2018. "Changes in Third-Party Content on European News Websites after GDPR." Technical report, Reuters Institute for the Study of Journalism.
Lukic, K., K. M. Miller, and B. Skiera. 2023. "The Impact of the General Data Protection Regulation (GDPR) on the Amount of Online Tracking." SSRN 4399388.
Maex, S. A. 2022. "Modern Privacy Regulation, Internal Information Quality, and Operating Efficiency: Evidence from the General Data Protection Regulation." PhD dissertation, Temple University.
Martin, N., C. Matt, C. Niebel, and K. Blind. 2019. "How Data Protection Regulation Affects Startup Innovation." *Information Systems Frontiers* 21 (6): 1307–1324.
McDowall, D., R. McCleary, and B. Bartos. 2019. *Interrupted Time Series Analysis*. Oxford University Press.
Miller, A. R. 2024. "Privacy of Digital Health Information." In *The Economics of Privacy*, edited by Avi Goldfarb and Catherine Tucker. Chicago, IL: University of Chicago Press. This volume.
Miller, A. R., and C. Tucker. 2009. "Privacy Protection and Technology Diffusion: The Case of Electronic Medical Records." *Management Science* 55 (7): 1077–1093.
Miller, A. R., and C. E. Tucker. 2011. "Encryption and the Loss of Patient Data." *Journal of Policy Analysis and Management* 30 (3): 534–556.
noyb. 2022. "noyb Aims to End "Cookie Banner Terror" and Issues More than 500 GDPR Complaints." https://noyb.eu/en/noyb-aims-end-cookie-banner-terror-and-issuesmore-500-gdpr-complaints.
Peukert, C., S. Bechtold, M. Batikas, and T. Kretschmer. 2022. "Regulatory Spillovers and Data Governance: Evidence from the GDPR." *Marketing Science* 41 (4): 318–340.
Phillips, N. 2019. "Keep it: Maintaining Competition in the Privacy Debate." Remarks for Internet Governance Forum.
Polinsky, A. M., and S. Shavell. 2000. "The Economic Theory of Public Enforcement of Law." *Journal of Economic Literature* 38 (1): 45–76.
Prasad, A., and D. R. Perez. 2020. "The Effects of GDPR on the Digital Economy: Evidence from the Literature." *Informatization Policy* 27 (3): 3–18.
Presthus, W., and K. F. Sønslien. 2021. "An Analysis of Violations and Sanctions following the GDPR." *International Journal of Information Systems and Project Management* 9 (1): 38–53.
Presthus, W., and H. Sørum. 2019. "Consumer Perspectives on Information Privacy following the Implementation of the GDPR." *International Journal of Information Systems and Project Management* 7 (3): 19–34.
Presthus, W., and H. Sørum. 2021. "A Three-Year Study of the GDPR and the Consumer." In *14th IADIS International Conference Information Systems 2021. International Association for Development of the Information Society*.
Ravichandran, D., and N. Korula. 2019. "Effect of Disabling Third-Party Cookies on Publisher Revenue." Technical report, Google Inc.

Romanosky, S., R. Telang, and A. Acquisti. 2011. "Do Data Breach Disclosure Laws Reduce Identity Theft?" *Journal of Policy Analysis and Management* 30 (2): 256–286.

Schmitt, J., K. M. Miller, and B. Skiera. 2021. "The Impact of Privacy Laws on Online User Behavior." arXiv preprint arXiv:2101.11366.

Schneider, M. J., S. Jagpal, S. Gupta, S. Li, and Y. Yu. 2018. "A Flexible Method for Protecting Marketing Data: An Application to Point-of-Sale Data." *Marketing Science* 37 (1): 153–171.

Skiera, B., K. Miller, Y. Jin, L. Kraft, R. Laub, and J. Schmitt. 2022. "The Impact of the General Data Protection Regulation (GDPR) on the Online Advertising Market." https://www.gdpr-impact.com/.

Sobolewski, M., and M. Paliński. 2017. "How Much Consumers Value On-Line Privacy? Welfare Assessment of New Data Protection Regulation (GDPR)." University of Warsaw Faculty of Economics Sciences Working Paper.

Sørum, H., and W. Presthus. 2020. "Dude, Where's My Data? The GDPR in Practice, from a Consumer's Point of View." *Information Technology and People* 34 (3): 912–929.

TrustArc. 2018. *GDPR Compliance Status: A Comparison of US, UK and EU Companies*. Technical report. TrustArc.

Urban, T., D. Tatang, M. Degeling, T. Holz, and N. Pohlmann. 2020. "Measuring the Impact of the GDPR on Data Sharing in Ad Networks." In *Proceedings of the 15th ACM Asia Conference on Computer and Communications Security* (ASIA CCS '20). ACM.

Venkatesan, R., S. Arunachalam, and K. Pedada. 2022. "Short Run Effects of Generalized Data Protection Act on Returns from AI Acquisitions." Working paper. https://conference.nber.org/conf_papers/f161612.pdf.

Wang, P., L. Jiang, and J. Yang. 2023. "The Early Impact of GDPR Compliance on Display Advertising: The Case of an Ad Publisher." *Journal of Marketing Research* (April 11).

Wang, X., F. Xu, and F. Zhang. 2022. "Consumer Privacy in Online Retail Supply Chains." SSRN 3912642.

Williams, A. R., and C. M. Bowen. 2023. "The Promise and Limitations of Formal Privacy." *WIREs Computational Statistics* (May 9). https://wires.onlinelibrary.wiley.com/doi/abs/10.1002/wics.1615.

World Bank. 2021. *World Development Report 2021: Data for Better Lives*. The World Bank.

Yom-Tov, E., and Y. Ofran. 2022. "Implementation of Data Protection Laws in the European Union and in California Is Associated with a Move of Clinical Trials to Countries with Fewer Data Protections." *Frontiers in Medicine* 9.

Yuan, B., and J. Li. 2019. "The Policy Effect of the General Data Protection Regulation (GDPR) on the Digital Public Health Sector in the European Union: An Empirical Investigation." *International Journal of Environmental Research and Public Health* 16 (6).

Zhao, Y., P. Yildirim, and P. K. Chintagunta. 2021. "Privacy Regulations and Online Search Friction: Evidence from GDPR." SSRN 3903599.

Zhuo, R., B. Huffaker, kc claffy, and S. Greenstein. 2021. "The Impact of the General Data Protection Regulation on Internet Interconnection." *Telecommunications Policy* 45 (2): 102083.

Zolas, N., Z. Kroff, E. Brynjolfsson, K. McElheran, D. N. Beede, C. Buffington, N. Goldschlag, L. Foster, and E. Dinlersoz. 2020. "Advanced Technologies Adoption and Use by US Firms: Evidence from the Annual Business Survey." NBER Working Paper 28290. Cambridge, MA: National Bureau of Economic Research.

5 Privacy of Digital Health Information

Amalia R. Miller

5.1 Introduction

Health information merits special attention within the economics of privacy because the stakes of its protection are especially high. Some of the most sensitive and revealing facts about a person pertain to their physical and mental health. Having those facts disclosed publicly can cause a person to experience both direct discomfort and indirect harms through various ways in which other people respond to the information. If patients are unable to trust medical providers to keep their information private, they may be unwilling to undergo testing or seek medical treatment, or they may withhold key information about symptoms and risk factors.

Health information is also important for privacy scholars because of its special policy treatment. The US lacks any national law that protects privacy for all types of personal data, yet federal laws addressing the privacy and security of health information have been in place for years. The most prominent of these is the 1996 Health Insurance Portability and Accountability Act (HIPAA) that produced the 2003 Privacy and Security Rules (45 CFR § 160 and 164). Further data security provisions were added in the 2009 Health IT for Economic and Clinical Health (HITECH) Act and protec-

Amalia R. Miller is a professor of economics at the University of Virginia, a research fellow of IZA Institute of Labor Economics, and a research associate of the National Bureau of Economic Research.

This chapter is based on a presentation at the Fall 2022 NBER Economics of Privacy Conference. I am grateful to the conference organizers, Avi Goldfarb and Catherine Tucker, and to other faculty and graduate student participants at the conference, for stimulating comments and feedback. For acknowledgments, sources of research support, and disclosure of the author's material financial relationships, if any, please see https://www.nber.org/books-and-chapters/economics-privacy/privacy-digital-health-information.

tions for genetic information were adopted in the 2008 Genetic Information Non-discrimination Act (GINA).[1] National laws protect health privacy around the world (OECD 2022), and broad-based privacy rules typically categorize health information as particularly sensitive and require stricter protections.[2]

Health privacy policy has become increasingly important and complex as advances in computing have spurred the collection, storage, and analysis of massive amounts of personal health data. Digitization of health information makes that information easier to share and harder to protect, which increases the individual risks to health privacy. At the same, widespread digitization of health information has unique potential to increase human welfare, through improvements in healthcare delivery quality and efficiency and through data-driven innovation in medical devices and personalized medicine that can better target treatments which extend and improve lives. This dual nature of health information digitization therefore presents policy makers with a significant challenge in devising health privacy rules in a way that balances the costs and benefits of amassing and exploiting digital health data.

Economic approaches, both theoretical and empirical, can be particularly valuable for assessing these trade-offs and for evaluating the effects of different approaches to health privacy policy. This chapter therefore offers a conceptual framework for the economics of health information privacy, surveying the existing literature, and highlighting open areas of inquiry. Section 5.2 delineates the various forms of harm that individuals might experience from having their health information revealed against their wishes and categorizes those harms into types. In principle, the potential harms from improper disclosure can be weighed against the benefits of allowing unrestricted use of digital health data, discussed in Section 5.3, to determine the socially optimal level of privacy protection. In practice, uncertainty about, and heterogeneity in, both costs and benefits of health privacy make it impossible to find a single universally optimal level of protection. Section 5.4 considers economic justifications for various government interventions in health privacy, based on efficiency and fairness grounds, and links them

1. Information about substance use disorders and treatments at federally funded programs are under stricter privacy protections (42 CFR § 2.11 Part 2). The US also has targeted privacy rules outside of health. The Financial Privacy Rule, created as part of the Financial Modernization Act of 1999 (the Gramm-Leach-Bliley Act, or GLBA), can also cover some health information, and the 1970 Fair Credit Reporting Act (FCRA) addresses privacy and accuracy in credit reports. Federal privacy rules also cover children (the Children's Online Privacy Protection Act, COPPA) and educational data (the Family Educational Rights and Privacy Act, FERPA). Use and dissemination of personal information by federal government agencies is regulated under the 1974 Privacy Act.

2. These laws include the European 2016 General Data Protection Regulation (GDPR), discussed in Chapter 4 of this volume (Johnson 2022), and the 2019 Brazilian General Data Protection Law (LGPD).

to specific policy provisions and rules. Variation in these policies across places and time has provided valuable opportunities for empirical researchers to measure the effects of health privacy laws as implemented. Section 5.5 reviews this empirical economics literature, aiming to draw insights to inform health privacy policy and shed light on privacy issues in other sectors with less history of empirical variation.

5.2 Costs of Health Privacy Loss

A natural starting point for assessing the economic value of protecting individual health privacy is measuring the potential harm that a person can suffer from having their personal information disclosed against their wishes. Measuring that potential harm, however, is complicated by the variety of specific harms that are commonly raised in health privacy research and advocacy (e.g., IOM 2009; Gostin 1994), listed in Table 5.1. We will consider these harms in turn, distinguishing first between elements of the list that reflect direct, or primary, harms that happen from the disclosure itself, regardless of whether or how the data is eventually used (items 1–3, discussed in Section 5.2.1), and the indirect, or secondary, harms that result from how other people react to or use the data (items 4–11, discussed in Section 5.2.2). Although much has been written about these harms, most of the writing has been either theoretical or anecdotal, so relatively little is known about their magnitudes or prevalence.

Table 5.1 **Potential individual harms from health privacy loss**

Direct harms	
1	Feelings of shame, embarrassment
2	Feelings of betrayal, trust violation
3	Feelings of invasion, surveillance, loss of freedom, autonomy
Indirect market harms	
4	Labor market harms (e.g., hiring, salary, promotion, termination)
5	Insurance (e.g., health, disability, life, long-term care) market harms
6	Harms in other product markets, e.g., higher prices
7	Targeted advertising—if manipulative, annoying, intrusive
Indirect non-market harms	
8	Social stigma, isolation
9	Harms to reputation, personal and family relationships
10	Increased risk of identity theft, other theft, impersonation, fraud
11	Increased civil or criminal legal exposure

5.2.1 Direct Harm from Health Privacy Loss

People may experience direct harms from violations of their health data privacy because knowledge of the data disclosure can induce feelings of shame or embarrassment about their information being revealed to others (item 1). The extent of this harm will depend on the nature of the information, the recipients of the information, and each person's attitude toward that information.

The second direct harm is from feeling a trust has been violated by the person or organization that revealed the information. This harm is also subjective, and likely to be particularly important in the healthcare sector, where preserving the confidentiality of patient information is a long-standing professional norm.[3] Violations of this norm can erode trust in particular providers and in the healthcare system more generally (Mechanic 1998), which can reduce healthcare seeking and treatment.[4] The salience of privacy in the healthcare provision relationship is reflected in much of the literature on health privacy discussing "patients" (rather than "consumers") and in greater legal restrictions on the use and transfer of health information by healthcare providers and health insurance plans (the focal "covered entities" in HIPAA and state health privacy laws). It is possible to maintain trust while also disclosing some private information, for example when patients are informed in advance about how their data will be used and when they give affirmative consent to those uses. However, if disclosure and consent procedures are perfunctory as a precondition for service, and offer no option to withhold consent, they can themselves be damaging to trust, particularly if the data uses extend beyond the direct functions of medical care provision.

People may also value the ability to keep certain health information private because it enhances their sense of freedom. Having one's information widely available can feel invasive, coercive, or controlling, even when there are no explicit penalties or consequences (item 3). This applies to surveillance either by private companies or by government agencies, and extensive information flows between the two sectors make those concerns impossible to fully disentangle.[5]

These first three items are grouped together as direct harms because they happen within the individual and are not tied to specific responses to their private information from others. This is true despite privacy being inherently a relationship concept, about setting boundaries with other people (Nissen-

3. For physicians, the text of the revised Hippocratic Oath includes a promise to "respect the privacy of my patients, for their problems are not disclosed to me that the world may know."

4. Alsan and Wanamaker (2018) illustrate the severe and lasting consequences of trust violations related to failures of healthcare researchers to provide full disclosure and obtain informed consent.

5. See, e.g., Qian et al. (2022), for discussion of the state's expansive use of digital surveillance tools in China.

baum 2004). Because they depend on circumstances and context, including the relationships among people giving and receiving data, the direct harms are unlikely to be universal in any meaningful sense. As a result of this heterogeneity and instability, the interiority and subjectivity of the direct harms make them particularly challenging to quantify or convert to money value.

5.2.2 Indirect Harm from Health Data Use

The economics literature on privacy has typically focused on the indirect or secondary harms from information flows (e.g., Acquisti, Taylor, and Wagman 2016), which can be mediated by market forces (items 4–7) or not (items 8–11). Within the health privacy sphere, the areas of greatest policy attention are job (item 4) and insurance (item 5) markets, because those are markets in which health information can be especially damaging to individuals, and where individuals report feeling the greatest level of concern about potential disclosure (e.g., Institute of Medicine [IOM] 2009).

Disclosure of personal information about physical or behavioral health conditions can make a worker less attractive to employers, which can have negative labor market effects in areas of hiring, compensation, promotion, and termination (item 4). The use of health information as a basis for differential treatment in labor markets can be considered a form of discrimination and examined using economic models developed to study discrimination by race or gender. For example, employers may use health information for statistical discrimination (Phelps 1972), because of its value in predicting worker productivity or labor supply. This use of health information could be profitable for employers, but it might also be inefficient if employers overreact to health information because they are less able to assess future productivity of workers with those conditions (Aigner and Cain 1977) or if they have biased beliefs about, and limited experience with, such workers.

Even when health information is irrelevant for productivity, it is also possible that employers have preferences related to worker health and use health information to engage in taste-based discrimination at the expense of profit maximization (Arrow 1973; Becker 1957). This can be because employers (or customers or fellow employees) have preferences against hiring or working with people with certain health conditions, or because the health conditions are informative proxies about other nonproductive characteristics, such as sexual orientation, over which they have such preferences (e.g., Badgett 2007). Discrimination by health status is also closely related to discrimination by disability status (see, e.g., Baldwin and Johnson 2006 for a survey), but not the same, for example, because not all sensitive health information is related to a current disability. Regardless of the underlying motivations, workers who anticipate adverse employer reactions to their health information will prefer to keep that information private.

Markets for insurance—health, life, disability, long-term care (item 5)—are another major setting in which health information can be relevant to firm profits and firms might penalize individuals with certain health conditions or risks. In these markets the assumption is typically that health information is used solely for its predictive value, rather than for animus-based discrimination. This in no way diminishes the harm experienced by people with medical information that implies higher expected insurance claims when they are charged higher premiums or restricted in their insurance offerings. Although not directly relevant to the individual harm, the profit motive for using health information in insurance markets, as with labor markets, nevertheless presents challenges for health privacy regulation in these markets, for both conceptual and practical reasons. The theoretical concern is that some privacy rules might reduce overall welfare and the practical concern is that firms will be more motivated to circumvent the rules, with no role for market forces to limit discrimination. These will be discussed further in Section 5.4 on regulation.

Health insurance and employment are also tightly connected in the US, where 57 percent of the non-elderly population is covered by an employment-based plan (KFF 2022). This means that employers are often concerned about expected medical claims. This is particularly the case for self-funded plans,[6] where employers are financially responsible for claims.[7] It can also apply to employers who buy insurance in group markets and are exposed to some degree of "experience rating" where premiums can increase based on past claims,[8] which increases the cost to the employer of providing health benefits. An implication of this connection is examined empirically, for example, in Gruber (1994), where mandated health insurance coverage of maternity affected employment outcomes for women. The close connection between employment and health insurance also entails extensive information sharing, which further connects the privacy concerns across the two settings.

Unlike the direct harms in the prior subsection, these indirect harms can have significant financial impacts, which makes them potentially easier to quantify. This is certainly true for an individual who is denied a job or charged a higher price for insurance because of a specific piece of health information. However, attribution can also be challenging in assessing indirect health privacy harms. For health conditions that affect productivity or medical costs, it is often difficult to disentangle the impact of the health information itself, separately from the observable consequences of that information. More generally, it is often difficult to identify the incremental

6. Self-funded health plans are more commonly offered at larger employers and account for a growing majority of enrollees in employment-based health plans (Miller, Eibner, and Gresenz 2013; Claxton et al. 2022).

7. Greenhouse and Barbaro (2006) report on an internal memo at Walmart recommending hiring fewer unhealthy workers as means of reducing healthcare spending.

8. The practice of experience rating has been largely proscribed in the individual and small group markets under the ACA.

impact of any specific piece or set of health information on labor or insurance market outcomes, relative to what could have been inferred from the rest of the available data. Little is known about the aggregate importance of these harms at a population level, or even within specific subpopulations based on medical diagnoses.[9]

What is known, from surveys and focus groups, is that individuals frequently cite privacy concerns about information disclosure to their employers or insurers as paramount, because of heightened fear of discrimination in those markets (IOM 2009).[10] There is also evidence that these concerns are reflected in behavior. The potential for negative predictive health information to be used against individuals in future market transactions lowers people's willingness to seek out actionable health information, such as HIV status (Vermund and Wilson 2002) and genetic testing (Gostin 1991; Hellman 2003; Oster, Shoulson, and Dorsey 2013). Some individuals report engaging in overt efforts to acquire the relevant information in a way that is shielded from their insurers or employers, for example by paying privately for testing (Oster et al. 2008; Miller and Tucker 2018) or testing outside of clinical settings (Figueroa et al. 2015).

Outside of health, most economics research on privacy has focused on other product markets (item 6) and the use of information about an individual's willingness to pay for a product for price discrimination or for targeted advertising or product recommendations (item 7). For examples outside of health, see Acquisti, Taylor, and Wagman (2016), Ichihashi (2020), Acemoglu et al. (2022), and references therein. Health information can plausibly be used for these purposes as well, either for marketing health services or for health-related goods, though it is unclear that health information would be especially useful outside of those products. The harm in this case is also less obvious. Targeted advertising (and personalized product matching and recommendations) that is based on health information is indeed harmful if it is annoying or manipulative or if it causes further disclosure of health information to third parties. An example of manipulation is implied, for example, in the claim in Duhigg (2012) that retailers target advertisements to new parents because they are "exhausted and overwhelmed" and therefore open to trying new brands. But there can also be a positive side to personalization, even when based on health information, if it improves match quality and helps consumers find products and services most valuable to them. As with labor and insurance markets, empirical researchers face sig-

9. Going beyond the effects of individual data disclosures, an aggregate reduction in consumer privacy could also affect market-level outcomes, raising equilibrium prices and lowering consumer surplus under certain market conditions (e.g., Taylor and Wagman 2014). Information flows can also affect concentration, but the direction of the impact is uncertain, and privacy rules can increase concentration in some industries (e.g., Campbell, Goldfarb, and Tucker 2015; Johnson, Shriver, and Goldberg 2023).

10. For substance use disorders, housing markets are also a key area of concern for discrimination, addressed in research and policy.

nificant challenges in attempting to link any specific release or inference of health information to outcomes in these other markets, which is further complicated by the availability of similar information from other sources. Empirical work in this area could be exceptionally valuable.

Nonmarket factors include social stigma or isolation (item 8) and damage to personal and family relationships (item 9). Mental illness, substance abuse, and HIV status are concrete examples of health information that have been shown to disrupt family relationships, but it is also possible that relationships could be damaged by disclosure of other acute or chronic medical conditions. While responses to these disclosures can have a significant impact on individual well-being, they are impossible to regulate directly, other than by preventing the flow of information. For market transactions, policy makers have the added ability to regulate the use of personal information, which is an important feature of health privacy rules that generates overlap with antidiscrimination and civil rights laws (see Section 5.4 for further discussion).

The two final categories of potential harm relate to potentially illegal behavior. The first category (item 10) is that disclosure of personal medical information, primarily from data breaches or involuntary loss, can increase a person's likelihood of being a victim of identity theft (medical or otherwise). This highlights the importance of addressing data security concerns, and preventing even unintentional disclosures, in maintaining health privacy. The other category (item 11) is that health information could potentially contribute to a trail of evidence used in a legal (civil or criminal) investigation or proceeding. This concern may arise because the health information provides evidence of wrongdoing (e.g., illegal drug use, child abuse or neglect, violent crimes) or because the medical treatment is itself illegal (e.g., reproductive healthcare such as abortion that violates state level restrictions).[11] As discussed in Section 5.4 below, these uses of health information are typically exempted from health privacy protections, under varying conditions.[12]

5.2.3 Quantifying the Costs of Health Privacy Loss

Although it is relatively straightforward to list the various potential harms to individuals from lost health privacy, measuring the value of those harms presents substantial challenges. Part of the injury is subjective, and the objective parts can be hard to detect. Both subjective and objective harms are also likely to vary significantly across people and data types, and

11. The latter category could take on heightened importance in the wake of the 2022 US Supreme Court decision in *Dobbs v. Jackson Women's Health Organization* overturning prior limits on states' abilities to ban or regulate abortions. See, for example, recent news coverage in Hill (2022), Nix and Dwoskin (2022), and Kelly, Hunter, and Abril (2022).

12. For example, HIPPA-covered entities can provide health information in response to a court order or, after meeting notification requirements, in response to a subpoena. Data sharing with law enforcement is more strictly limited under rules for Confidentiality of Alcohol and Drug Abuse Patient Records (42 CFR § 2).

over time, and to depend on the nature and context of the disclosure. This makes it difficult to value the harm at the individual level for any specific disclosure or at the population level from overall reductions in protection.

Perhaps unsurprisingly, relatively little is known about the empirical distribution of individual or aggregate harms from health privacy loss. Major reports on health privacy rarely cite values for these harms, in total or for specific elements, and instead focus on consumer attitudes (e.g., IOM 2009, HHS 2017). For attitudes, public opinion polls typically find high fractions of respondents who report feeling concerned about their health privacy (e.g., majorities in surveys by 1999 and 2005 surveys by Forrester Research and a 2005 survey by the California Healthcare Foundation, cited in IOM 2009), but not universally (the 2014 Truven Health Poll cited in HHS 2017 had rates under 20 percent). When asked to consider hypothetical choices to protect their online information across data types, subjects in Skatova et al. (2019) consistently reported placing the highest value on protecting the privacy of medical and financial records.

Outside of health privacy, researchers have attempted to go beyond stated preferences to examine situations in which subjects make consequential choices about information sharing to infer privacy preferences. These results illustrate the difficulty of converting information on stated preferences into economic measures of value. The field experiment in Athey, Catalini, and Tucker (2017) illustrates an example of the "privacy paradox" in which individuals express strong privacy preferences yet disclose personal information for small rewards. Lin (2022) infers privacy preferences using non-response rates to personal questions in a survey, similar to the analysis of observational survey data in Goldfarb and Tucker (2012). What is unusual in Lin (2022) is that the experimental treatments are designed to separately measure two components of privacy tastes—the intrinsic value (roughly corresponding to preventing the direct harms in Section 5.2.1 of this chapter) and the instrumental value (indirect harms in Section 5.2.2). Although the mean intrinsic value is low in the sample, the paper finds substantial variation across participants. Other experiments find further evidence of heterogeneity in privacy choices, even within individuals, where choices vary with contextual factors and framing (e.g., Adjerid, Acquisti, and Loewenstein 2019; Athey, Catalini, and Tucker 2017; Acquisti, Brandimarte, and Loewenstein 2015).[13]

Aggregate information on health privacy loss from data breaches is available because of mandatory reporting, but official statistics cover only the volume and type of data, and not the costs or consequences to individuals

13. This heterogeneity in privacy concerns is also found in focus group discussions. For example, attitudes about privacy and security in mobile health applications are highly variable across people, information types, and context (Atienza et al. 2015). Goldfarb and Tucker (2012) also find significant heterogeneity in privacy-preserving behavior across demographic groups and over time.

of the breach.[14] Survey responses in Ponemon (2013) indicate that medical identity theft is increasingly common in the US (affecting an estimated 0.8 percent of adults), with victims incurring an average out-of-pocket cost of $6,718 and experiencing other adverse consequences such as lost health insurance, time and effort devoted to resolving or correcting the issue, and lower trust in healthcare providers. The Ponemon survey also reveals another important feature of medical identity theft, which is that security breaches at healthcare providers and insurers are not, in fact, the primary sources of information. Instead, a significant majority of victims attribute the crime to their having knowingly shared their information (30 percent) or to a family member accessing their medical credentials without their consent (28 percent).

Despite the conceptual and practical challenges, there is significant value from empirical measures of the distribution of actual and perceived costs that individuals face from different aspects of health privacy risk. This is because (as discussed in Section 5.3) privacy protections are not costless. Optimal privacy policy should therefore ideally focus on preventing the most serious potential harms and addressing the areas of most widespread concern.

5.3 Digitization and Costs of Health Privacy Protection

Although privacy risks are present with any form of medical record keeping, they are substantially higher for digital records than for paper files. Electronic records are much cheaper and easier to store, access, and transfer. This greater portability of digital records threatens data confidentiality, by making intentional disclosures less expensive, as well as data security, by potentially enabling massive data breaches carried out by distant attackers. Electronic health information is also easier to combine with other data sources, to manipulate, and to analyze, which increases the risks of indirect harms from how the information is used after disclosure. It is not surprising, therefore, that the increased impetus for health privacy in the late 1990s was closely tied to the diffusion of electronic medical records and health information exchange, particularly among medical providers and payors, and that the HIPAA Privacy and Security Rules focused on entities that transfer information in electronic form. If protecting privacy rights entails allowing individuals to decide for themselves what information to conceal from others (Posner 1981), then stronger protections of health privacy will require restrictions on the volume, flows, and usage of digital health data, and will reduce the amount of health data available to companies. Data elements and uses that are not directly and sufficiently beneficial to consumers will become

14. The Department of Health and Human Services (HHS) maintains a public listing at https://www.hhs.gov/hipaa/for-professionals/breach-notification/breach-reporting/index.html.

more expensive to access or will no longer be available. For that reason, the primary cost of strong privacy protection comes from reducing the gains that would otherwise be generated by greater use of digital health data.

What are the benefits of digital health information? Advances in information technology and computing have significantly lowered costs of data collection and use and driven a shift to digital record keeping and processing across the economy (Goldfarb and Tucker 2019). As an industry, healthcare has been slow to transition away from paper records, despite arguments that electronic medical records (EMRs) have potential to both improve healthcare quality, by reducing errors due to inaccurate or incomplete information about patients (IOM 2000), and to lower administrative costs (Hillestad et al. 2005). Several reasons have been posited for the slow diffusion of EMRs, including privacy concerns, as well as positive externalities from EMR adoption from quality improvements and information sharing across organizations (Miller and Tucker 2009). The 2009 HITECH Act allocated over $25 billion of federal government funding to provider incentives for health IT adoption. At the time of its passage, only 2 percent of US hospitals had an EMR system in place that met the government's "meaningful use" criteria (Jha et al. 2010).

A substantial literature examines the impact of adoption of digital health records by medical providers in the periods before and after the HITECH Act. Studies have found significant improvements in quality, particularly for the most vulnerable patients and complex cases (Gresenz et al. 2017; Miller and Tucker 2011a; Derksen, McGahan, and Pongeluppe 2022; McCullough, Parente, and Town 2016; Freedman, Lin, and Prince 2018), though the gains have not been universal across providers or patient groups (e.g., Spetz, Burgess, and Phibbs 2014; Agha 2014; Hitt and Tambe 2016).[15] Lin, Lin, and Chen (2019) sheds some light on the heterogeneous effects of EMRs across hospitals. The study finds no effects of technology alone, but significant quality improvements from achieving "meaningful use" criteria of the HITECH Act. Lin, Lin, and Chen (2019) also finds larger quality improvements at small and rural hospitals, suggesting an important role for health IT in reducing health disparities. The estimated effects of EMRs on hospital operating costs are also heterogeneous across hospitals, with the benefits from adoption favoring hospitals located in areas with a stronger labor market presence of IT workers (Dranove et al. 2014).

In addition to the stand-alone benefits that accrue to EMR adopters and their patients, there can also be benefits from participating in health data exchanges with other providers (Walker et al. 2005). Indeed the "meaningful use" criteria for system interoperability were aimed at promoting network

15. Also see Atasoy, Greenwood, and McCullough (2019) and Bronsoler, Doyle, and Van Reenen (2022) for reviews of the literature on the effects of health IT on clinical quality, productivity, and healthcare utilization.

benefits from data exchange. These benefits cross the boundaries of individual firms, but still accrue to the patients whose data is shared. Empirical studies have found evidence supporting these spillover gains from health information exchange in both quality and costs. Janakiraman et al. (2022) find quality improvements at emergency departments in the form of shorter inpatient stays and lower patient readmission rates, while Lammers, Adler-Milstein, and Kocher (2014) find a reduction in duplicate testing for patients who visit multiple hospitals. Despite these gains, data exchange can be particularly hampered by privacy concerns (McGraw et al. 2009).

While information exchange among medical providers can improve healthcare operations, the social gains from health data use extend beyond the healthcare system and the data subjects themselves. These uses are well illustrated in the 12 "national priority purposes" for which the HIPAA Privacy Rule permits disclosure and use of personal health information without express permission.[16] These purposes include compliance with legal requirements and regulations, operation of government insurance programs, regulatory oversight and enforcement, and for law enforcement and crime prevention purposes. Of these, public health activities and research uses are likely to have the most significant economic impacts.

The need for timely and extensive data on health conditions for effective public health operations stands in conflict with absolute individual rights to privacy. Health privacy regulations, including HIPAA and state laws, typically relax disclosure rules for public health uses such as disease surveillance and contact tracing programs to monitor and contain outbreaks of infectious diseases. These uses, and the vital importance of free-flowing health data, were especially salient in the government response to the COVID-19 pandemic (e.g., Halpern 2020; Buckman, Adjerid, and Tucker 2023).[17] Even outside of epidemic control, privacy protections often need to be relaxed to promote public health, such as registries for noncommunicable disease. Other examples including limiting patients' control over their prescription information to curb opioid abuse through drug monitoring programs (Maclean et al. 2020) and limiting parental control over child health information to protect abused and neglected children.

Perhaps the largest social benefit from digital health data comes from its use as an input into health research and development. Digital health data, whether generated from clinical encounters and insurance claims, from sources outside of the healthcare system, or by merging existing public and

16. See, e.g., https://www.hhs.gov/hipaa/for-professionals/privacy/laws-regulations/index.html, which describes the aim as "striking the balance between the individual privacy interest and the public interest need for this information."

17. Lawmakers reacted to the threat to health privacy from these expanded public health data uses by introducing a specific COVID-19 Public Health Emergency Privacy Act. The bill was introduced in the Senate in January 2021 (see text at https://www.congress.gov/bill/117th-congress/senate-bill/81) and in the House in February 2021 (text at https://www.congress.gov/bill/117th-congress/house-bill/651/text).

private sources, can advance health research by significantly lowering the costs of conducting large-scale studies that study novel treatments and measures. Massive data sets with health information can be especially valuable for research into rare conditions and for assessing heterogeneous effects across detailed sub-groups, making it a key input into the development and deployment of personalized medicine, where disease prevention, diagnosis, and treatment are all tailored to the patient's individual genetic, social, and environmental characteristics (Miller and Tucker 2017, 2018).[18]

Large quantities of health data are also needed to exploit novel information processing tools, such as machine learning and artificial intelligence, for healthcare applications (Price and Cohen 2019; Smalley 2017; Sanders et al. 2019; Yu, Beam, and Kohane 2018; Shilo, Rossman, and Segal 2020; Goldfarb, Taska, and Teodoridis 2020; Bates and Syrowatka 2022). Better use of health information can also lead to process improvements within healthcare delivery systems, through internal quality improvement program evaluations and utilization reviews.[19] One conception of this is the idea of the "learning health system" (IOM 2007, 2013; Friedman et al. 2015), whose activities can fall outside of formal research, but nevertheless contribute to improving performance and health outcomes.

Although the precise economic value of the resulting medical innovation is hard to measure, and even harder to predict for future discoveries, its potential is enormous, because of the immense economic value of extending lives and improving health (e.g., Murphy and Topel 2003, 2006). HIPAA's Privacy Rule includes provisions aimed at reducing the barriers to using previously collected health data for research purposes. These include the possibility to waive consent with approval from an Institutional Review Board (IRB) or Privacy Board,[20] to disclose a limited data set with a data use agreement, or to exclude the health information from protected status by rendering it anonymous and stripped of its personal identifiers (or de-

18. A prominent public investment in this area is the Precision Medicine Initiative at the US National Institutes of Health (NIH) and the resulting *All of Us* Research Program (All of Us Research Program Investigators 2019).

19. It is also important to note concerns that big data and algorithms can potentially exacerbate existing inequalities, by race or other protected groups, including in healthcare (HHS 2017). Alternatively, increased use of computer algorithms and decision support in healthcare could improve outcomes more for traditionally disadvantaged groups, by reducing the impact of human biases (as found in Bartlett et al. 2022 in financial services). As noted elsewhere in this chapter, digitization in healthcare, by increasing standardization and reducing error rates, has been found to produce greater gains for disadvantaged populations, such as larger improvements in survival rates of Black infants in Miller and Tucker (2011a), lower amputation rates for Black patients in Ganju et al. (2020), and improved quality measures at smaller and rural hospitals in Lin, Lin, and Chen (2019). Further empirical evidence is needed to understand whether and how more advanced data applications affect health disparities.

20. The regulations governing IRB's and ethical guidelines for protecting the privacy of research subjects are addressed in the Federal Policy for the Protection of Human Subjects, known as the Common Rule, adopted by 20 federal agencies and departments. See https://www.hhs.gov/ohrp/compliance-and-reporting/common-rule-agencies-contacts/index.html.

identified).[21] Despite these allowances, evidence suggests that even the limited burdens imposed by the HIPAA Privacy Rule have been detrimental to health research (IOM 2009).[22]

An increasing volume of health data is now being generated outside of clinical settings from a growing number of mobile health devices and applications used by consumers directly to manage their physical and mental health conditions or to invest in general wellness and disease prevention (e.g., HHS 2017, EDPS 2015). Some of these applications are used to exchange data with healthcare providers, or under their supervision, which could help expand access to healthcare for people in rural and underserved areas, while others are used with no connection to formal healthcare providers. Although these applications can significantly increase the amount of health data at risk of disclosure, even consumers with strong preferences for health data privacy and security express a willingness to sacrifice on those dimensions to benefit from the convenience and quality improvements (Atienza et al. 2015).

The reuse of personal health information for marketing purposes is more controversial. While it is true that health data used for personalized advertising, pricing, or product recommendations can be unfavorable to consumers (as discussed in Section 5.2.2), that is not universally the case. Consumers can also benefit from improved match quality in seeing more relevant advertisements and learning about products they are more likely to want to purchase. Using health data as an input to better predictions of product matches is similar in spirit to personalized medicine, though in a different context, and can similarly have a public good component from more data sharing from one person improving the quality of matches for others (e.g., Loertscher and Marx 2020). However, unlike medical applications that improve health, better predictions in other markets can sometimes be used in ways that benefit firms at the expense of some consumers or to infer hidden health information. For those uses, the spillovers across people from increased data sharing, and improved predictions, would be negative. Whether consumers benefit or suffer harm from personalized marketing depends on the nature of the marketing they receive and on their subjective preferences about the underlying health information and the promoted products.

Consumers can also benefit indirectly from the value their data provides

21. This de-identification can be accomplished by an expert or through the Safe Harbor method of removing 18 types of personal identifiers. Heightened privacy concerns around the use of government data, and greater awareness of re-identification risk from previously anonymized data (Komarova, Nekipelov, and Yakovlev 2018), have led to renewed debate about the adequacy of HIPAA's provisions for health research (e.g., IOM 2009). Outside of health, revised disclosure methods to improve privacy protection have been implemented in producing Census data products for the public, possibly at the expense of statistical accuracy (Abowd and Schmutte 2019; Hotz et al. 2022).

22. Outside of health, Miller, Ramdas, and Sungu (2021) discuss costs (and advantages) of using informed consent to collect individual Internet browsing histories for research.

to advertisers if a robust market for consumer health data supplies revenue to developers to create new digital health-related products and offer them to consumers for free or at low cost. In that case, consumers are effectively compensated for their data through useful digital products (e.g., Kummer and Schulte 2019). A recent analysis of over 15,000 free mobile health (medical or health and fitness) apps available through Google Play found that 88 percent included programming code that could collect user data, with 88 percent of data collection operations sending information to external third parties for tracking, analytics, or advertising (Tangari et al. 2021).[23] While it is unclear if these benefits are particularly high for sensitive medical information, the increasing depth and scope of personal information used in digital advertising means that health-related information is increasingly being amassed from sources unrelated to healthcare, including Internet browsing and mobile device location services.[24] It can also be increasingly possible to infer health information from non-health data, as was done in Merchant et al. (2019), using textual analysis of social media posts to predict health conditions and treatments found in EMR records. Because health information is so tightly enmeshed with other types of information, strict privacy rules that cover any health information, regardless of source or confidence level, could operate effectively as broad-based restrictions and raise the costs of collecting and using of all forms of personal data.

5.4 Economic Foundations for Health Privacy Regulations

As the previous two sections illustrate, decisions about when to keep health information private and when to disclose it produce a wide variety of private and social effects. This variety is reflected in the various concepts of privacy employed in the theoretical literature in economics on privacy (discussed in Bonatti 2022, Chapter 3 of this volume) as well as in the various approaches to privacy protection employed by policy makers. This section connects theory to policy by presenting economic foundations for different types of privacy rules.

Decisions about disclosing health information are made by consumers, who are the subjects of the information, and by firms, who control and man-

23. An earlier study of 211 diabetes apps on Google Play found that fewer than 1 in 5 had a privacy policy and only 4 said they would obtain user permission for data sharing (Blenner et al. 2016). A smaller study of apps for smoking cessation and depression found that 80 percent transmitted data to Facebook or Google services, but fewer than half of those notified users in their privacy policies (Huckvale, Torous, and Larsen 2019).

24. See, for example the August 2022 FTC case against Kochava, in which the data broker was alleged to have sold geolocation information that could be used to trace individual visits to "sensitive" locations, including abortion clinics. Also note the "Socioeconomic Health Risk" product offered by LexisNexis Risk Solution, described at https://www.lexisnexis.com/risk/downloads/literature/health-care/Socioeconomic-Health-Risk-Score-br.pdf as a way to "predict health risk more precisely—without medical claims data."

age it. Although there can be significant overlap in their interests, the alignment is imperfect. Individuals typically bear the main costs from improper disclosure and misuse of their information, making them prefer a higher level of privacy and security than firms do. A natural starting point for resolving disagreements between firms and individuals about information privacy is through private contracts and bargaining, as in Coase (1960). In the ideal case, when the Coase Theorem holds, bargaining delivers the efficient level of privacy, balancing the costs and benefits between the parties, regardless of the initial allocation of property rights. In that case, government intervention would be unnecessary (if it leaves the final allocation unchanged) or harmful (if it were binding). Unfortunately, it is unlikely that the Coase Theorem will hold.

Bargaining over health privacy is impossible if the initial allocation of ownership rights is ambiguous. Companies that create, collect, and maintain health data have plausible claims to property rights, as do individuals who are its subjects. Without specific information to the contrary, people might assume a higher level of protection than is being offered. One function of privacy laws is therefore resolving the ambiguity. This entails setting a default initial allocation of ownership rights, either to consumers or to firms. It can also entail establishing notification and consent rules to ensure that consumers are explicitly informed about relevant privacy terms before they make decisions about sharing their health information or using products or services that will generate a trail of personal health data. An even weaker form of this policy is the Federal Trade Commission (FTC) guidance on best practices for mobile health app developers that recommends clear communication with consumers about privacy data collection and privacy policy but is otherwise focused on data security.[25]

While providing detailed information to consumers about the different potential uses of their data is an important first step, it may not be enough to enable them to make optimal decisions about their own desired levels of privacy. This is because privacy choices and risks can be complex and uncertain, involving hypothetical outcomes that are hard for people to assess. Furthermore, health data can be persistently informative over a lifetime and the disclosure risks can increase as science and technology advance (see Miller and Tucker 2018 on the evolving privacy risk from genetic data). It seems inevitable that some people would struggle to understand and optimize over these risks. Outside of healthcare, researchers find empirical support for concerns about nonstandard decision-making in privacy choices in their sensitivity to framing and provision of extraneous reassuring information (e.g., Athey, Catalini, and Tucker 2017; Adjerid, Acquisti, and Loewenstein

25. See https://www.ftc.gov/business-guidance/resources/mobile-health-app-developers-ftc-best-practices.

2019). This suggests a potential role for some paternalistic government interventions to protect individuals from mistakenly giving up too much privacy at the time of initial information disclosure. This could be accomplished, for example, by nudging people toward more privacy-preserving choices through default options (Bhargava and Loewenstein 2015), or possibly by mandating or supplying education to citizens about privacy issues and access to counseling and decision support services.

Even when consumers are well informed and fully comprehend their privacy choices, consent requirements at the initial contracting stage may still not be sufficient to ensure efficient privacy levels if the range of privacy options offered to them is severely restricted. This can happen when consumers need to accept a take-it-or-leave-it list of allowed disclosures as a precondition to obtaining medical treatment or using data-intensive products. When it comes to online activity, Acquisti, Brandimarte, and Loewenstein (2020) argue that consumers face prohibitive costs to constraining digital tracking. To the extent that the limited set of privacy options comes from coordination among competitors or the exercise of market power, it could be addressed under antitrust policy. However, this is unlikely on its own to ensure privacy-preserving options for consumers who value them. Simply assigning property rights to consumers could also be ineffectual if they agree to transfer the rights as part of the terms of trade. Instead, if there are categories of re-disclosures or uses that are harmful to a significant majority of consumers, there could be a role for government in limiting the allowed uses, i.e., preventing certain trades from happening, even when both sides are willing. This could increase overall welfare even if there is a loss from the forgone trade. Health privacy rules that require explicit patient authorization for every re-disclosure of their data have that form, as do rules that set time limits on authorizations, in that they preclude agreements that provide blanket or perpetual authorization. These provisions are notably absent from the HIPAA Privacy Rule, for example, which has been criticized for its leniency because it only requires notification of privacy practices, but not that patients are given specific options to limit disclosures (Rothstein 2007).

Asymmetric information about what happens to data after the initial disclosure presents another challenge to private bargaining. Once a consumer discloses information to a company, they are unable to monitor how the company handles the data in their possession, what information they re-disclose to third parties, or how the information is further transferred and used after it moves beyond the boundaries of the initial company that directly interacted with them. The data may be sold or transferred for some in-kind benefit or as part of a merger or acquisition of the original company. Violations of contractual restrictions on data use could easily go undetected, which limits consumers' ability to obtain recourse through legal or reputational channels. Here, again, the government has an important role in providing the necessary structure to enforce property rights over privacy, which includes both detecting and penalizing violations.[26] This motivates rules that increase consumer information about harmful data loss (through breach notification requirements), as well as standards and mandates for information security requirements that apply to companies that collect or use health data as well as ones that develop and manufacture devices and products that do the same.

In areas of both privacy and security, there could also be a role for government in imposing tighter restrictions than the market would provide to address negative spillovers from data sharing across people. These can arise among close family members, as in the cases of genetic information in Miller and Tucker (2018) and children's HIV status in Derksen, McGahan, and Pongeluppe (2022), but they are not limited to those cases. In the model of data markets studied in Acemoglu et al. (2022), data spillovers come from information about one person revealing information about others, which can lead to inefficiently low levels of privacy.

Even when people have an interest in sharing personal health information with healthcare or other service providers, they may still want to keep it secret from other firms or people, where it can be used against them. Health privacy rules that limit all data collection or re-disclosure may be too broad because they prevent even positive data uses. At the same time, by focusing on the party making the disclosure (and sending the data), they may not do enough to align incentives and prevent the most severe financial risks associated with health data loss. Another approach to privacy protection is therefore to regulate how companies, primarily employers and insurance providers, can use personal health information, by restricting the types of personal information they can acquire or consider.

Health privacy rules that focus on data use by employers or insurers operate as anti- discrimination rules that treat health characteristics as protected categories. A prime example is the 2008 Genetic Information Non-discrimination Act (GINA) that treats genetic information as a protected category. Other federal laws that ban discrimination based on health-related information include the 1978 Pregnancy Discrimination Act, the 1990 Americans with Disabilities Act (ADA), the 2010 Patient Protection and Affordable Care Act (ACA)'s ban on individual insurance market consideration of information on preexisting health conditions. The provisions in HIPAA (outside the Privacy and Security Rules) restricting the treatment of preexisting conditions in group health plans would also fit in this category. Restrictions on data use are not focused on the informational aspect, but they can function similarly. Interestingly, the equal protection requirements of these rules could increase

26. There may also be a role for public enforcement of privacy rules. For the general literature on public versus private enforcement, see, for example, Landes and Posner (1975) and Polinsky and Shavell (2000).

the amount of health information workers disclosure to their employers, particularly if they seek workplace accommodations under the ADA.[27]

Antidiscrimination rules can increase market efficiency if the source of the discrimination was based on bias or animus against people with certain genetic or health conditions, but they can be a source of inefficiency if they block companies from using economically relevant information. When insurers are not able to incorporate information on health conditions in setting premiums or coverage levels, that could significantly improve access to insurance for individuals with higher expected health costs, but it could worsen access for people without those conditions if their premiums are raised. At a market level, making health information invisible (or non-actionable) to insurers effectively creates an information asymmetry, because the information is known to consumers. This can cause problems of adverse selection if people with fewer medical risks opt to reduce their insurance purchases or if companies attempt to steer consumers using non-price features to different contracts based on health status (Handel, Hendel, and Whinston 2015; Oster et al. 2010; Einav, Finkelstein, and Cullen 2010; Akerlof 1970; Rothschild and Stiglitz 1976). This has a potential efficiency cost in reducing the size of the market.

Similar distortions can occur in labor markets if the antidiscrimination rule causes average expected productivity, overall or for identifiable groups, to drop so much that hiring is curtailed (e.g., Herman and Katz 2006). Companies may try to circumvent antidiscrimination rules that focus on specific types of health information by increasing attention to non-protected data elements that function as proxies. The use of proxies can have its own perverse effects, as seen in the findings of increased racial disparities in labor markets from regulations delaying employer access to criminal background information (Doleac and Hansen 2020; Agan and Starr 2018) and of labor market effects of the Pregnancy Discrimination Act affecting all women of childbearing ages (Gruber 1994). It is notable that in both cases the affected groups are themselves protected classes under labor market antidiscrimination rules; this points to the general challenge of enforcing these rules and of detecting violations.

Policy debates around restricting the use of health information in insurance markets therefore tend to center on the trade-off between the inefficiency produced by increasing the potential role for adverse selection and the distributional aim of providing financial support to people with adverse health shocks (Posner 1981).[28] Yet even when motivated by fairness con-

27. Because of this, title I of the ADA also features requirements that employers preserve the privacy of information they receive about employee's health conditions. The requirements are not limited to materials produced by healthcare providers or that contain information on medical diagnoses or treatments and include information such as accommodation requests.

28. There can also be moral hazard concern from rules that prevent insurers from pricing based on health status, because they lower individual incentives to make "self-protective" investments in preventative care, a healthy diet, and regular exercise (Ehrlich and Becker 1972).

cerns, the distributional aims of health privacy rules have been argued to serve efficiency goals. One basis for this is similar to the idea behind social insurance more generally, namely, that the *ex post* redistribution that happens after negative health shocks are realized provides *ex ante* insurance to the population from the financial risk of experiencing those shocks (a form of insurance that private markets are ill equipped to supply). A second argument for the efficiency of redistribution based on negative health status is if people have altruistic preferences and care about the well-being of people in poor health, wanting them to have access to healthcare and gainful employment. While those preferences can be expressed through voluntary contributions to private charities, the well-being of the disadvantaged group takes on the characteristics of a public good—non-excludable and non-rivalrous. In that case, private charity will under-provide, and there can be a social gain from increasing the level of support. A counterpoint to these arguments is that health privacy rules, or indeed health status, may not be the best way to target the neediest populations, as was found in the analysis of the federal disability insurance program in Deshpande and Lockwood (2022).

Health privacy rules typically include special restrictions on the use of personal health information for marketing purposes. Nevertheless, in recognition of the potential value to consumers of some targeted marketing of health and insurance products based on their health data, these uses are not typically banned. Even the HIPAA Privacy Rule allows for certain limited marketing uses of personal health data without prior authorization, such as communication about products and services at their current provider or relevant to their course of treatment or disease management.

Outside of the specific exceptions, however, permission from patients is needed before their HIPAA-protected health information can be used, transferred, or sold for marketing purposes. This includes data from certain medical and wellness tracking devices and apps that are used under physician direction, but it leaves most consumer health products outside of the scope of federal privacy rules.[29] Some mobile medical apps are regulated by the Food and Drug Administration, but the requirements are for security and not confidentiality. The FTC acts against companies that violate the terms of their privacy or security policies, or that make false claims about their data practices, under general consumer protection rules against unfair or deceptive practices.[30] Taken together, these rules leave a substantial amount of health information outside of federal privacy rules. Extending the full set of HIPAA protections to these other sources of health information would impose significant costs on companies that collect, disseminate, or share

29. State health privacy rules sometimes have broader scope of covered entities or stricter provisions, but they also tend to focus on healthcare providers rather than general health information.

30. Recent health privacy cases, listed on the FTC webpage at https://www.ftc.gov/legal-library/browse/cases- proceedings, include the 2022 action against Kochava, Inc., and the settlements with Flo Health in 2021 and with SkyMed in 2020.

health data, and could reduce the quality and variety of health products that rely on consumer data.

Finally, it is important to note that health privacy laws often include provisions aimed at increasing the flow of health information. One way they do this is by granting to consumers greater rights of access to information about their own health that is held by companies. These provisions fit with the idea of health privacy laws as providing a form of consumer protection and are discussed more in Section 5.5.3 below. Another important set of provisions is the exemptions and carve-outs from other privacy rules that are aimed at allowing for health data applications that serve the public good (like the "national priority purposes" in HIPAA), discussed in Section 5.3. In addition to these relaxations of existing privacy rules, the government also provides significant public subsidies to support voluntary participation and health data sharing for research purposes and makes data sharing compulsory for public health registries and administrative oversight.

Furthermore, because the initial provision of health information, or contracting decision, involves a voluntary choice by consumers, it is theoretically possible that stronger privacy protections, such as those that limit data re-disclosure or discriminatory uses, could serve to increase the initial supply of information. This can happen if the legal rules provide reassurance and structure that make people willing to provide information and use data-demanding products. Absent this reassurance, people may avoid seeking care, invest in costly efforts to mask or obscure their identities when seeking treatment, or provide limited or misleading information for their records (as discussed in Section 5.2.2).

5.5 Insights from Empirical Studies of Health Privacy Regulation

Theoretical predictions about the effects of privacy laws depend fundamentally on factors that are hard to measure in advance, creating a pressing need for empirical analysis to guide ongoing policy debates. This section discusses four key insights from the empirical literature on health privacy regulation.

5.5.1 Privacy Rules Can Inhibit Digitization

The first insight from the economics literature on health privacy policy is empirical confirmation of the prediction that privacy laws can inhibit digitization of health information. This is the main finding in Miller and Tucker's (2009) analysis of new adoption of electronic medical records (EMRs) in US hospitals between 1996 and 2005. Controlling for hospital and year fixed effects, as well as a variety of time-varying factors related to the hospital and local area, strict health privacy rules governing disclosure of patient data are found to have significantly slowed the diffusion of EMRs, reducing annual adoption at hospitals by over 24 percent.

The mechanism through which privacy laws depressed EMR adoption is from the elimination of the positive network effects that would otherwise cause EMR adoption by one hospital in a health services area to increase the likelihood of adoption by other hospitals in the same area. This channel is consistent with the privacy laws reducing the net benefit of EMRs to hospitals by increasing the costs of sharing data, effectively creating a regulatory barrier preventing hospitals from realizing the value of the technological innovation in EMRs that reduces the cost of exchanging patient data. This result does not imply that privacy regulation did not also serve a role in reassuring some patients and increasing their comfort with digital health data collection and sharing, only that the positive effect on consumers was small relative to the negative effect on firms.

Empirical variation in privacy rules comes primarily from states adopting laws that preceded the HIPAA Privacy Rule. These rules exceeded the relatively weak provisions in HIPAA related to data re-disclosure (Rothstein 2007). Because they were not preempted by HIPAA, they continued to be operative after its enactment, unless modified at the state level (Pritts 2001; Pritts et al. 2009). As shown in Figures 1 and 2 of Miller and Tucker (2009), these laws were geographically dispersed across the country, but more common in larger states with higher average income levels. The Miller and Tucker (2009) paper therefore also addresses the concern that their presence may be endogenous, by repeating the analysis using state political representation to instrument for privacy laws, confirming the significant negative effect of privacy laws on EMR adoption, operating through spillovers from other local adoption.

This core finding is again replicated and then extended in Miller and Tucker (2011a), which further examines the welfare impact of delayed EMR adoption by studying its effects on neonatal mortality. Miller and Tucker (2011a) focuses on newborn health because it is a key measure of health system performance on which the US routinely underperforms relative to other high-income countries. It is also a setting in which EMRs can also be particularly valuable by helping medical specialists monitor and access patient data needed to track and manage the progress of high-risk pregnancies and births.

Using 11 years of panel data derived from vital statistics records of every live birth and infant death in the nation, Miller and Tucker (2011a) finds that hospital adoption of EMRs is associated with significant reductions in neonatal mortality, after controlling for a wide range of maternal, pregnancy, hospital, and county-level controls, as well as location and year fixed effects. A 10 percent increase in basic EMR adoption in a county is associated with a reduction of neonatal deaths of 16 per 100,000 live births, with larger reductions coming when EMR adoption is coupled with adoption of an obstetric-specific IT system. Consistent with predictions, the improvements in neonatal survival were largest for pregnancies with perinatal complications and premature births and not present for pregnancies with no prenatal care (and therefore no prior data to access). EMRs also had no effects on mortality from causes that are not affected by information flows, including congenital defects, sudden infant death syndrome, and accidents.

To address concerns about the potential endogeneity of adoption decisions by hospitals, the study uses state-level health privacy laws as a source of instrumental variables for EMR adoption. The instruments include indicators for having in place a variety of health privacy provisions (as discussed in Section 5.4.1), as well as interactions between re-disclosure rules and the latent value of health data exchange (using the size of the hospital, its membership in a system of hospitals, and the number of other hospitals in the area; each of these is also included as controls in the main equation). The first-stage estimates reveal that disclosure rules are the most important provisions that slow EMR adoption overall, with effect sizes that are larger for hospitals with more local opportunity for data exchange (with more hospitals in the area) and smaller at large hospitals that may have less need for data sharing. The IV estimates confirm the OLS finding that health IT adoption improves neonatal survival rates.

These results, together with other studies of health IT, discussed in Section 5.3, suggest significant social costs from delayed EMR adoption on hospital quality.[31] Although these studies have focused on the adoption and use of existing technologies, the effect of privacy laws is unlikely to be limited to those outcomes. To the extent that privacy laws affect expected adoption rates for health IT, they can affect investments in innovation and the future evolution of technology (similar to the dynamic effects from vaccine policy in Finkelstein 2004).

5.5.2 Different Privacy Rules Produce Different Effects

A second insight from the empirical literature is that different approaches to health privacy policy can produce different effects. This result is perhaps best illustrated in Miller and Tucker (2018), which studies the effects of different types of state laws addressing genetic privacy. Although health privacy laws often cover genetic information, there is additional policy and advocacy focus on genetic privacy because of the heightened privacy risks from genetic information disclosure (Hellman 2003; Oster et al. 2010). Genetic data can reveal a significant amount of information about a person and their biological relatives. Unlike Internet browsing or phone location histories, genetic information is persistently informative over a person's lifetime, and the meanings and uses of the information are likely to expand in unpredictable ways as biological science advances. At the same time, genetic information is increasingly valuable in healthcare for disease prevention and

31. Derksen, McGahan, and Pongeluppe (2022) further illustrate the conflict between respecting privacy preferences and harnessing the value of IT in healthcare delivery. EMR adoption in Malawian clinics lowered AIDS mortality through improved tracing of HIV-positive patients for follow-up care; the largest benefits were among patients who asked not to be traced.

treatment, and it is a key input in the development of more personalized medicine (e.g., All of Us Research Program Investigators 2019).

Miller and Tucker (2018) studies individual decisions to undergo genetic testing for cancer risks, using data from over 80,000 people surveyed across the 2000, 2005, and 2010 waves of the National Health Interview Surveys (NHIS) Cancer Control Modules. Patients with known genetic markers for cancer risk (such as BRCA1 or BRCA2 mutations) can receive tailored care, such as more frequent screenings or preventative medication (such as raloxifene or tamoxifen) or surgery (such as prophylactic mastectomy). Yet testing rates are very low in the population (under 1 percent), and even among populations with elevated risk factors from family history who have discussed genetic testing with their physician (only 20 percent). Availability of genetic testing services at hospitals is also limited, covering only about 11 percent of hospitals in the American Hospital Association (AHA) survey.

Concerns about increased privacy risks and potential discriminatory uses of genetic information have been proposed as possible reasons for the low testing rates and as a motivation for specific privacy rules that address genetic data to reassure patients and increase their willingness to seek testing. At the same time, the results from Miller and Tucker (2009) and (2011a) suggest that privacy rules may lower availability of testing at hospitals if they face increased compliance costs or perceive the data to be less valuable.

The analysis in Miller and Tucker (2018) therefore empirically examines the separate effects of three different dimensions of genetic privacy laws: (1) explicit notification requirement on privacy risks as part of informed consent; (2) requirements that companies obtain individual consent before data re-disclosure, effectively assigning ownership rights to individuals over their data; and (3) restrictions on downstream uses of data through antidiscrimination rules. State laws typically include one or more of these protections, while GINA (which comes into effect at the end of the sample period) focuses on the third related to discriminatory uses.

Consistent with the countervailing mechanisms inherent in privacy rules, Miller and Tucker (2018) finds different empirical effects of the different dimensions of privacy policy. The policy of requiring clear and detailed notification of privacy risks is associated with lower testing rates, but policies that strengthen patients' ownership and control over their data are associated with increased adoption. Restrictions on third-party discriminatory uses, at the state level or federal level from GINA, are not found to have any detectable impact on testing rates. While the finding that ownership rights increase testing is promising for the potential role of privacy rules to reassure the public, the implications from the other results are more concerning. The importance of notification requirements appears to come in large part from lower supply of testing at hospitals, but it may also come from the greater salience of privacy at the time of testing decisions or from better guiding consumers in making informed choices about their information.

Similarly, the lack of an effect of antidiscrimination laws on testing could reflect the difficulties that consumers anticipate in detecting illegal discrimination and enforcing of future claims. This null effect differs from findings in the literature on the effects of the ADA, which prohibits discrimination by disability status (DeLeire 2001; Acemoglu and Angrist 2001; Jolls 2004) and of the pregnancy discrimination act (Gruber 1994). One potential source for that difference is that those studies focused on labor market effects rather than on data generation and disclosure.

5.5.3 Privacy Rules Can Sometimes Increase Data Flows

In contrast to the theoretical concerns that privacy rules increase the costs of information exchange and lower the value of health IT, supported by the empirical findings in Miller and Tucker (2009 and 2011a) that privacy rules lower EMR adoption, another insight from the literature is that privacy rules can increase IT adoption and data use in some circumstances.

One mechanism for this is that privacy laws provide reassurance to patients about data security and limits on reuse, making them more willing to undertake medical testing or seek treatments that will create sensitive records. This mechanism was supported empirically for genetic testing in Miller and Tucker (2018). It was also argued as a reason why privacy rules could help promote health information exchange (McGraw et al. 2009), as found in Adjerid et al. (2016) when combined with financial incentives for adoption. The findings in Buckman, Adjerid, and Tucker (2023) for COVID-19 vaccination rates similarly support the idea that privacy concerns can reduce healthcare seeking for some patients, and that legal health privacy protections (in their case the right to remove identifying information from the vaccine registry) can provide the needed reassurance.

A second mechanism is that privacy laws that strengthen consumers' ownership rights over their health information can increase the production and use of health data by making it easier to extract data from the control of organizations that generate and use it. Giving patients more control over their data can increase data flaws because patients sometimes want their data to be transferred and shared more easily than providers do. When patient records belong to healthcare providers, it becomes a form of proprietary information that some firms want to keep siloed away from competitors. One such motivation for hospitals is to "lock-in" existing patients for follow-on care. Miller and Tucker (2014) find empirical support for this in the lower rates of external health data exchange among hospitals that are part of larger systems. This pattern is present despite the fact that those hospitals tend to have greater technological capacity for health IT and engage in significantly more internal data exchange within their systems.[32] The effect is larger for hospitals with patients who are otherwise more mobile (having non-HMO insurance coverage), with higher paid staff, and with specialty

32. Concerns about corporate data control being used to foreclose competition arise outside of healthcare as well, for example, in debates about car repairs (Magliozzi 2022).

services (such as cardiology or oncology), suggesting that the reduction in external data exchanges come from a strategic motivation to retain patients.

Notwithstanding these considerations, the "meaningful use" requirements for health IT data compatibility and exchange in the original HITECH Act were focused solely on the technological capacity and ability to exchange data. This proved insufficient when providers and vendors had financial incentives to block data flows (Pear 2015). This was addressed in part in the 21st Century Cures Act of 2016 (Cures Act), which updated the HITECH Act (effective April 2021) to prohibit data blocking by technology vendors or healthcare providers.

These results point to an important aspect of health privacy rules that is sometimes neglected in the literature. Although the rules often aim to restrict information flows and prevent unwanted disclosures, those are not their only goals. Privacy rules often originate from a consumer protection perspective and aim at bolstering individual property rights over personal data. This is reflected in US federal laws described above and in the GDPR provisions related to individual rights of data access and erasure and to data portability.[33]

Advancing the goals of increasing consumer control over their data can increase information flows and improve efficiency if it reduces inefficient data hoarding by companies. This idea is central to the theory of Jones and Tonetti (2020), who focus on the non-rivalrous aspect of data use. The idea also receives empirical support in the finding in Baker, Bundorf, and Kessler (2015) that rules that increase consumer access to their health data—in their case, state laws that capped the charges that healthcare providers could impose for copies of paper medical records—led to increased adoption of EMRs at hospitals.

5.5.4 Is Regulating Technology Enough?

A final theme from the empirical literature is that a focus on technological solutions alone is not enough to protect privacy. This was seen above when "meaningful use" rules for technological capability were not enough to ensure meaningful flow of patient data across providers. It is further illustrated in Miller and Tucker's (2011b) study of health data security.

The technology of interest in that paper is data encryption, which can preserve privacy in the event of a breach, by rendering the information unreadable to anyone without the key. Data security rules in several states recognize this feature by exempting breached data from mandatory disclosure requirements if encryption was in place. Miller and Tucker (2011b) first confirm the motivation for devoting special attention to the security of electronic health records, by showing that digitization of hospital records

33. Data access rights are also included in state-level broad-based privacy laws in California and Virginia.

indeed increases the loss of patient data through publicized data breaches, and then studies the role of data encryption in preventing data loss. State policies that exempt encrypted data from breach notification rules are found to have their intended effect of increasing the adoption of data encryption at hospitals. However, the paper also finds that encryption alone does not reduce the amount of data lost. Instead, public reports of lost data are higher at hospitals with encryption. To address concerns that this relationship could come from hospitals with higher-value data being both more likely to adopt encryption and more likely to be targeted, Miller and Tucker (2011b) also estimates effects of encryption using the legal variation as a source of exogenous variation. Again, the results confirm that encryption increases data loss. The reason for this surprising effect is that encryption increases data loss from internal fraud and from lost equipment.

This result highlights a key challenge in regulating data privacy and security. Technical solutions can be effective for firms, but focusing policy on them can be counterproductive if it draws attention away from human factors that also contribute to data protection. This is analogous to the multi-task principal-agent problem in employment contracts (Holmstrom and Milgrom 1991) and an example of the general problem of unintended consequences of regulation. There is also a lesson specific to privacy regulation. Technological change is the key source of the increased risks of privacy loss, so understanding and addressing technology is essential to managing the risk. However, the solutions will not come from technology alone. Privacy problems are inherently about human behaviors; effective privacy policy needs to keep human factors, such as cost and incentives, at its center. This is true even for data security, where firms and consumers share some common interest in data protection. Incentives must play an even larger role in addressing confidentiality and intentional disclosures.

5.6 Conclusion

The economic approach to digital health privacy presented in this chapter is a complement to approaches from other fields centered on legal rights and principles or on technological challenges and solutions. The approach is characterized by its consideration of costs and benefits of different data uses and restrictions and it is grounded in both theory models and empirical evidence of how firms and individuals make decisions and how markets operate. These features make the economic literature on health privacy particularly promising for providing a foundation for assessing the impacts of existing health privacy rules, and for predicting effects of new rules. Although the focus of this chapter is on health privacy, the increasing prevalence of health- related information outside of traditional medical and insurance settings presents new challenges for policy makers, raising questions about the desirability of expanding the scope of existing health privacy rules or enacting broad-based privacy rules. Economic research in health privacy can therefore serve to inform pressing policy debates and to advance scientific understanding of the fundamental trade-offs between preserving privacy and harnessing the value of IT and data-driven innovation in healthcare.

This chapter concludes by noting some promising avenues for further research on health data privacy. The first is to address the continuing need for measures of the value of health privacy. In addition to assessing external effects of privacy protections, data disclosures, and breaches on individuals and firms, it is also important to quantify the subjective elements. For that, it will be particularly useful to develop approaches based on revealed preferences (i.e., consequential choices) to study the size and distribution of individual tastes for different types of health data collection and uses. A second avenue for new research is the examination, theoretical and empirical, of the evolving privacy policy landscape, tracking and analyzing new privacy rules as they are crafted and enacted. In addition to studying rule changes, it will also be important to study how existing rules are interpreted and enforced.[34] The third avenue is to study the underlying impetus for privacy policy reform, which is the diffusion of new computing technologies that is producing a proliferation of health-related data. As discussed in the chapter, a significant volume of this data is being collected, maintained, and used outside of traditional healthcare settings that are often subject to stricter privacy protections. This data is heterogeneous in its content (pertaining to diseases, health conditions, or treatments; or to wellness, fitness, and lifestyle) and source (inputted directly by individuals, collected from devices) and varies significantly in its value, sensitivity, and regulatory treatment. As such, it provides a range of opportunities for researchers to study the interactions between privacy policies and the development, spread, and impact of emerging technologies.

References

Abowd, J. M., and I. M. Schmutte. 2019. "An Economic Analysis of Privacy Protection and Statistical Accuracy as Social Choices." *American Economic Review* 109 (1): 171–202.

Acemoglu, D., and J. D. Angrist, 2001. "Consequences of Employment Protection?

34. In the US, a listing of FTC cases, including those related to privacy within and outside of healthcare, can be found at https://www.ftc.gov/legal-library/browse/cases-proceedings. Fines and penalties imposed on organizations and individuals under the European GDPR can be found, e.g., at https://www.enforcementtracker.com/ and https://www.privacyaffairs.com/gdpr-fines/. Examples of economic research on effects of enforcement actions outside of health privacy include Miller (2010) on airline collusion and Miller and Segal (2012 and 2019) on employment discrimination.

The Case of the Americans with Disabilities Act." *Journal of Political Economy* 109 (5): 915–957.
Acemoglu, D., A. Makhdoumi, A. Malekian, and A. Ozdaglar, 2022. "Too Much Data: Prices and Inefficiencies in Data Markets." *American Economic Journal: Microeconomics* 14 (4): 218–56.
Acquisti, A., L. Brandimarte, and G. Loewenstein. 2015. "Privacy and Human Behavior in the Age of Information." *Science* 347 (6221): 509–514.
Acquisti, A., L. Brandimarte, and G. Loewenstein. 2020. "Secrets and Likes: The Drive for Privacy and the Difficulty of Achieving It in the Digital Age." *Journal of Consumer Psychology* 30 (4): 736–758.
Acquisti, A., C. Taylor, and L. Wagman. 2016. "The Economics of Privacy." *Journal of Economic Literature* 54 (2): 442–92.
Adjerid, I., A. Acquisti, and G. Loewenstein. 2019. "Choice Architecture, Framing, and Cascaded Privacy Choices." *Management Science* 65 (5): 2267–2290.
Adjerid, I., A. Acquisti, R. Telang, R. Padman, and J. Adler-Milstein. 2016. "The Impact of Privacy Regulation and Technology Incentives: The Case of Health Information Exchanges." *Management Science* 62 (4): 1042–1063.
Agan, A., and S. Starr. 2018. "Ban the Box, Criminal Records, and Racial Discrimination: A Field Experiment." *Quarterly Journal of Economics* 133 (1): 191–235.
Agha, L. 2014. "The Effects of Health Information Technology on the Costs and Quality of Medical Care." *Journal of Health Economics* 34: 19–30.
Aigner, D. J., and G. G. Cain. 1977. "Statistical Theories of Discrimination in Labor Markets." *ILR Review* 30 (2): 175–187.
Akerlof, G. 1970. "The Markets for 'Lemons': Quality Uncertainty and the Market Mechanism." *Quarterly Journal of Economics* 84 (3): 488–500.
All of Us Research Program Investigators. 2019. "The 'All of Us' Research Program." *New England Journal of Medicine* 381 (7): 668–676.
Alsan, M., and M. Wanamaker. 2018. "Tuskegee and the Health of Black Men." *Quarterly Journal of Economics* 133 (1): 407–455.333
Arrow, K. 1973. "The Theory of Discrimination." In *Discrimination in Labor Markets*, edited by Orley Ashenfelter and Albert Rees. Princeton University Press.
Atasoy, H., B. N. Greenwood, and J. S. McCullough. 2019. "The Digitization of Patient Care: A Review of the Effects of Electronic Health Records on Health Care Quality and Utilization." *Annual Review of Public Health* 40: 487–500.
Athey, S., C. Catalini, and C. Tucker. 2017. "The Digital Privacy Paradox: Small Money, Small Costs, Small Talk." NBER Working Paper 23488. Cambridge, MA: National Bureau of Economic Research.
Atienza, A., C. Zarcadoolas, W. Vaughon, P. Hughes, V. Patel, W-Y. S. Chou, and J. Pritts. 2015. "Consumer Attitudes and Perceptions on mHealth Privacy and Security: Findings from a Mixed-Methods Study." *Journal of Health Communication* 20 (6): 673–679.
Badgett, M. L. 2007. *Sexual Orientation Discrimination: An International Perspective*. London: Routledge.
Baldwin, M. L., and W. G. Johnson. 2006. "A Critical Review of Studies of Discrimination against Workers with Disabilities." In *Handbook on the Economics of Discrimination*, edited by W. M. Rodgers. Northampton, MA: Edward Elgar Publishing.
Baker, L. C., M. K. Bundorf, and D. P. Kessler. 2015. "Expanding Patients' Property Rights in Their Medical Records." *American Journal of Health Economics* 1 (1): 82–100.
Bartlett, R., A. Morse, R. Stanton, and N. Wallace. 2022. "Consumer-Lending Discrimination in the Fintech Era." *Journal of Financial Economics* 143 (1): 30–56.

Bates, D. W., and A. Syrowatka. 2022. "Harnessing AI in Sepsis Care." *Nature Medicine* 28 (7): 1351–1352.

Becker, G. S. 1957. *The Economics of Discrimination*. University of Chicago Press.

Bhargava, S., and G. Loewenstein. 2015. "Behavioral Economics and Public Policy 102: Beyond Nudging." *American Economic Review* 105(5): 396–401.

Blenner, S. R., M. Köllmer, A. J. Rouse, N. Daneshvar, C. Williams, and L. B. Andrews. 2016. "Privacy Policies of Android Diabetes Apps and Sharing of Health Information." *JAMA* 315 (10): 1051–1052.

Bonatti, A. 2022. "Theory and Privacy." In *Economics of Privacy*, edited by A. Goldfarb and C. Tucker. University of Chicago Press.

Bronsoler, A., J. Doyle, and J. Van Reenen. 2022. "The Impact of Health Information and Communication Technology on Clinical Quality, Productivity, and Workers." *Annual Review of Economics* 14.

Buckman, J. R., Idris Adjerid, and Catherine Tucker. 2023. "Privacy Regulation and Barriers to Public Health." *Management Science* 69 (1): 342–350.

Campbell J., A. Goldfarb, C. Tucker. 2015. "Privacy Regulation and Market Structure." *Journal of Economics & Management Strategy* 24 (1): 47–73.

Claxton, G., M. Rae, A. Damico, E. Wager, G. Young, and H. Whitmore. 2022. "Health Benefits In 2022: Premiums Remain Steady, Many Employers Report Limited Provider Networks for Behavioral Health: Study Examines Employer-Sponsored Health Benefits in 2022." *Health Affairs* 10–1377.

Coase, R. H. 1960. "The Problem of Social Cost." *Journal of Law and Economics* 3: 1–44.

DeLeire, T. 2001. "Changes in Wage Discrimination against People with Disabilities: 1984–93." *Journal of Human Resources 36 (1)*: 144–158.

Derksen, L., A. McGahan, and L. Pongeluppe. 2022. "Privacy at What Cost? Using Electronic Medical Records to Recover Lapsed Patients Into HIV Care." Working Paper.

Deshpande, M., and L. M. Lockwood. 2022. "Beyond Health: Non-health Risk and the Value of Disability Insurance." *Econometrica* 90 (4): 1781–1810.

Doleac, J. L., and B. Hansen. 2020. "The Unintended Consequences of 'Ban the Box': Statistical Discrimination and Employment Outcomes When Criminal Histories Are Hidden." *Journal of Labor Economics* 38 (2): 321–374.

Dranove, D., C. Forman, A. Goldfarb, and S. Greenstein. 2014. "The Trillion Dollar Conundrum: Complementarities and Health Information Technology." *American Economic Journal: Economic Policy* 6 (4): 239–70.

Duhigg, C. 2012. "See How Companies Learn Your Secrets." *New York Times*, February 6.

Ehrlich, I., and G. S. Becker. 1972. "Market Insurance, Self-Insurance, and Self-Protection." *Journal of Political Economy* 80 (4): 623–648.

Einav, L., A. Finkelstein, and M. R. Cullen. 2010. "Estimating Welfare in Insurance Markets Using Variation in Prices." *Quarterly Journal of Economics* 125 (3): 877–921.

European Data Protection Supervisor (EDPS). 2015. "Mobile Health: Reconciling Technological Innovation with Data Protection." May 21. https://edps.europa.eu/sites/edp/files/publication/15-05-21_mhealth_en_0.pdf.

Figueroa, C., C. Johnson, A. Verster, and R. Baggaley. 2015. "Attitudes and Acceptability on HIV Self-Testing among Key Populations: A Literature Review." *AIDS and Behavior* 19 (11): 1949–1965.

Finkelstein, A. 2004. "Static and Dynamic Effects of Health Policy: Evidence from the Vaccine Industry." *Quarterly Journal of Economics* 119 (2): 527–564.

Freedman, S., H. Lin, and J. Prince. 2018. "Information Technology and Patient

Health: Analyzing Outcomes, Populations, and Mechanisms." *American Journal of Health Economics* 4 (1): 51–79.
Friedman, C., J. Rubin, J. Brown, M. Buntin, M. Corn, L. Etheredge, C. Gunter, M. Musen, R. Platt, W. Stead, and K. Sullivan. 2015. "Toward a Science of Learning Systems: A Research Agenda for the High-Functioning Learning Health System." *Journal of the American Medical Informatics Association* 22 (1): 43–50.
Ganju, K. K., H. Atasoy, J. McCullough, and B. Greenwood. 2020. "The Role of Decision Support Systems in Attenuating Racial Biases in Healthcare Delivery." *Management Science* 66 (11): 5171–5181.
Goldfarb, A., B. Taska, and F. Teodoridis. 2020. "Artificial Intelligence in Health Care? Evidence from Online Job Postings." *AEA Papers and Proceedings* 110: 400–404.
Goldfarb, A., and C. Tucker. 2012. "Shifts in Privacy Concerns." *American Economic Review* 102 (3): 349–53.
Goldfarb, A., and C. Tucker. 2019. "Digital Economics." *Journal of Economic Literature* 57 (1): 3–43.
Gostin, L. 1991. "Genetic Discrimination: The Use of Genetically Based Diagnostic and Prognostic Tests by Employers and Insurers." *American Journal of Law & Medicine* 17: 109.
Gostin, L. O. 1994. "Health Information Privacy." *Cornell Law Review* 80: 451.
Greenhouse, S., and M. Barbaro. 2006. "Wal-Mart to Add Wage Caps and Part-Timers." *New York Times*, Oct. 2.
Gresenz, C. R., S. Laughery, A. R. Miller, and C. E. Tucker. 2017. "Health IT and Ambulatory Care Quality." SSRN Working Paper #2665664.
Gruber, J. 1994. "The Incidence of Mandated Maternity Benefits." *American Economic Review* 84 (3): 622–641.
Halpern, S. 2020. "Can We Track COVID-19 and Protect Privacy at the Same Time?" *New Yorker Magazine*, April 27.
Handel, B., I. Hendel, and M. D. Whinston. 2015. "Equilibria in Health Exchanges: Adverse Selection versus Reclassification Risk." *Econometrica* 83 (4): 1261–1313.
Hellman, D. 2003. What Makes Genetic Discrimination Exceptional?" *American Journal of Law & Medicine* 29 (1): 77–116.
Hermalin, B. E., and M. L. Katz. 2006. "Privacy, Property Rights and Efficiency: The Economics of Privacy As Secrecy." *Quantitative Marketing and Economics* 4 (3): 209–239.
Hill, K. 2022. "Deleting Your Period Tracker Won't Protect You." *New York Times*, June 30.
Hillestad, R., J. Bigelow, A. Bower, F. Girosi, R. Meili, R. Scoville, and R. Taylor. 2005. "Can Electronic Medical Record Systems Transform Health Care? Potential Health Benefits, Savings, and Costs." *Health Affairs* 24 (5): 1103–17.
Hitt, L. M., and P. Tambe. 2016. "Health Care Information Technology, Work Organization, and Nursing Home Performance." *ILR Review* 69 (4): 834–859.
Holmstrom, B., and P. Milgrom. 1991. "Multitask Principal-Agent Analyses: Incentive Contracts, Asset Ownership, and Job Design." *Journal of Law, Economics, & Organization* 7: 24–52.
Hotz, V. J., C. R. Bollinger, T. Komarova, C. F. Manski, R. A. Moffitt, D. Nekipelov, A. Sojourner, and B. D. Spencer. 2022. "Balancing Data Privacy and Usability in the Federal Statistical System." *Proceedings of the National Academy of Sciences* 119 (31): e2104906119.
Huckvale, K., J. Torous, and M. E. Larsen. 2019. "Assessment of the Data Sharing and Privacy Practices of Smartphone Apps for Depression and Smoking Cessation." *JAMA Network Open* 2 (4): e192542–e192542.

Ichihashi, S. 2020. "Online Privacy and Information Disclosure by Consumers." *American Economic Review* 110 (2): 569–95.
Institute of Medicine (IOM). 2000. *To Err Is Human: Building a Safer Health System*. Washington, DC: National Academy Press.
Institute of Medicine (IOM). 2007. *The Learning Healthcare System: Workshop Summary*. Washington, DC: National Academies Press.
Institute of Medicine (IOM). 2009. *Beyond the HIPAA Privacy Rule: Enhancing Privacy, Improving Health through Research*. Washington, DC: National Academies Press.
Institute of Medicine (IOM). 2013. *Best Care at Lower Cost: The Path to Continuously Learning Health Care in America*. Washington, DC: National Academies Press.
Janakiraman, R., E. Park, E. M. Demirezen, and S. Kumar. 2022. "The Effects of Health Information Exchange Access on Healthcare Quality and Efficiency: An Empirical Investigation." *Management Science* 69 (2): 791–811.
Jha, A. K., C. M. DesRoches, P. D. Kralovec, and M. S. Joshi. 2010. "A Progress Report on Electronic Health Records in US Hospitals." *Health Affairs* 29 (10): 1951–1957.
Johnson, G. 2022. "Economic Research on Privacy Regulation: Lessons from the GDPR and Beyond." In *The Economics of Privacy*, edited by A. Goldfarb and C. Tucker. University of Chicago Press.
Johnson, G. A., S. K. Shriver, and S. G. Goldberg. 2023. "Privacy and Market Concentration: Intended and Unintended Consequences of the GDPR." Forthcoming. *Management Science*.
Jolls, C. 2004. "Identifying the Effects of the Americans with Disabilities Act Using State-Law Variation: Preliminary Evidence on Educational Participation Effects." *American Economic Review* 94 (2): 447–453.
Jones, C. I., and C. Tonetti. 2020. "Nonrivalry and the Economics of Data." *American Economic Review* 110 (9): 2819–58.
Kelly, H., T. Hunter, and D. Abril. 2022. "Seeking an Abortion? Here's How to Avoid Leaving a Digital Trail." *Washington Post*, June 26.
KFF. 2022. "Health Insurance Coverage of Nonelderly 0-64." Accessed October 12. https://www.kff.org/other/state-indicator/nonelderly-0-64/?currentTimeframe=0&sortModel=%7B%.22colId%22:%22Location%22,%22sort%22:%22asc%22%7D.
Komarova, T., N. Nekipelov, and E. Yakovlev. 2018. "Identification, Data Combination, and the Risk of Disclosure." *Quantitative Economics* 9 (1): 395–440.
Kummer, M., and P. Schulte. 2019. "When Private Information Settles the Bill: Money and Privacy in Google's Market for Smartphone Applications." *Management Science* 65 (8): 3470–3494.
Lammers, E. J., J. Adler-Milstein, and K. Kocher. 2014. "Does Health Information Exchange Reduce Redundant Imaging? Evidence from Emergency Departments." *Medical Care* 52 (3): 227–34.
Landes, W. M., and R. A. Posner. 1975. "The Private Enforcement of Law." *The Journal of Legal Studies* 4 (1): 1–46.
Lin, T. 2022. "Valuing Intrinsic and Instrumental Preferences for Privacy." *Marketing Science 41 (4): 663–681.*
Lin, Y. K., M. Lin, and H. Chen. 2019. "Do Electronic Health Records Affect Quality of Care? Evidence from the HITECH Act." *Information Systems Research* 30 (1): 306–318.
Loertscher, S., and L. M. Marx. 2020. "Digital Monopolies: Privacy Protection or Price Regulation?" *International Journal of Industrial Organization* 71: 102623.

Maclean, J. C., J. Mallatt, C. J. Ruhm, and K. Simon. 2020. "Economic Studies on the Opioid Crisis: A Review." NBER Working Paper 28067. Cambridge, MA: National Bureau of Economic Research.

Magliozzi, R. 2022. "'Car Talk' Host: Independent Auto Shops Deserve the Right to Repair Your Car." *Washington Post, September 28*.

McCullough, J. S., S. T. Parente, and R. Town. 2016. "Health Information Technology and Patient Outcomes: The Role of Information and Labor Coordination." *RAND Journal of Economics* 47 (1): 207–236.

McGraw, D., J. X. Dempsey, L. Harris, and J. Goldman. 2009. "Privacy as an Enabler, Not an Impediment: Building Trust into Health Information Exchange." *Health Affairs* 28 (2): 416–427.

Mechanic, D. 1998. "The Functions and Limitations of Trust in the Provision of Medical Care." *Journal of Health Politics, Policy and Law* 23 (4): 661–686.

Merchant, R. M., D. A. Asch, P. Crutchley, L. H. Ungar, S. C. Guntuku, J. C. Eichstaedt, S. Hill, K. Padrez, R. J. Smith, and H. A. Schwartz. 2019. "Evaluating the Predictability of Medical Conditions from Social Media Posts." *PloS One* 14 (6): e0215476.

Miller, A. R. 2010. "Did the Airline Tariff Publishing Case Reduce Collusion?" *Journal of Law and Economics* 53 (3): 569–586.

Miller, A. R., C. Eibner, and C. R. Gresenz. 2013. "Financing of Employer Sponsored Health Insurance Plans before and after Health Reform: What Consumers Don't Know Won't Hurt Them?" *International Review of Law and Economics* 36: 36–47.

Miller, A. R., K. Ramdas, and A. Sungu. 2021. "Browsers Don't Lie? Gender Differences in the Effects of the Indian COVID-19 Lockdown on Digital Activity and Time Use." SSRN Working Paper #3930079.

Miller, A. R., and C. Segal. 2019. "Do Female Officers Improve Law Enforcement Quality? Effects on Crime Reporting and Domestic Violence." *Review of Economic Studies* 86 (5): 2220–2247.

Miller, A. R., and C. Segal. 2012. "Does Temporary Affirmative Action Produce Persistent Effects? A Study of Black and Female Employment in Law Enforcement." *Review of Economics and Statistics* 94 (4): 1107–1125.

Miller, A. R., and C. Tucker. 2009. "Privacy Protection and Technology Diffusion: The Case of Electronic Medical Records." *Management Science* 55 (7): 1077–1093.

Miller, A. R., and C. Tucker. 2011a. "Can Health Care Information Technology Save Babies?" *Journal of Political Economy* 119 (2): 289–324.

Miller, A. R., and C. Tucker. 2011b. "Encryption and the Loss of Patient Data." *Journal of Policy Analysis and Management* 30 (3): 534–556.

Miller, A. R., and C. Tucker. 2014. "Health Information Exchange, System Size and Information Silos." *Journal of Health Economics* 33: 28–42.

Miller, A. R., and C. Tucker. 2017. "Frontiers of Health Policy: Digital Data and Personalized Medicine." *Innovation Policy and the Economy* 17: 49–75.

Miller, A. R., and C. Tucker. 2018. "Privacy Protection, Personalized Medicine, and Genetic Testing." *Management Science* 64 (10): 4648–4668.

Murphy, K. M., and R. H. Topel. 2003. *Measuring the Gains from Medical Research: An Economic Approach*. University of Chicago Press.

Murphy, K. M., and R. H. Topel. 2006. "The Value of Health and Longevity." *Journal of Political Economy* 114 (5): 871–904.

Nissenbaum, H. 2004. "Privacy as Contextual Integrity." *Washington Law Review* 79: 119.

Nix, N., and E. Dwoskin. 2022. "Search Warrants for Abortion Data Leave Tech Companies Few Options." *Washington Post*, August 12.

Organization for Economic Co-operation and Development (OECD). 2022. Health Data Governance for the Digital Age: Implementing the OECD Recommendation on Health Data Governance. Paris: OECD Publishing. https://doi.org/10.1787/68b60796-en.

Oster, E., E. R. Dorsey, J. Bausch, A. Shinaman, E. Kayson, D. Oakes, I. Shoulson, and K. Quaid. 2008. "Fear of Health Insurance Loss among Individuals at Risk for Huntington Disease." *American Journal of Medical Genetics Part A* 146 (16): 2070–2077.

Oster, E., I. Shoulson, and E. Dorsey. 2013. "Optimal Expectations and Limited Medical Testing: Evidence from Huntington Disease." *American Economic Review* 103 (2): 804–30.

Oster, E., I. Shoulson, K. Quaid, and E. R. Dorsey. 2010. "Genetic Adverse Selection: Evidence from Long-Term Care Insurance and Huntington Disease." *Journal of Public Economics* 94 (11–12): 1041–1050.

Pear, R. 2015. "Tech Rivalries Impede Digital Medical Record Sharing." *New York Times*, May 26.

Phelps, E. S. 1972. "The Statistical Theory of Racism and Sexism." *American Economic Review* 62 (4): 659–661.

Polinsky, A. M., and S. Shavell. 2000. "The Economic Theory of Public Enforcement of Law." *Journal of Economic Literature* 38 (1): 45–76.

Ponemon Institute. 2013. *Survey on Medical Identity Theft*. https://www.ponemon.org/research/ponemon-library/security/2013-survey-on-medical-identity-thef-2.html.

Posner, R. A. 1981. "The Economics of Privacy." *American Economic Review* 71 (2): 405–409.

Price, W. N., and I. G. Cohen. 2019. "Privacy in the Age of Medical Big Data." *Nature Medicine* 25 (1): 37–43.

Pritts, J. L. 2001. "Altered States: State Health Privacy Laws and the Impact of the Federal Health Privacy Rule." *Yale Journal of Health Policy, Law, and Ethics* 2 (2): 327–64.

Pritts, J. L., S. Lewis, R. Jacobson, K. Lucia, and K. Kayne. 2009. "Privacy and Security Solutions for Interoperable Health Information Exchange: Report on State Law Requirements for Patient Permission to Disclose Health Information." https://www.healthit.gov/sites/default/files/disclosure-report-1.pdf.

Qian, I., M. Xiao, P. Mozur, and A. Cardia. 2022. "Four Takeaways from a Times Investigation into China's Expanding Surveillance State." *New York Times. Published June 21, 2022. Updated July 26, 2022.* https://www.nytimes.com/2022/06/21/world/asia/china-surveillance-investigation.html.

Rothschild, M., and J. Stiglitz. 1976. "Equilibrium in Competitive Insurance Markets: An Essay on the Economics of Imperfect Information." *Quarterly Journal of Economics* 90 (4): 629–649.

Rothstein, M. A. 2007. "Health Privacy in the Electronic Age." *Journal of Legal Medicine* 28 (4): 487–501.

Sanders, S. F., M. Terwiesch, W. J. Gordon, and A. D. Stern. 2019. "How Artificial Intelligence Is Changing Health Care Delivery." *NEJM Catalyst* 5 (5).

Shilo, S., H. Rossman, and E. Segal. 2020. "Axes of a Revolution: Challenges and Promises of Big Data in Healthcare." *Nature Medicine* 26 (1): 29–38.

Skatova, A., R. L. McDonald, S. Ma, and C. Maple. 2019. "Unpacking Privacy: Willingness to Pay to Protect Personal Data. Working Paper. doi: 10.31234/osf.io/ahwe4.

Smalley, E. 2017. "AI-Powered Drug Discovery Captures Pharma Interest." *Nature Biotechnology* 35 (7): 604–606.

Spetz, J., J. F. Burgess, and C. S. Phibbs. 2014. "The Effect of Health Information Technology Implementation in Veterans Health Administration Hospitals on Patient Outcomes." *Healthcare* 2 (1): 40–47.

Tangari, G., M. Ikram, K. Ijaz, M. A. Kaafar, and S. Berkovsky. 2021. "Mobile Health and Privacy: Cross Sectional Study." *BMJ* 373: n1248.

Taylor, C., and L. Wagman. 2014. "Consumer Privacy in Oligopolistic Markets: Winners, Losers, and Welfare." *International Journal of Industrial Organization* 34: 80–84.

US Department of Health and Human Services (HHS). 2017. "Health Information Privacy beyond HIPAA: A 2018 Environmental Scan of Major Trends and Challenges." December 13. https://ncvhs.hhs.gov/wp-content/uploads/2018/05/NCVHS-Beyond- HIPAA_Report-Final-02-08-18.pdf.

Vermund, S. H., and C. M. Wilson. 2002. "Barriers to HIV Testing—Where Next?" *Lancet* 360 (9341): 1186–1187.

Walker, J., E. Pan, D. Johnston, J. Adler-Milstein, D. W. Bates, and B. Middleton. 2005. "The Value of Health Care Information Exchange and Interoperability: There Is a Business Case to be Made for Spending Money on a Fully Standardized Nationwide System." *Health Affairs* 24 (Suppl1): W5–10.

Yu, K. H., A. L. Beam, and I. S. Kohane. 2018. "Artificial Intelligence in Healthcare." *Nature Biomedical Engineering* 2 (10): 719–731.

Author Index

Subject Index

Page numbers followed by *f* refer to figures.